T0302126

Service Business Development

How can manufacturers of capital goods succeed in service business development? What are the potential network approaches for manufacturing companies planning on extending their service business? Over the last decade, the business environment of capital goods manufacturers has changed dramatically. Few capital goods manufacturers are able to outrun the competition with pure product-related technologies and innovation alone. For this reason they have added services to products as a way of responding to eroding margins and the loss of strategic differentiation through product innovation and technological superiority. Based on over 12 years of research, this book provides academics and business professionals with a thorough overview of the strategies available for value creation through service business development. It features case studies and covers a wide range of topics, including emerging issues such as service business in small- and medium-sized companies, business innovation through services and the impact of rapidly growing Asian markets.

THOMAS FISCHER has been a research associate at the Institute of Technology Management at the University of St. Gallen. His research interests lie in service business development, service innovation and the internationalisation of the value chain in manufacturing companies. He completed his Ph.D. in 2010.

HEIKO GEBAUER is Associate Professor at the Swiss Federal Institute of Aquatic Science and Technology (Eawag) and at the Institute of Technology Management at the University of St. Gallen. His research focuses on service and innovation management in infrastructure sectors, service business development in manufacturing companies and value creation in public transit services. He is also an adjunct professor at the Service Research Center at the Karlstad University in Sweden.

ELGAR FLEISCH is Professor of Technology Management and Director of the Institute of Technology Management at the University of St. Gallen. He is also Professor of Information Management at the Swiss Federal Institute of Technology Zurich (ETHZ). His research focuses on the economic impacts and infrastructures of ubiquitous computing. He is co-chair of research of Auto-ID Labs, co-founder of several university spin-offs and serves as a member of multiple management boards and academic steering committees.

Service Business Development

Strategies for Value Creation in Manufacturing Firms

THOMAS FISCHER, HEIKO GEBAUER AND
ELGAR FLEISCH

CAMBRIDGE
UNIVERSITY PRESS

CAMBRIDGE
UNIVERSITY PRESS

University Printing House, Cambridge CB2 8BS, United Kingdom

One Liberty Plaza, 20th Floor, New York, NY 10006, USA

477 Williamstown Road, Port Melbourne, VIC 3207, Australia

314-321, 3rd Floor, Plot 3, Splendor Forum, Jasola District Centre, New Delhi - 110025, India

79 Anson Road, #06-04/06, Singapore 079906

Cambridge University Press is part of the University of Cambridge.

It furthers the University's mission by disseminating knowledge in the pursuit of education, learning and research at the highest international levels of excellence.

www.cambridge.org
Information on this title: www.cambridge.org/9781107022454

© Thomas Fischer, Heiko Gebauer and Elgar Fleisch 2012

First published 2012
Reprinted 2013

A catalogue record for this publication is available from the British Library

Library of Congress Cataloging in Publication data
Fischer, Thomas, 1959–
 Service business development : strategies for value creation in manufacturing firms /
 Thomas Fischer, Heiko Gebauer, Elgar Fleisch.
  pages cm
 Includes bibliographical references and index.
 ISBN 978-1-107-02245-4 (hardback)
 1. Manufacturing industries–Management. 2. Service industries. 3. Customer
 services. I. Gebauer, Heiko, 1976– II. Fleisch, Elgar. III. Title.
 HD9720.5.F567 2012
 658.4′012–dc23
 2012002187

ISBN 978-1-107-02245-4 Hardback

Contents

List of figures	*page* viii	
List of tables	x	
List of exhibits	xii	
Preface	xv	
Acknowledgements	xviii	
List of abbreviations	xx	

1 Introduction — 1
1.1 Motivation — 1
1.2 Challenges of service business development — 21
1.3 Central questions — 37
1.4 Methodology — 40
1.5 Structure — 41

2 Basic concepts of service business development — 43
2.1 Organisational capabilities necessary for service business development — 43
2.2 Service strategies for manufacturing companies — 70
2.3 Strategic fit between service strategy and operational capabilities — 79

3 Dynamic capabilities for service business development — 87
3.1 Exploitation or exploration: two distinct approaches for service business development — 87
3.2 Phases of the exploitation and exploration approaches — 90
3.3 Dynamic capabilities required in the exploitation approach — 91
3.4 Dynamic capabilities necessary for succeeding with exploration — 98

4 A case study: using the exploitation approach to develop a service business — 106
4.1 Phase 1: integrating basic services into the product price — 106
4.2 Phase 2: separating product and service businesses to increase the profit and revenue generated by service — 107

4.3 Phase 3: exploiting service expansion in the primary customer
activity chain   112

5 A case study: using the exploration approach to develop
   a service business   113
   5.1 Background of the company   113
   5.2 Initial situation and triggers for developing the service business   114
   5.3 Exploring service opportunities and reconfiguring the business logic 116

6 Developing service business via the exploitation
   approach   122
   6.1 Service strategies associated with the exploitation approach   122
   6.2 Case studies of changes in service strategy   136
   6.3 Operational capabilities for service strategies   141
   6.4 Service strategy changes as the antecedent to providing solutions   142

7 Configurations of service strategies and operational
   capabilities supporting the exploitation approach   145
   7.1 Operational capabilities for after-sales service providers   146
   7.2 Operational capabilities for customer support service providers   153
   7.3 Operational capabilities for development partners   167
   7.4 Operational capabilities for outsourcing partners   182
   7.5 Operational capabilities for solution providers   192

8 Network perspective   199
   8.1 Dimensions of business networks   199
   8.2 Types of business networks   201
   8.3 Vertical after-sales service networks   204
   8.4 Horizontal outsourcing service networks   207
   8.5 Vertical life-cycle solution networks   213
   8.6 Horizontal solution networks   215

9 International aspects of service business development   217
   9.1 Global approaches to service business development   217
   9.2 Service business development in the Chinese market   232

10 Service business development for small and medium
   suppliers   248
   10.1 Approaches for service business development   248
   10.2 Co-evolvement of organisational capabilities   253

11 Service business development in small and medium OEMs   267
   11.1 The exploitation approaches used by SMEMs   267
   11.2 SMEMs selling directly to a limited number of customers   267
   11.3 SMEMs selling to a large number of customers via distributors 275

12 Summary   281
    12.1 Highlights   281
    12.2 Recommendations for further research   285

Bibliography   286
Index   296

Figures

1.1 Moving from being a product manufacturer
to a service provider   *page* 6
1.2 Service revenues   9
1.3 Share of service revenues   10
1.4 EBIT products and services   13
1.5 The development of revenues at IBM   17
1.6 The service paradox   22
2.1 Challenges and payoffs in the service business   45
2.2 Downstream analysis   51
2.3 An example of a life-cycle cost analysis   51
2.4 Excel spreadsheet for evaluating the service
potential of the installed base   52
2.5 The service opportunity matrix   54
2.6 Typology of service strategies and service opportunities   55
2.7 Service opportunities for moving towards integrated
solutions   57
2.8 The product service continuum   71
2.9 Service strategies in manufacturing companies   74
2.10 Supporting service activities in the capital goods
value chain   75
2.11 Service strategies and transition trajectories via the
addition of service   77
2.12 Framework for describing new service-based
business concepts   78
3.1 Exploitation and exploration in relation to the
service opportunities   88
3.2 A comparison of the phases used to explore or exploit
service opportunities   91
4.1 Organisational structures   107
4.2 Financial indicators   109
5.1 Hilti System Solutions   114

5.2 The Hilti business model and corporate strategy 115
5.3 The service packages included in the new business model 119
6.1 Service strategies for exploiting service opportunities 123
6.2 The pattern followed when service strategy is changed in relation to the service opportunities available 131
6.3 Effects of Stage 2 on service profitability and revenue 134
6.4 Preliminary operational capabilities for each service strategy 142
6.5 Solution providers as combination of different service strategies 144
7.1 Organisation of the BU when products are separated from services 157
7.2 The process for selling solutions 197
8.1 The dimensions of the four types of business networks 201
8.2 Illustration of an after-sales (customer-support) service network 205
8.3 Illustration of a horizontal outsourcing network 208
8.4 Vertical life-cycle service network 214
8.5 Horizontal solution network 216
9.1 Service offerings and organisational elements 219
9.2 The integrated and ethnocentric global service approach 222
9.3 The integrated and polycentric global service approach 225
9.4 The separated and polycentric global service approach 228
9.5 The separated and geocentric global service approach 231
9.6 Service revenues achieved in China and Europe 233
9.7 Role profiles of service technicians and managers 238

Tables

0.1 Overview of the research activities undertaken   *page* xvi

1.1 Service categories involved in service business development   4

1.2 Comparison of margins in OEM and service businesses   12

1.3 Milestones in the development of IBM   18

1.4 The questions addressed   38

2.1 The complexity of product and service business   45

2.2 Ratio between a new order intake for products and the installed product base   47

2.3 Cognitive phenomena limiting the rationale for developing service business   49

2.4 Transition line from products to services   59

2.5 Six steps for managing a service network   61

2.6 Phases for overcoming the service paradox   62

2.7 Actions for improving service profitability   65

2.8 Actions for implementing the chosen source of competitive advantages and strategic intent   67

2.9 Additional overview of service strategies   80

2.10 A comparison of product-orientated and service-orientated corporate cultures   81

2.11 Service orientation in human resource management   82

2.12 Advantages and disadvantages of separation and integration   84

2.13 Basic types of service orientation of organisational structures   85

3.1 Characteristics of the exploitation and exploration approaches   89

3.2 Dynamic capabilities necessary for exploiting service opportunities   96

3.3 Dynamic capabilities necessary for exploring service opportunities   102

5.1 Transferring the automotive fleet management concept
to the construction industry 118
6.1 Value propositions and service offerings of service
strategies 124
6.2 Summary of the six service strategies 128
6.3 Summary of the stages observed when service strategy is
changed 133
6.4 Risks involved when changing service strategy 135
7.1 The operational capabilities required by providers of
after-sales service 152
7.2 The operational capabilities required by providers of
customer support service 168
7.3 The operational capabilities required by development
partners 180
7.4 The operational capabilities necessary for outsourcing
partners 190
8.1 Description of the business networks 202
9.1 Overview of the four approaches used to provide global
service 221
9.2 Human resource management in China 240
9.3 Advantages and disadvantages of current logistics
concepts for spare parts 242
10.1 The three approaches used by suppliers to develop
their service business 252
10.2 Summary of the dynamic capabilities associated with
each approach 262
10.3 Summary of the operational capabilities associated
with each approach 264
11.1 Capability development in SMEMs selling directly
to a few strategic customers 270
11.2 Capability development in SMEMs selling via
distributors to a large number of customers 278

Exhibits

1.1 Ericsson's movement towards providing services   *page* 7
1.2 The moves made by IBM towards improved service and
    new value creation logic   19
1.3 IBM's and General Electric's dynamic capabilities for
    service business development   23
1.4 The challenges of dynamic capabilities   25
1.5 Examples of strategic changes made in service business
    development   27
1.6 Challenges of achieving strategic fit in service business
    development   30
1.7 Magna's movement towards services   34
1.8 SKF's movement towards services (SKF 2004 to 2010)   35
6.1 Providing solutions to manufacturing industries   143
7.1 Bucher Foodtech's service organisation and human
    resource management   148
7.2 Deutz's service values and proximity of its service
    organisation to customers   149
7.3 The development of repair services at Mikron   151
7.4 The service values and human resource issues
    of Mettler-Toledo   154
7.5 AgieCharmilles' measurement and reward system   156
7.6 Intra-firm collaboration at Trumpf   158
7.7 Endress+Hauser's proximity to customers   159
7.8 The service development process used by Heidelberg   161
7.9 The service business of Carl Zeiss IMT   165
7.10 The service culture and human resource management at
    Bystronic Glass   170
7.11 Ericsson's acquisition of an R&D service organisation   173
7.12 The service organisation at Sulzer Innotec   174
7.13 Magna-Steyr's proximity to customers and development
    of the concept of 'total vehicle service'   176

7.14 Service development at Bühler Die Casting 178
7.15 The service business of Voith Railservice 182
7.16 IT support used by ABB's maintenance management
service 188
7.17 The customer-focused organisational structures
of Bosch Packaging 193
7.18 The customer-focused organisational structures
of Mettler-Toledo 194
7.19 The key account management used by solution providers 195
7.20 The service packages offered by Ericsson Operating
Systems 197
8.1 The vertical service network operated by GF
AgieCharmilles 204
8.2 Acquisition activities at Voith Industrial Services 209
8.3 Bilfinger Berger's mergers and acquisitions 211
8.4 Acquisitions made by Bosch Packaging 212
9.1 The global service approach used by Bystronic 225
9.2 The spare parts logistics concept used by GF
AgieCharmilles 245
10.1 The radical leap taken by Fraisa towards a new value
constellation downstream in the value chain 251
10.2 Escatec's financial seeking behaviour in existing
buyer and new supplier–buyer relationships 257
10.3 Scenarios at Fraisa 260
11.1 Service business development at Hunkeler 273

Preface

Our research aims at improving theory-building (theoretical extension and replication) as well as offering managerial guidance for extending the service business of manufacturing companies. The first phase involved describing and comparing narratives on the extension of the service business in manufacturing companies, as shown in Table 0.1. Comparing such narratives improved the transferability of the qualitative findings, which laid the foundation for developing hypotheses and testing them empirically (Phase 2).

The qualitative studies in Phase 1 show evidence of the 'service paradox' phenomenon: manufacturing companies invest in extending their service business but are not able to earn the corresponding returns. Determinants in overcoming the service paradox and improving revenues and profits include (1) managerial motivation, (2) a market-orientated and clearly defined service development process, (3) focusing service offers on the customer's own value proposition, (4) initiating a marketing relationship, (5) defining a clear service strategy, (6) establishing a separate service organisation, and (7) creating a service culture. These determinants were subjected to more detailed qualitative investigations regarding service development processes, organisational structures and behavioural and cultural implications. Companies seem to acknowledge, for example, that although they have no general service development process or organisational structure, each type of service and/or service strategy nevertheless has specific considerations.

The development and testing of hypotheses in Phase 2 revealed specific patterns in the changes made to service strategy, namely from after-sales service strategy to customer-support service strategy, and from customer-support service strategy to development partner or outsourcing partner strategy. These service strategies require a specific alignment with organisational design elements such as service orientation in the corporate culture (values and behaviour), human resources (recruitment development and compensation) and organisational

Table 0.1: *Overview of the research activities undertaken*

	Phase 1 1997–2007	Phase 2 2008–2011
Goals and research methodology	Building theories for understanding the service paradox; exploring determinants for increasing service revenues and profits Qualitative studies using interviews, focus groups and action research A variety of manufacturing industries enhances the transferability of the findings	Testing theories of specific determinants and antecedents for increasing service revenues and profits Quantitative studies using a variety of surveys, benchmarking approaches and different empirical methods, such as cluster analysis, factor analysis and structural equation modelling
Theoretical contributions	Determinants for overcoming the service paradox Service development processes for different service categories Behavioural and cultural elements and organisational structures supporting the extension of the service business Types of organisational structures supporting the service business extension	Configuration of environmental strategy and strategy structure Patterns of changes in service strategy Impact the service orientation of the corporate culture has on business performance Measurement validation for service orientation of corporate culture (values and behaviour of managers and employees) Interaction between service differentiation, innovativeness and customer centricity for driving competitive advantages Role of dynamic capabilities (sensing, seizing and reconfiguring) in extending the service business
Practical implications	Guidelines, process models and procedures for moving from products to services	Description of potential service strategies in terms of value propositions and service offerings Description of alignments between service strategies and design elements of the organisation Description of how dynamic capabilities contribute to the approach (exploitation vs. exploration) taken to the service business

structures (proximity to customers and distinguishing products from services).

At the cultural level, a positive association between the service orientation of the corporate culture and the business performance was corroborated empirically and, at the strategic level, the positive role of differentiating service to achieve competitive advantages was corroborated. In addition, the differentiation of services in existing concepts, such as innovativeness and customer centricity, was also incorporated. Service differentiation strengthens the positive impacts of innovativeness and customer centricity on business performance.

All these contributions enhance the theory-building of operational capabilities. These, in turn, overcome the service paradox and ensure service revenues and profits. The insights gained by the operational capabilities (e.g. sensing service opportunities, seizing the sensed opportunities and reconfiguring operational capabilities) are supplemented by the dynamic capabilities that play a key role in determining whether service business is extended via the exploitation or exploration approach. The former uses services to enhance the existing value constellations incrementally; the latter uses services for defining new value constellations, thereby allowing companies to make radical leaps towards a new strategic stage.

The chapters following concentrate on these qualitative findings and offer key insights and recommendations on the managerial level for extending the service business.

Acknowledgements

This book is the result of our research work at the Institute of Technology Management (ITEM-HSG) at the University of St. Gallen, Switzerland. The work offered us the opportunity of collaborating closely with companies from various industries and academic institutions over the last twelve years. The interdisciplinary nature of the research, and being able to focus on addressing actual business problems, is truly appreciated. Our work was only possible because of the contribution of several companies and industrial partners, who kindly provided us with the case studies that we required. We are indebted to the company representatives and thank them for their valuable time, support, commitment and feedback.

Thanks are due to the other Ph.D. students who contributed significantly to the research topics and made valuable contributions to the research field as a whole. We would like to thank in particular Ms Katharina Hildenbrand, Ms Regine Schröder, Mr Bernold Beckenbauer, Mr Carlos Bravo-Sanchez and Mr Felix Pütz. Further, we would like to express our deep gratitude to Ms Elisabeth Vetsch-Keller for her outstanding organisational support and Ms Maureen Sondell for her linguistic revision services.

Being allowed to conduct part of our research as visiting scholars at the Institute for Manufacturing (IfM) at the University of Cambridge, England, and the Service Research Centre at the Karlstad University, Sweden, is appreciated immensely. Thank you, Prof. Mike Gregory and Prof. Andy Neely, for being the faculty sponsor of Mr Thomas Fischer. And thank you, Prof. Bo Edvardsson, Prof. Anders Gustafsson and Prof. Lars Witell for many inspiring discussions and the valuable feedback we received.

Our gratitude extends to the Swiss National Science Foundation, the Commission for Technology & Innovation and the University of St. Gallen for their financial support of our research projects. This book compiles research findings that the authors have conducted over the last 12 years. We are thankful to our international co-authors for their support during this long journey of discovery. Various related findings of the work presented in this book have been published in academic journal articles and they are reproduced with the kind permission of the co-authors. Portions of Chapters 3 and 6 appeared in the following two articles published in the *Journal of Service Management*:

Fischer, T., Gebauer, H., Ren, G., Gregory, M. and Fleisch, E. (2010). 'Exploitation or exploration in service business development? Insights from a dynamic capabilities perspective', *Journal of Service Management* **21** (5): 591–624.

Gebauer, H., Fischer, T. and Fleisch, E. (2010). 'Exploring the interrelationship among patterns of service strategy changes and organizational design elements', *Journal of Service Management* **21** (1): 103–29.

The analysis of the global approach to the service business was originally published as:

Kuzca, G. and Gebauer, H. (2011). 'Global approach to the service business in manufacturing companies', *Journal of Business & Industrial Marketing* **26** (7): 472–83.

The research on the impact of the Chinese culture on service management approaches was published in the following three articles:

Gebauer, H. (2007). 'Lösungsansätze zum Personalmanagement in chinesischen Serviceorganisationen', *Zeitschrift für wirtschaftlichen Fabrikbetrieb* **11**: 736–40.

(2007). 'Extending the service business in China? Experience of Swiss companies', *Singapore Management Review* **29** (1): 59–72.

Gebauer, H., Kuzca, G. and Wang, C. (2011). 'Spare parts logistics for the Chinese market', *Benchmarking: An International Journal*, **18** (6): 748–68.

Abbreviations

CAD	computer-aided design
CAS	computer-aided sales and services
CEO	chief executive officer
ECAD	electronic computer-aided design
ERP	enterprise resource planning
IT	information technology
OEM	original equipment manufacturer
PDM	product data management
PLM	product life-cycle management
R&D	research and development
SBU	strategic business unit
SLA	service-level agreement
SMEM	small- and medium-sized OEM

1 | Introduction

1.1 Motivation

1.1.1 Service business development as a response to commoditisation tendencies

Over the last decade, the business environment of capital goods manufacturers has changed dramatically. Unlike consumer goods, capital goods are durable and capital-intensive products; manufacturers sell their products and/or capital goods to other companies. Capital goods manufacturers are involved in business-to-business relationships; in the value chain, they can be positioned as manufacturers of machines and equipment or suppliers of modules and components (i.e. 1st, 2nd or 3rd tier suppliers).

Capital goods manufacturers invest substantially in product innovation, develop proprietary new product technologies, try relentlessly to reduce the time to market of their products and attempt to achieve cost optimisations. However, few capital goods manufacturers are able to outrun the competition with pure product-related technologies and innovation alone (Matthyssens and Vandenbempt, 2008; Vandenbosch and Dawar, 2002). Moreover, capital goods manufacturers often face the situation where the marginal rate of R&D investments is considered to be diminishing. In order to achieve similar competitive advantages as in the past it means that companies have to invest all the more in R&D. Maintaining R&D investments at the same level would make transferring technological advantages to the price of the product more difficult. Capital goods have become commodities (Grönroos, 1990; Matthyssens and Vandenbempt, 2008). This, in turn, puts pressure on product margins and profitability. As a direct consequence, many categories of capital goods have reached competitive equality leading to a situation where technological advantages are becoming increasingly difficult to maintain as a lasting strategy.

In some industries, capital goods are even sold at cost price: the intensive level of the competition leads to a situation in which product prices are very close to the actual manufacturing costs. The underlying idea of selling at cost price is to attract more customers and thereby increase the market share of the installed base. 'Installed base' is a specific term used in the capital goods manufacturing industry to describe the products that are currently being used by their customers. Once the customers use their products, companies can then start to provide services that lead to increased revenues and margins from their service business (Brax, 2005; Gebauer and Fleisch, 2007; Jacob and Ulaga, 2008). The actual profit comes from the service business since the products are sold at cost price.

Adding services to the products, along with extending the total offering through services, are potential ways of responding to eroding product margins and the loss of strategic differentiation through product innovation and technological superiority. The extension of the total offering via services has been conceptualised in the literature through notions such as 'servitisation' (Vandermerwe and Rada, 1988), 'transition from products to services' (Oliva and Kallenberg, 2003), 'going downstream in the value chain' (Wise and Baumgartner, 1999), 'product-service systems' (Tukker, 2004), 'moving towards high-value solutions, integrated solutions and systems integration' (Davies, 2004; Windahl and Lakemond, 2010) and 'manufacturing/service integration' (Schmenner, 2009). These views converge on the concept of 'service business development', which can be defined as increasing the value contribution of services in the capital goods industry.

Generally speaking, service business development covers the strategic movement from being a pure manufacturer of capital goods to a provider of innovative combinations of products and services. Pure manufacturers develop, manufacture and sell capital goods. Providing innovative combinations of products and services suggests that companies develop, manufacture and provide products; develop and deliver services; integrate and combine products and services creatively for tailor-made solutions. Such an innovative combination leads to high-value unified responses to the needs of customers (Davies *et al.*, 2007; Sawhney, 2006).

Extension of service offerings

It is arguable that the development of service business corresponds to an extension of the service offerings. The extension of the service offerings includes basically the following service categories (see Table 1.1):

- *Customer service*: extending the service offerings often starts with customer service. The aim of customer service is to augment the product offering. General strategic options involve increasing the logistical precision of the delivery of the product, customer integration in customising the product offering, customer adaptation of the product features and standardised customer service (Wouters, 2004). Customer service influences the client's overall level of satisfaction and strengthens not only the confidence of the customer but also the credibility of the manufacturing company. Services that are typically embraced are information, delivery, billing and documentation. Such services improve the quality of the relationship with the customer (Mathieu, 2001a).
- *Product-related services*: product-related services cover the provision of basic service for the installed base, e.g. spare parts, repair, inspections and basic training, to ensure that the product functions correctly. Product-related services also cover more advanced services such as preventive maintenance service, process optimisation and training and maintenance contracts (Gebauer, 2008; Oliva and Kallenberg, 2003). Basic services simply ensure the functionality of the product whereas more advanced services aim at the prevention of any product breakdown. The aim is to optimise the efficiency and effectiveness of the product when it is utilised by the customer. Both the basic and the advanced services for the installed base address the operational needs of the customer. The service offering could be extended further by supplying services supporting their business needs.
- *Services supporting business needs*: these services reach beyond the operational needs of the customer and address their business needs. The services involved are very diverse and different in nature. They are closely associated with Kotler's (1994) concept of business services, Oliva and Kallenberg's (2003) process-orientated services and Davies' (2004) description of operational services and system integration. The services are based on the customer's requirements for integrating products and services into a customised and functioning system. They involve providing assistance and advice in, for example, technical questions, feasibility studies, design and construction and R&D. Using such services, companies can design and construct products and systems using the competencies developed in-house and by the customer. Customers benefit directly from development competencies: it is indeed these competencies that keep

Table 1.1: *Service categories involved in service business development*

	Customer service	Product-related service	Services supporting business needs
Goals	- Improving the quality of the customer relationship	- Ensures the functionality of the product. Basic services enable companies to react as soon as possible to product breakdowns - Increases the efficiency and effectiveness of the product. Advanced services aimed at the prevention of product breakdowns	- Reaching beyond the operational needs of the customer
Examples	- Services related to information, delivery, billing, documentation	- Basic services for the installed base (e.g. spare parts, repair, inspections and basic training) - Advanced services for the installed base (e.g. preventive maintenance service, process optimisation, training and maintenance contracts)	- Outsourcing services - Business consulting - Technical consulting services (e.g. R&D, design and construction, feasibility studies)

competitors at bay and deter them from catching up. Both the companies and their customers possess a unique position of competency that is difficult to duplicate (Davies 2004; Wernerfelt 1984). The collaborative process of co-creation allows customers to learn of the capabilities possessed by the manufacturers. The manufacturers, in turn, are then able to advise them in the design and construction of their processes. Furthermore, services can also cover 'outsourcing', whereby companies take over part of the processes on behalf of the customer. The manufacturing company assumes the operating risk and full responsibility for the customer's operating processes. Outsourcing services allow manufacturers and their customers to co-create an in-depth understanding of the operational requirements of the process output (Gebauer *et al.*, 2010).

These service categories fulfil the various needs of the customer. They ensure the functionality and performance of the product when used in the customer's production process, cover its operation and maintenance whilst in use and, finally, take the business considerations of the customer into account. The needs of the customer with regards to operating and maintaining the product are closely coupled to the question of outsourcing. Developing service business appears, therefore, in part to be the 'other side of the coin' of the outsourcing discussion (Hobday *et al.*, 2005). Customers reduce their set competencies, thus becoming more flexible and highly specialised: they concentrate on their core competencies alone. It means that they turn to outsourcing activities and demand more services (Oliva and Kallenberg, 2003).

**Moving from being a product manufacturer
to a service provider**
Service business development can be a potentially competitive strategy for manufacturing companies (capital goods manufacturers) to compensate for the lack of technological opportunities for product differentiation (Bowen *et al.*, 1989; Martin and Horne, 1992; Vandermerwe and Rada, 1988). It proceeds along a continuum from *product manufacturer* towards *service provider* (Belz *et al.*, 1997; Oliva and Kallenberg, 2003).

- A product manufacturer considers services as a supplement, i.e. an add-on to the product. Service revenue is quite low: most of the value contribution stems from the product and the few services, such as installation, documentation and spare parts, which are offered. The value contribution of these services is relatively low.
- A service provider relies mainly on creating value through the provision of services. Service profits and revenues drive the overall profitability of the company. A large number of services are offered, including product-related services and customer-support services (such as maintenance contracts, consulting services, financial services, etc.) (Belz *et al.* 1997; Oliva and Kallenberg, 2003).

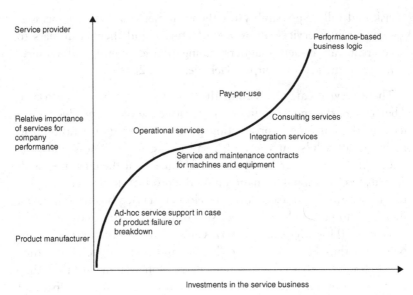

Figure 1.1: Moving from being a product manufacturer to a service provider

Moving from being a product manufacturer to a service provider requires more than investments in the service business to change the business logic, as illustrated in Figure 1.1. A product manufacturer offering a few services might either integrate services into the price of the product or charge the customers for the service support as and when needed, e.g. product-related services such as spare parts and field services. In such a situation, the value contribution of services is relatively low. Moving towards the role of service provider can help convince customers to pay a fixed price for the service desired: the customer is thereby provided with an annual service contract that covers all of the service costs associated with maintaining the product (Cohen *et al.*, 2006).

A further step in developing the business logic towards being a service provider is paying only for the performance of the product. ABB, a specialist in industrial automation, for example, offers its customers traditional product-related services such as spare parts, field services and maintenance services but also an 'Automation Performance Management Service'. ABB guarantees specific performance levels of the industrial automation equipment it provides. Performance levels are determined by the reliability of the industrial automation equipment and the service excellence achieved in the provision of spare parts, field services and maintenance. Customer payments depend on whether ABB meets the performance goals or not. Alternatively, the business logic could involve paying only for services used by the customer. In the aircraft industry, for example, Rolls-Royce and General Electric sell 'power-by-the-hour'. Customers pay a fixed tariff for the hours that the air engines actually run. This covers all of the costs involved, including the air engine, installation and after-sales services (e.g. repair, maintenance, modernisations and spare parts) (Glueck *et al.*, 2007).

Whereas Figure 1.1 illustrates the general movement from being a product manufacturer to a service provider, Exhibit 1.1 illustrates Ericsson Operating Systems as an example of this movement.

Exhibit 1.1: Ericsson's movement towards providing services

Despite fundamental changes in the world of telecommunication, Ericsson Operating Systems has been one of the most successful businesses in the branch in the last decade. At the level of the business model, an emerging digital value network is replacing the traditional value chain. Whilst technologies such as broadband, multimedia and wideband allow new services and solutions to be introduced, they also raise the questions of reducing costs, using service to ensure quality worldwide, making profits, being the first to create revenue as well as building new skills in order to be successful. To cope with such potential questions, Ericsson set up a Global Services Division in 1999. Its creation was a major step that the top management called 'the evolution of services at Ericsson'. The evolution of services began by selling products and giving away services, and culminated with the total solution being sold as a service. Accordingly, business logic implies payment being made either for the actual performance or pay-per-use. Bearing this vision of the evolution of services in mind, the top management triggered Ericsson's transition from being a product manufacturer towards being a service provider. In 2010, Ericsson generated about 39 per cent of its revenue through the provision of services.

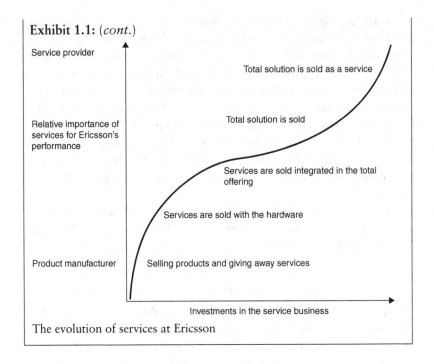

Exhibit 1.1: (*cont.*)

The evolution of services at Ericsson

1.1.2 Economical and strategical arguments for moving towards services

The rationale for service business development can be divided into *economical* and *strategical* arguments (Oliva and Kallenberg, 2003).

Economical arguments: these highlight the financial potential of services (Cohen *et al.*, 2006). The financial potential of services embraces three different aspects: (1) using service revenue as a performance indicator for moving toward services, (2) services are more profitable than products and (3) service business is less volatile than product business.

Using service revenue as a performance indicator for moving toward services

Services can yield an attractive share of revenue. One example is the report of the longitudinal development in the share of service revenue in the German machine and equipment industry (VDMA, 2008), in which the share of revenue generated by services increased, on average, from 13 per cent in 1991 to 27 per cent in 2007. Similar increases

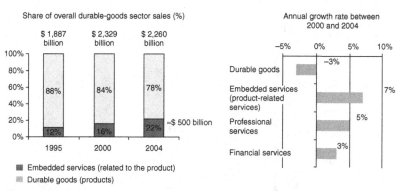

Figure 1.2: Service revenues

Source: Auguste *et al.* (2006, p. 43).

in the share of service revenue have been observed in the sales of durable goods (Auguste *et al.*, 2006). The data reported indicates that the share of revenue attributed to embedded services (product-related services) increased from 12 per cent in 1995 to 16 per cent in 2000: it was reported to have reached 22 per cent in 2004. The growth rate suggests that embedded services achieve the highest growth rates when compared to the sales of durable goods. They outperform other service business such as professional and financial services (Auguste *et al.*, 2006), both of which represent service categories that could also be offered by manufacturers of durable goods. Professional services correspond to business consulting and integration services (see Figure 1.2).

Whilst the above figures of 27 per cent and 22 per cent are averages, the share of revenue that can be attributed to the provision of services varies significantly from company to company. Figure 1.3 illustrates that although the majority of companies (38.7 per cent) generate less than 10 per cent of their total revenue through services, a few companies achieve more than 40 per cent of their total revenue this way (11.1 per cent). The share of revenue created by services has a positive relationship to the overall profitability of manufacturing companies. Homburg *et al.* (2000a) suggest similar numbers: 70.4 per cent of industrial marketing companies in their sample create up to 15 per cent of their total revenue through services and 11.3 per cent of the companies generate more than 40 per cent of their total revenue this way. Meiren (2006) argues that 66 per cent of companies create less than

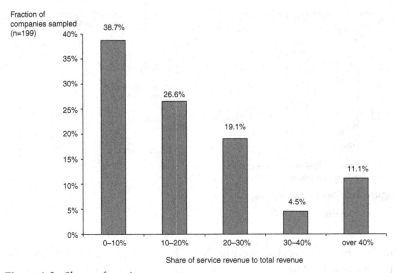

Figure 1.3: Share of service revenues
Source: Gebauer and Fleisch (2007); Ren and Gregory (2007).

20 per cent of their total revenue through services and only 9 per cent create more than 40 per cent of their revenues through services. It is important to note that the calculation of shares of service revenues can differ. For example, some studies integrate spare parts revenues into the service revenue, whereas other studies consider spare part revenue as product revenues.

Such attractive service revenues indicate that the service market is often considered as being greater in magnitude than the actual product market. Wise and Baumgartner (1999, p. 135) argue that 'in many industries today, the sale of a product accounts for only a small portion of overall revenues. Providing services to customers is where the real money is.' Similarly Jack Welch, the former CEO of General Electric, argued that 'the [service] market is bigger than we ever dreamt' (Mathieu, 2001a, p. 451). Consider, for example, the following three industries: locomotive, automobile and personal computers. The ratio between customer expenditure on the product and services throughout its life-cycle ranges from 1 to 5 and 1 to 20. It means that a customer who invests 1 million euros in a new locomotive will spend about 20 million euros on services. These include not only services necessary throughout the life cycle of the locomotive but also services related to railway infrastructures and administration (Wise and Baumgartner, 1999).

It is also important to note that the share of revenue generated by service can sometimes be misleading. The financial flow and mechanisms within a company affect service revenues. The financial flow is related to the legal structure of the company and its activities in different international markets. The financial flow for services goes directly to the company if a company serves markets through its own subsidiaries. Conversely, the financial flow for services is only partly returned to the company if the company serves markets mainly through distributors and independent dealers. The financial flow is influenced by the international markets in which the manufacturing companies are active. Manufacturing companies that increase exports to the emerging markets of China, India and South America will experience an automatic decrease in their share of service revenue. Services such as maintenance, repairs and installations are a mark-up for local labour costs. Although the products are sold for the same price worldwide, the price for providing service differs according to the local labour costs. Labour costs in the emerging markets are about one-tenth of those in the mature markets. Consequently, the service revenue generated in emerging markets is much lower than that in mature (i.e. developed) markets.

Service revenue is also dependent on the types of services offered; potential side effects of the various types of services have to be considered. Companies moving towards maintenance services experience a positive development of revenues that can be attributed to maintenance activities but might create less revenue through spare parts, repair and inspection services. In general, revenues from unscheduled and scheduled service activities seem to compensate each other to a certain degree.

Despite these few drawbacks, services can nevertheless yield an attractive share of the revenue generated by the capital goods industry.

Services are more profitable than products
Services offer higher margins than products (Oliva and Kallenberg, 2003). The average product margin in the German machine and equipment manufacturing industry was reported to be just 1 per cent

Table 1.2: *Comparison of margins in OEM and service businesses*

Industry	Margin in OEM business	Margin in services	Margin leverage (service/OEM business)
Paper machines	1–3 per cent	10–15 per cent	5
Power equipment	2–5 per cent	15–20 per cent	4
Metallurgy equipment	−3 to +6 per cent	15–20 per cent	4
Rail vehicles	3–6 per cent	8–10 per cent	2
Machine tools	1–12 per cent	5–15 per cent	2

Source: Ren and Gregory (2007).

(VDMA, 2004), whereas services such as repair, maintenance contracts and assembly, on the other hand, provide margins of more than 10 per cent. Ren and Gregory (2007) estimate the product and service margins achieved in five industries: paper machines, power equipment, metallurgy equipment, rail vehicles and machine tools. The results illustrate that the margin leverage, where margin leverage = margin in services/margin in OEM (original equipment manufacturer) business, ranges between two and five: the service margins are two to five times higher than those of products. The product and service margins achieved in these five industries are shown in Table 1.2.

Combining the higher service margin with the service revenues leads to the situation that the share of profit attributed to services is estimated as ranging from 40 to 90 per cent (Glueck *et al.*, 2007). It means, for example, that up to 90 per cent of the profits of companies providing equipment such as elevators and transportation comes from their service business.

Managers should be nonetheless be critical when faced with the argument that services are *always* more profitable than products. An interesting example here is IBM (see Exhibit 1.2). The gross margins for global technology services and global business services are lower than those for software and systems and technology. Whilst IBM is an example of service business within the IT sector, other industries also show evidence that the direct profitability created by services differs, depending on the types of services being offered. In the machine

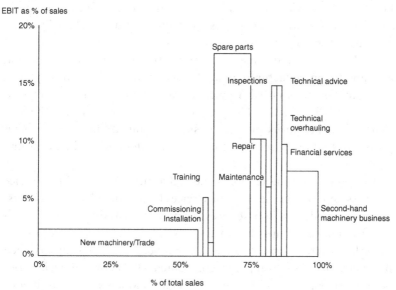

Figure 1.4: EBIT products and services
Source: Mercer (2003).

and equipment manufacturing industries, for example, the margins of providing spare parts are much greater than those of the product, whereas installations are often provided free of charge and create lower margins than the products (see Figure 1.4). In the case of spare parts, those that are manufactured by the company itself should be differentiated from those that are purchased (i.e. standard parts). The margins created by manufactured parts are three to five times higher than those of standard parts. This leads, in turn, to the emergence of the important side issue of 'making or buying' in the context of adding value. Companies that increasingly reduce the amount of added value will also lose essential margins and the corresponding profits in the spare parts business. The intensity of the competition in the case of labour-related services depends on how well the competencies used for delivering the services are imitated. Triggers for reducing the risks for imitating service competencies rely on the co-creation of services.

Services as a more stable source of revenue
Revenue from services offers not only more attractive margins but also a more stable source of income. Compared to the volatile product

business, the service business is often either counter-cyclical or more resistant to the economic cycles that influence investment. Product-related services in particular (i.e. maintenance contracts, etc.) represent a stable source of income for manufacturing companies. Wärtsilä, a renowned manufacturer of ship power systems and power plants, for example, experienced an increase in service sales of 16 per cent between 2009 and 2010. This increase was counter-cyclical to the pronounced decline in its product business (minus 29 per cent for ship power and minus 5 per cent for power plants) during the prevailing financial crises.

It is important to note, nonetheless, that the volatility of the service business depends on the types of services being offered. A typical illustration is modernisation services: customers investing in new products leading to an upswing in the new product business experience a marked decrease in the demand for modernising existing installed products. Vice versa, companies confronted with a downswing in product investments, where their customers are more restrictive in investing in new products, typically experience an increase in the demand for modernisation services. Services such as finance and designing customer solutions or installations follow the same investment cycles as products and should therefore be excluded from the argument that the service business is less volatile than the product business. Maintenance services are arguably less volatile once the product is sold: if the investment cycle is depressed then customers do not buy new products but still spend money on maintenance services that ensure the functionality of the products purchased previously.

Strategic argument: the strategic argument is twofold and involves (1) services that are used for differentiating the total offering and (2) service strategies that create sustainable competitive advantages (Mathieu, 2001b; Matthyssens and Vandenbempt, 1998).

Services used for differentiating the total offering

Services can be used for differentiating a total offering. Malleret (2006) argues that it becomes more difficult to compare the offerings of different suppliers when products and services are combined in customer-specific high-value solutions (Davies, 2004). It results in there being less direct competition on price, which improves profitability. The usage of services to create sustainable competitive advantages is related to the argument that services enable differentiation to be made in the total offering. Maintenance services, for example, are related to the total life cycle cost, which is increasingly becoming the major determining factor in purchasing decisions made by customers. Using the life cycle cost as the main decision criteria makes the offering completely transparent, leading to the situation where customers simply choose the provider with the lowest life cycle cost. A similar argument applies to operational services in terms of taking over the responsibility for customer processes. Operational services involve selling the performance of the customer process instead of product and service combinations (Windahl *et al.*, 2004). If customers of car painting equipment, for example, simply compare the price for one painted car and the number of cars painted using the equipment, they can easily choose the manufacturer with the most reasonable prices. It means that not all services can be taken into consideration: it would make comparing different total offerings more difficult, and could lead to less price competition and improved profitability. In order to understand this issue, research should explore the differentiation of service in the total offering from the perspective of the buying behaviour of the customer.

Service strategies creating sustainable competitive advantages
The intangibility of services means that they can generate competitive advantages that may be more sustainable (Simon, 1992). Competencies for providing services are created jointly between manufacturing firms and their customers; they serve as a barrier to the acquisition of resources and can be translated as being an entry barrier for competitors. This barrier means that the service competency of manufacturing firms makes it more difficult, both directly and indirectly, for competitors to catch up. In such a case, manufacturing firms possess a service competency position that is unique and difficult to duplicate, and leads to sustainable competitive advantages.

1.1.3 Service business development as a trigger for changing the logic of value creation

Closely related to the strategic argument that services create competitive advantages is the assumption that the development of service business can change the logic of 'value creation'. Value creation logic has been dominated by the 'value chain' concept, which implies that value creation takes place through adding value to supplier inputs at each stage of the value chain (Porter, 1985). Nowadays, there is a trend to break free from this value chain perspective and to consider, instead, the value-creating processes of the customer system. It means that the emphasis of the logic of value creation is shifting from the production to the user phase: from viewing products and services as output and seeing them as input; from one-time transactions to long-term relationships between supplier and customer (Normann, 2001). The co-creation of competencies means that service business development has also the potential of departing from the traditionally industrial logic of producing value (Ramírez, 1999).

An effective first step that could be taken is reconsidering the business logic from the former perspective of service business development: a strategy that is widely considered as being a potential route to success (Reinartz and Ulaga, 2008; Wise and Baumgartner, 1999). Focusing on service business development means achieving competitive advantages and generating new revenues and profits through concentrating on long-term relationships and constant interaction with customers over the product utilisation phase. This moves the focus of value creation downstream, towards the customer (Wise and Baumgartner, 1999).

A prominent success story is the strategic move taken by IBM towards services and a new value creation logic. Transforming IBM from a product company to one that co-creates solutions for customer problems is the result of IBM's strategic move towards services. The development of the service business was based on the radical shift in viewing strategy not as being about how to beat the competition in the first place but as understanding the needs of the customer and removing barriers in order to help them with solutions that add value to their products.

This transition towards services started in the early 1990s when IBM was facing one of its biggest crises as a company. Competitors, such as Sun Microsystems and Compaq, left IBM behind; investors doubted whether IBM had the ability to re-emerge as a major force in the computer industry. Faced with this situation, IBM came to the insight that the future of the computer industry was not in computers per se. In 1991, IBM was a $64.8 billion company of which less than $6 billion

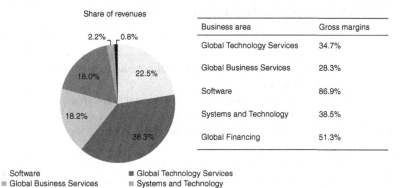

Figure 1.5: The development of revenues at IBM

came from non-maintenance services. Now, just ten short years later, the service business creates half of the revenue, with information technology services being the single largest source of revenue in the IBM portfolio (IBM, 2010). Even more dramatic is the shift in the source of income. In 2000, services accounted for 40 per cent of pre-tax income (approx. $4.5 billion) whereas hardware accounted for only 24 per cent (approx. $2.7 billion) and software for 25 per cent (approx. $2.8 billion). Financial activities are the source of the remaining 11 per cent (approx. $1.2 billion).

The transition started with old-fashioned, painstaking hard work and serious management commitment, as Table 1.3 illustrates. The serious commitment to the service business laid the foundation for growth, one customer at a time. Customer growth stems from one basic principle: a clear understanding of their needs. IBM formed the distinct and specialised service organisation ISSC (Integrated System Solution Corporation, which was the precursor to IBM Global Services) and the IBM Consulting Group in 1991. Further major milestones include:

- The development of a first comprehensive service strategy for the whole company in 1993.
- The formation of IBM Global Services by combing IBM service businesses with the IBM Consulting Group in 1996.
- The addition of hosted storage and storage management to the portfolio of services delivered via network in 2000.

Table 1.3: *Milestones in the development of IBM*

Year	
1991	Disciplined management and financial systems are built for the service business Experts in recruiting and training are brought into all areas: from IT consulting to systems architecture and web services
1992	IBM develops its first comprehensive company-wide service strategy IBM Japan Services Company is formed
1993	IBM Global Network is created, linking more than 20 separate IBM-managed networks worldwide
1994	15,000 new people are employed, mostly within sales and service sectors An incentive-based compensation system that pays greater rewards to star performers at all company levels is implemented New training programmes to increase skills and career development are implemented
1995	IBM's services businesses and the IBM Consulting Group combine to form IBM Global Services
1996	IBM Global Services hires 15,000 new employees. IBM Australia takes over Telstra's data centre, creating the largest data centre in the southern hemisphere
1997	IBM Global Services sign more than $30 billion in new business deals. Of 38 contracts worth $100 million or more, nearly half are from outside the United States IBM's service market leadership increases: the 126,000 employees who work in services can draw on all the technology and human assets of IBM, including an R&D community with a strong record of innovation (they have just marked their sixth straight year of US patent leadership)
1998	IBM's service advantages come from applying technology to solve problems. This requires the creation of new capabilities for customers in a quick and cost-effective manner
1999	IBM sells its data network infrastructure and connectivity operations (the IBM Global Network) to AT&T for $5 billion IBM extends its lead as the world's largest provider of IT services. Revenue grows by 11 per cent; customers are committed to more than $38 billion in new contracts; the backlog of engagements (work that will be done and invoiced this year as well as in the future) grows by 18 per cent to more than $60 billion

Table 1.3: *(cont.)*

Year

| 2000 | E-business service revenue increases by 60 per cent, to more than $3 billion. Add the factors to all the other services revenues that can be attributed to e-business, such as consulting, business intelligence and strategic outsourcing, and our e-business services revenue easily doubles
IBM Global Services adds hosted storage and storage management to its portfolio of services delivered via network. Revenue from e-business services grows by more than 70 per cent |
| 2001 | IBM services revenue surpasses IBM hardware revenue for the first time: global services (40.7 per cent), hardware (38.9 per cent), software (15.1 per cent), global financing (4.0 per cent), enterprise investments/other (1.3 per cent) |

Source: IBM (2001, p. 24).

Exhibit 1.2: The moves made by IBM towards improved service and new value creation logic

Revenues from IBM services surpassed those from IBM hardware in 2001 for the first time; since then IBM has invested intensively in software businesses. In 2010, software created around 23 per cent of their total revenue and services around 56.5 per cent. Services are divided into two parts: Global Technology Services and Global Business Services. The former accounted for 38.3 per cent and the latter for 18.2 per cent. Systems & Technology created about 18.0 per cent and the remaining revenue share of 0.8 per cent is attributed to global financing and other business activities (see figure below and Figure 1.5). It is interesting to note that IBM's service business (Global Business Services and Global Technology Services) departs from the argumentation that services are more profitable than products: examination of the gross margins suggests that Systems & Technology and Software outperform Global Business Services and Global Technology Services.

With respect to IBM's pre-tax income in 2010, hardware accounted for only 8 per cent ($1.6 billion) and financing for 9 per cent ($2.0 billion). Most of the income was generated by software (44 per cent, i.e. approx. $9.1 billion) and services (39 per cent, i.e. approx. $8.1 billion).

Exhibit 1.2: (*cont.*)

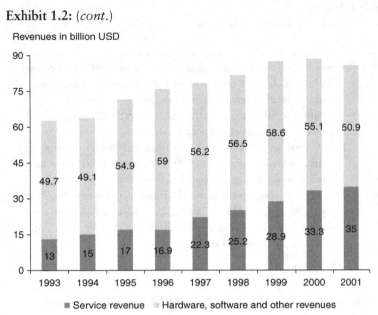

Revenues in billion USD

IBM – revenue shares and gross margins in 2010
Note: Total revenue of 99.8 billion USD. IBM (2010).

The underlying rationale of these various steps lies in establishing a strategic leadership framework. This defines the strategy process clearly in terms of assigning the company's general managers the task of constantly identifying (1) performance gaps between the results expected and those achieved, and (2) opportunity gaps between current business results (e.g. revenue growth per customer in existing markets) and those achievable with a new business design (e.g. by providing solutions to generate new revenues and thereby profits). This strategy process guarantees the constant orientation of IBM towards identifying new opportunities for bringing value to customers and for delivering that value at a profit (Harreld *et al.*, 2007). For IBM, the transformation from making and selling products to selling a capability such as services (Gerstner, 2002) meant adding new capabilities to its existing competencies in technology and quality to improve service to customers, to reintegrate the organisation around the needs of the customer by bringing together experts to solve problems and, most importantly of all, to shift its strategy approach radically. The latter included designing a process of strategic insight to identify opportunities systematically and a process of strategic execution that involves the alignment of people, structure, culture and processes to seize opportunities (Harreld *et al.*, 2007).

1.2 Challenges of service business development

Exhibit 1.2, showing the moves made by IBM towards improved service, offers two insights. Firstly, companies should not wait until a fundamental crisis is reached before moving into the service business and, secondly, that developing service business is a complex strategic task that requires strong commitment and great investments. Whilst it is not difficult to achieve solid commitment when the future of the company is jeopardised, it is much easier to deploy significant sums for investment when sufficient financial resources are available.

Service business development, as suggested in Exhibit 1.2, involves major investments in reconfiguration on multiple organisational levels. Despite the economic and strategic benefits already demonstrated associated with developing service business, companies are often confronted with the empirical phenomenon of the 'service paradox' (see Figure 1.6). This paradox suggests that companies need to invest substantially in extending the service business, but that these investments do not generate the higher returns expected (Gebauer *et al.*, 2005; Neely, 2008). The service paradox is caused by the 'service jungle', or 'servitisation failures', whereby companies increasingly offer services without having the necessary portfolio management responsible for developing, promoting, selling and providing them (Belz *et al.*, 1997). Service business development business can lead to a conflict with the product business, which, in turn, could reduce the company's overall performance (Brax, 2005). Ulaga and Reinartz (2011) refer to a study conducted by Bain & Company. According to this study, only 21 per cent of companies have real success with their services strategy (Baveja *et al.*, 2004).

The service paradox suggests that instead of moving along the continuum from being product manufacturers towards being service providers, companies fail to stay on the transition track. They are unsuccessful in their service efforts and are confronted with the situation in which the high investment in extending service business leads

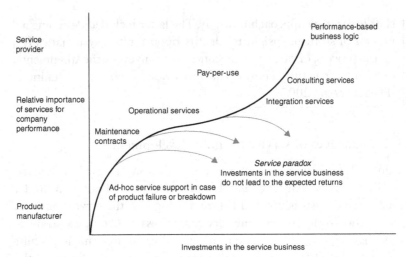

Figure 1.6: The service paradox

to increased service offering and higher costs but does not generate the corresponding higher returns expected.

The service paradox can be attributed to the following major challenges that are faced in service business development:

1. Developing the dynamic capabilities required for initiating and maintaining the service business development.
2. Implementing the changes in service strategy necessary during the development of the service business.
3. Aligning the service strategies and organisational variables (operational capabilities).
4. Considering international aspects with respect to organisational variables (operational capabilities).
5. Applying a network perspective to services.

These challenges are not caused through failures in implementing existing theories but rather have their origin in theoretical deficits. These theoretical deficits are especially important when it comes to small- and medium-sized enterprises moving towards services and for manufacturing companies positioned as suppliers rather than as machine and equipment manufacturers. Research appears to neglect how the size and value chain positions of companies such as suppliers may affect their service business development. The service paradox can therefore also be attributed to additional challenges, namely:

6. Developing the service business from the perspective of the supplier.
7. Developing the service business from the perspective of small- and medium-sized machine and equipment manufacturers.

(1) Dynamic capabilities necessary for service business development

Developing a service business extends the existing set of capabilities for designing, manufacturing and selling capital goods (Baines *et al.*, 2009; Davies *et al.*, 2007). The extension and reconfiguration of existing operational capabilities require dynamic capabilities. It is these dynamic capabilities that enable companies to change existing operational routines and individual skills for developing the service business (Fischer *et al.*, 2010). Dynamic capabilities are a concrete set of mechanisms that allow managers to sense opportunities and threats from changes in the competitive environment, including potential shifts in technology, competition, customers and regulations continually, and to seize these changes through dynamic organisational realignment by reconfiguring existing competencies or learning new skills (Teece, 2007).

Dynamic capabilities are close to Chandler's (1990) notion of strategic capabilities. Strategic capabilities describe the competition for developing and penetrating both existing and new markets. Strategic (i.e. dynamic) capabilities enable companies to move into growing markets more quickly, and withdraw from declining ones more effectively, than competitors. Such capabilities refer to the effective monitoring of external markets and internal operations, adjusting strategies to suit the changing technological and market environments (Davies and Brady, 2000).

Exhibit 1.3: IBM's and General Electric's dynamic capabilities for service business development

The IBM example above illustrates the relevance of dynamic capabilities for service business development. The newly-designed strategy framework for its transformation towards services, along with the insight gained of strategic processes and execution, reflect the two fundamental dynamic capabilities of sensing and seizing of opportunities and threats. This framework, based on the constant analysis of performance and gaps in opportunity, ensures that IBM's business is orientated towards exploiting existing operational

Exhibit 1.3: (*cont.*)

capabilities and processes to succeed in established businesses and identifying and capturing value opportunities to explore new businesses (Harreld *et al.*, 2007). Involving 25,000 executives in the strategy process of helping to sense and seize opportunities in 140 geographical locations with constantly changing competitors and technologies has helped the elephant to dance (Gerstner, 2002).

The development of the radically new service-orientated business model at General Electric for its aviation business illustrates further the importance of dynamic capabilities in transforming the service business in practice. Upon launch of the new, more efficient and powerful GE90 aircraft engine in the mid 1990s, General Electric first intended to establish a price premium based on established business models: the high degree of uncertainty pertaining to maintenance costs, however, created a major obstacle in doing so. Consequently, General Electric used the opportunity to transform the product-orientated business model into one that was service orientated by offering customers 'power-by-the-hour', i.e. billing customers a fixed charge per hour flown, which included all maintenance costs. This led to a better cost position through improved cost and budget planning (Cohen *et al.*, 2006; Michel *et al.*, 2008). In order to transform the business model, General Electric required multiple dynamic capabilities to sense and seize the opportunities and navigate threats associated with the new business model; to create the operational capabilities required, such as expertise for more sophisticated billing and risk assessment models; to restructure internal organisational arrangements and, finally, to develop new cooperative structures with financial institutions.

Despite popular success stories, such as those illustrated in Exhibit 1.3, establishing dynamic capabilities for developing service business is far from easy. Capital goods manufacturers still have narrow search horizons in terms of scanning, searching and exploring service opportunities. They seem to have become prisoners of the deeply ingrained belief that service business development emphasises the provision of basic services alone.

At the industry level, this 'straightjacket' is evident in the composition of service revenue. The share of service revenue is mostly composed of four basic types of service, namely spare parts, inspection and repair, maintenance and training (VDMA, 2008). Few companies create significant revenues with more advanced services. But if other services do not create any revenue, the question is how companies can continue successfully with the development of their service business into the high-value solutions by employing system integration, operational services or business consulting (Davies, 2004).

At the individual company level, the examples of Comau, ThyssenKrupp and Dürr shown in Exhibit 1.4 indicate the difficulties companies face with the dynamic capabilities required for service business development. Comau failed to seize the structures, processes and incentives necessary for its service business model. ThyssenKrupp Services struggled to enhance and reconfigure the service business for a better integration with the other business units. Dürr ran into great difficulties when attempting to offer outsourcing services (by taking over the customer's painting and assembly process) and to reconfigure its business model.

Exhibit 1.4: The challenges of dynamic capabilities

The business model used by the Comau Group for supporting customers from product engineering via production systems to maintenance services led to an increase in the share of service revenue from 16 to 23 per cent between 2004 and 2010. The decline in corporate revenue of about 40 per cent (from 1.716 to 1.023 million euros) in the same period, however, indicates that the structures, processes and incentives utilised by Comau for designing its business model are not uncontroversial.

Comau – corporate revenue and share of service revenue

	2004	2007	2010
Total revenue (in million euro)	1.716	1.090	1.023
Share of service revenue	16 per cent	19 per cent	23 per cent

ThyssenKrupp moved into the service business by establishing ThyssenKrupp Services as a separate business division, of which ThyssenKrupp Industrial Services forms a part. Despite being highly profitable and financially successful (see table below), ThyssenKrupp Services decided to sell its industrial service business

Exhibit 1.4: (*cont.*)

because it failed to enhance and reconfigure the service business for better integration with the other business units. ThyssenKrupp Industrial Services, which posts annual sales of about 1.7 billion euros, is highly profitable but was considered to be by far the smallest unit in the segment and has the smallest synergies with the core business: it was sold to Wisag in 2009.

ThyssenKrupp – revenues and earnings (in million euro)

Business segments		2005/ 2006	2006/ 2007	2007/ 2008	2008/ 2009
Steel	Revenue	10.747	13.209	14.358	9.945
	Earnings before taxes	1.417	1.662	1.540	−486
Stainless	Revenue	6.437	8.748	7.420	4.486
	Earnings before taxes	423	777	126	−946
Technologies	Revenue	14.057	11.523	12.412	10.64
	Earnings before taxes	183	544	741	−868
Elevator	Revenue	4.298	4.712	4.930	5.308
	Earnings before taxes	391	− 113	741	558
Services	*Revenue*	*14.204*	*16.711*	*17.336*	*11.896*
	Earnings before taxes	*482*	*704*	*750*	*−271*

Dürr, a manufacturer of paint and assembly systems for the automotive industry, tried to adopt a service strategy based on outsourcing services but met great difficulties when attempting to do so. Such outsourcing services would enable Dürr to take over the customer's painting and assembly processes, and to reconfigure its business model. The changes faced were just too challenging; they finally led to the decision being taken of selling the service unit to Voith Industrial Services.

In spite of having a strong foundation in strategic management literature, dynamic capabilities have not been applied directly to service business development in manufacturing companies. More specifically, existing research neglects the following three capabilities (Teece, 2007):

- sensing service opportunities and threats;
- seizing the service opportunities sensed;
- reconfiguration by maintaining service competitiveness through enhancing, combining and protecting operational capabilities.

(2) Changes in strategy necessary for service business development
The dynamic capabilities of sensing, seizing and reconfiguring lay the foundation for initiating the change in strategy that is aimed at developing service business. Service business development does not follow a single service strategy: it requires changes being made to various service strategies (see Exhibit 1.5). Succeeding with changes in service strategy enhances the contribution services make to value. However, the potential for changing the strategy to extend the value contribution of services currently lacks guidance. In most cases, it is not clear which change in strategy might prove to be successful: under such circumstances, the enhancements that could be created in the value contribution of the services might be jeopardised.

Exhibit 1.5: Examples of strategic changes made in service business development

Burckhardt Compression changed from augmenting the product offering through customer service to offering services such as spare parts, maintenance and repairs for its installed base of compressors. This medium-sized company has manufactured compressors for the last three decades; the value contribution of services, until the mid 1990s, was limited to a share of the revenue of services and a profit of less than 10 per cent. Today, services generate about 23 per cent of corporate revenue and account for 32 per cent of corporate profit (Burckhardt Compression, 2009).

IBM implemented several changes in its service strategy, which led to business consulting offered by IBM Global Services. It is interesting to note that, according to its own income statement, the fraction of pre-tax income IBM attributed to services dropped from 41 per cent to 37 per cent between 2003 and 2007 in spite of the changes made in service strategies.

Exhibit 1.5: (*cont.*)

General Electric also followed a clear pattern of strategy changes to service, initiated in the early 1980s, as one of the main strategic initiatives taken under the leadership of Jack Welch. The changes included: acquiring financial service companies, exploring new service-based growth opportunities, supplementing products with services to reduce dependence on traditional industrial products and benefiting from the unique worldwide installed base. It resulted in services accounting for two-thirds of General Electric's total revenues at the end of the 1990s (Bartlett and Wozny, 1999). Further change made in recent years towards the use of its service-orientated business model (based on selling actual usage time of jet engines) ultimately led to a 50 per cent growth in revenue between 2004 and 2007.

Companies either struggle or fail to change their service strategy, thereby demonstrating important gaps in knowledge (Fischer *et al.*, 2010). Researchers focus on the static term of service strategy (e.g. Davies, 2004; Mathieu, 2001a), but there seems to be a steady change in the strategic role of services (Bowen *et al.*, 1989; Neu and Brown, 2008). Early literature on the strategic aspects of services in manufacturing companies considers services to be part of business strategy (Bowen, 1990; Kellogg and Nie, 1995). Services are typically considered as being part of a differentiation strategy rather than cost leaders.

Later literature begins to specify different types of service strategies. Davies (2004), for example, describes three service strategies (systems integration, operational services and business consulting) whereas Gebauer (2008) classifies service strategies into after-sales service providers, customer support service providers, outsourcing partners and development partners. These service strategies are tendered through various types of service offerings. They are, nevertheless, merely explored at a specific time and neglect development over time, hence they do not capture changes from one service strategy to another. It remains unclear how companies change their service strategy in practice, e.g. from system integration to business consulting, or from operational services to system integration. Companies are therefore challenged when faced with the question of the direction in which their service business should be steered.

(3) Alignment of service strategies and operational capabilities
Developing service business not only requires the strategic knowledge of direction ('where to go'), i.e. a plan or pattern with clear strategic paths, but also the capabilities for earning a living when using each service strategy. These capabilities reflect the concept companies have of operational capabilities in the running of their service business. General Electric's service initiative, for example, laid equal importance on extending the provision of service to its customers and on developing internal service-related attitudes when it changed from selling products to helping customers become more productive. The mindset of the employee was thus considered an essential part of the corporate culture when General Electric decided to extend its service business (Bartlett and Wozny, 1999).

As Exhibit 1.2 pertaining to the transition made by IBM towards services suggests, further typical operational capabilities mandatory to running service businesses include corporate culture, human resources, organisational structures, IT skills and service development processes. Companies should not only increase the service orientation in their operational capabilities but also, and more importantly, align their service strategy with organisational variables inherent in their operational capabilities (Neu and Brown, 2005). Organisational variables describe the characteristics of operational capabilities, which enable a company to earn a living through the provision of services: the service orientation of human resource management is an example of an operational capability to create service revenues and profits. The service orientation of human resource management can be enhanced through the addition of organisational variables such as recruitment, training and development of personnel as well as compensation and assessment.

Reconfiguring operational capabilities involves more than simply increasing the size of the service orientation. Reconfiguration aims at achieving an alignment between the service strategy and the organisational characteristics of operational capabilities. Without an alignment, companies risk a mismatch occurring between their service strategy and organisational arrangements (see Exhibit 1.6). Since alignment results from skill rather than luck, it is reasonable to regard it as being a strategic capability in generating economic rents (Powell, 1992). This strategic capability is closely coupled with the dynamic capabilities of 'seizing' and 'reconfiguring'. Accordingly, companies have to find a way of coalescing service strategy with organisational variables in such a way that they are internally consistent, complementary and mutually reinforcing.

Exhibit 1.6: Challenges of achieving strategic fit in service business development

The idea behind setting up a separate business unit for services is to create the momentum required for the service business to grow. Separating products from service business is seen as a trigger for increasing orientation towards service in organisational structures. The experience Siemens had with its former division Siemens Business Services (SBS) illustrates the difficulties of implementing organisational factors (e.g. separating SBS from other business units) to fit in with service strategy. SBS remained unprofitable, despite achieving an attractive growth in service revenue. The service revenues of SBS as a separate business unit were 5.4 billion euros whilst losses added up to 690 million euros in 2005 (Siemens, 2006).

Xerox struggled with the challenge of aligning the management of its human resources with its strategy. Early on in the development of its solutions business, Xerox tried to adapt human resources by hiring a team of external consultants to convert existing business to solutions sales overnight. This effort was doomed to fail: the mindset and skills required for the solutions business were just too different (Cornet *et al.*, 2000).

Heidelberg started to offer customers remote monitoring of their printing presses to reduce expensive machine downtime: it was unsuccessful initially, despite pricing the service significantly below the amount a single breakdown would cost. Heidelberg found it difficult to recognise the fact that adopting a strategy of offering complex customer-orientated services required modifying the sales force that, in turn, had to align with the strategy because decisions were then being made higher up in the customer's hierarchy. The problem was that although Heidelberg's sales force and field technicians were well equipped to promote standard service contracts to people in procurement and in charge of in-house maintenance, they felt uncomfortable meeting the customer's production managers and found themselves incapable of explaining the more complex remote monitoring services to them (Reinartz and Ulaga, 2008).

In research pertaining to service, 'very little is known about the organisational elements managers should consider and how they should be designed to enhance performance' (Neu and Brown, 2008, p. 234). The frequency of changes in the organisational structures necessary for service business development (Matthyssens and Vandenbempt, 1998; Neu and Brown, 2005; Oliva and Kallenberg, 2003) indicates an absence of rigorous descriptions of how distinct service strategies are interrelated with operational capabilities. It remains unclear which modifications are necessary, for example, if companies adopt a service strategy for system integration, an operational service strategy or a strategy focusing on business consulting (Davies, 2004). The typical modifications suggested in the literature, such as separating the service and product organisations, that increase service orientation in corporate culture or implement service development processes (Gebauer *et al.*, 2005; Oliva and Kallenberg, 2003) are not linked to distinct service strategies.

(4) Service strategies and capabilities from a network perspective
Manufacturers of capital goods may not be able to master internally all the activities and capabilities relevant to value creation when moving from products to solutions (combinations of products and services), as this rarely makes economical sense. Consequently, they increasingly resort to complex business networks that are currently replacing traditional, vertically-integrated relationships between suppliers and customers.

The literature, however, concentrates on the efforts made by single firms in moving from products to solutions. The transition from products to services described by Oliva and Kallenberg (2003), for instance, is derived from individual companies moving along the following stages: (1) consolidating services, (2) entering the installed base service market, (3) expanding to relationship-based and process-centred services, (4) taking over the operation of the end-user. Similarly, the shift illustrated by Neu and Brown (2005) from offering services as add-ons to products to the exact opposite, i.e. offering products as add-ons to services, relies on the individual efforts of four companies in the IT branch. The investigation of manufacturing companies moving to integrated systems, integrated solutions and further onto operational services carried out by Davies (2004) also concentrates on the efforts of single firms.

Companies should follow a business network approach because they rely on other companies to contribute to the products and service components forming the solution (Davies *et al.*, 2007). Companies identify, select and manage other network actors across different supply chains who then contribute to the solutions (Johnson and Mena, 2008; Pawar *et al.*, 2009). Yet existing studies have neither conceptualised nor analysed in depth the characteristics of business networks in this context. It remains unclear, from an empirical and a theoretical perspective, what types of business networks contribute to the provision of solutions and how companies can form and utilise business networks.

(5) International aspects of service strategies
and operational capabilities
Capital goods manufacturers sell their products worldwide and to a variety of markets. Performance measures from selling products worldwide cover the levels of the industry and the individual company. At the level of industry, other countries in the EU and North America are the traditional export markets of the European capital-goods industry. The Asian market, however, has been booming over the last few years. The German machine and equipment manufacturing industry, for example, already exports 28 per cent of its products to Asia, with China being the main destination. The same applies to manufacturing industries in other European countries such as France, Italy, Sweden and Switzerland.

An example at the level of the individual company is Wärtsilä, a Finnish company that creates about 38.5 per cent of its revenues in Asia; Europe and the Americas account for 27.8 per cent and 22.7 per cent, respectively. Service business has to be located close to the actual customer: global presence and availability are therefore two of the most important criteria for service support. Wärtsilä Services builds up its presence, competencies and logistics where the customers have their needs. Wärtsilä set up service organisations in 70 countries around the world comprising service locations and a total of 11,000 service employees (including 7,500 field service technicians) in order to be able to offer customers around-the-clock support in the fields of logistics, technical support and field service from a single source (Wärtsilä, 2010).

Under such circumstances, international aspects of service business development become critical success factors. The literature is relatively silent regarding recommendations for setting up a global service infra-structure: various approaches for managing global organisations (polycentric, ethnocentric and geocentric) are described but are rarely applied to global service organisations. Closely related to the manage-ment of global service organisations are open questions as to whether companies should use an export approach for the provision of services or enter international service markets indirectly or directly.

- A direct export of services basically takes place when the service resources are located in the domestic market and, when needed, the resources for repairing and/or maintaining the product are moved abroad to the client.
- An indirect market entry occurs when a company does not want to establish a local service centre that they own, either totally or in part, but nevertheless needs to ensure they are represented in the foreign market. 'Service licensing agreement' is a concept often used for indirect entry into a foreign market.
- A direct market entry is when the service firm establishes an organisa-tion that produces its own services in the foreign market in question. A sales organisation can comprise the first stage in such an organisation; a local service centre can be established later on (Grönroos, 1999).

The literature neglects to examine how service organisations should function in various global markets despite the fact that international-isation influences services in many ways. Recommendations for service business development in Asian and Chinese markets in particular are very rare.

(6) Service business development from the
perspective of the supplier
Previous research has mainly focused on understanding the extension of the service business of OEMs: the integrated solutions of Davies (2004), the transition line of Oliva and Kallenberg (2003), the inves-tigation by Sandberg and Werr (2003) on corporate consulting for customer solutions, the exploration by Johnstone *et al.* (2008) of product-service systems as well as the description given by Matthyssens and Vandenbempt (2008) of the movement from basic offerings to value-added solutions are all based on companies such as Alstom, Ericsson, Thales, Atkins, C&W, Heidelberger Printing Machines, Swiss Industrial Group, ABB, AT&T, IBM and Porsche.

These companies all enjoy advantages as they develop their service businesses. OEMs typically offer products with a long life cycle throughout which services can be offered. The entire market for services tends to revolve around two to five orders of magnitude greater than annual sales of capital goods (Wise and Baumgartner, 1999). OEMs have direct access to their own installed base and are in a superior market position for offering services. Nonetheless, little is known about how traditional *suppliers* develop their service business. The Canadian automotive supplier, Magna, and the Swedish supplier, SKF, are examples of suppliers that have been successful in moving towards services (see Exhibits 1.7 and 1.8).

Exhibit 1.7: Magna's movement towards services

Magna is an automotive supplier that supports vehicle manufacturers from the design stage right through to the stage where they are ready for serial production. The Magna tooling and engineering unit offers customers the opportunity of outsourcing certain development tasks. Despite an increase in the quality requirements of vehicle manufacturing companies such as BMW, Chrysler and Peugeot these tooling and engineering services have succeeded in making the product creation process more efficient. Magna targets automobile manufacturers with a broad range of development services for vehicle assembly/equipment, engine installation, design and electrics/electronics. Together with its customers, Magna acquires knowledge of optimising the development of vehicles with a view to their subsequent serial production.

Serial production refers to yet another service business. Magna offers the complete assembly of vehicles whereby Magna actually assemblies complete cars for its customers. Although still heavily reliant on selling components and systems (external production), both the complete vehicle assembly and tooling and engineering services represent important parts of Magna's revenues. The strategic aspects of creating partnerships with customers and co-creating competencies through their tooling and engineering and vehicle assembly services are more important than the purely financial contribution made by the services. These competencies generate resource positions that are hard for competitors to imitate: it becomes difficult for other automotive suppliers to enter into a relationship with the customer.

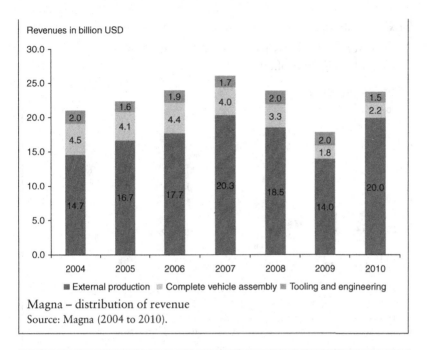

Magna – distribution of revenue
Source: Magna (2004 to 2010).

Exhibit 1.8: SKF's movement towards services (SKF 2004 to 2010)

SKF is a global supplier of products, solutions and services in the fields of ball bearings, seals, mechatronics, services and lubrication systems. SKF does business mainly through three divisions: *Industrial Division, Automotive Division* and *Service Division*. The *Industrial* and *Service Divisions* provide services to OEMs and aftermarket customers, respectively. The *Automotive Division* services automotive OEMs and aftermarket customers and the *Service Division* functions as a separate strategic business unit, offering various types of services such as:

- engineering consultancy;
- logistics;
- asset management;
- condition monitoring;
- mechanical maintenance;
- remanufacturing: industrial bearings, railway bearings units, machine tool spindles and aerospace including AKF (aerospace airlines aero-engine service);
- training (SKF Reliability Maintenance Institute).

Exhibit 1.8: (*cont.*)

The service business has become a major source of revenue at SKF and is highly profitable.

Billion Swedish Krona

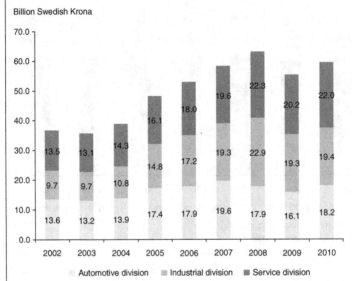

Automotive division   Industrial division   Service division

SKF – development of revenue

Operating margin

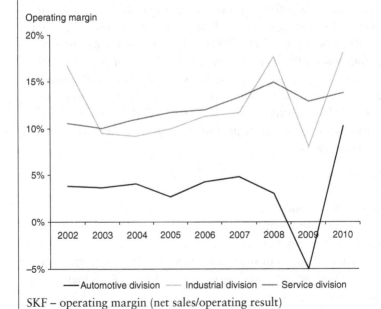

—— Automotive division ——— Industrial division ——— Service division

SKF – operating margin (net sales/operating result)

(7) Service business development from the perspective
of small- and medium-sized OEMs

Research neglects furthermore the ways in which the size of a firm may affect its service business development. Oliva and Kallenberg (2003) argue that companies have to enter the service market by way of serving their installed base. This finding cannot be easily transferred to small- and medium-sized OEMs since they offer and sell through distributors, deliver through installers and therefore have limited access to their installed base.

In order to provide services, small- and medium-sized OEMs are required to reconsider their sales channels, motivate distributors to offer services and arrange paybacks from customers to distributors and from distributors to the small- and medium-sized OEMs. Payback arrangements seem to be critical for service growth and profitability, as well as adding complexity to the belief that manufacturing companies should move from offering services for 'free' to charging for them (Gebauer *et al.*, 2005; Malleret, 2006; Oliva and Kallenberg, 2003; Reinartz and Ulaga, 2008). It is only natural that small- and medium-sized OEMs experience difficulties when moving downstream in the value chain since then they threaten their own customers, distributors and installers by becoming potential competitors. Another obstacle is the need to set up a separate service organisation with a specific responsibility for creating revenue (Oliva and Kallenberg, 2003). Small- and medium-sized OEMs might not reach the critical mass required by the service business to be profitable. In addition, a separate service organisation adds complexity to the structures of SMEs, creating high coordination costs and limiting flexibility. Thus, setting up separate service units can lead to investments that do not generate corresponding returns.

1.3 Central questions

Service business development seems to be a rational response that capital goods manufacturing companies can take in order to meet the current trends that demand a shift in the focus of value creation: from the production and one-off sales perspective to one that is long-term and establishes relationships with customers over the entire product utilisation phase. As outlined in Section 1.2 there is a lack of descriptions pertaining to (1) dynamic capabilities for initiating the service business

Table 1.4: *The questions addressed*

Business challenges	Deficits in theory	Questions
1. Companies do not have the dynamic capabilities required for service business development: scanning, searching and exploring service opportunities; formulating strategic responses and reconfiguring existing structures	The literature neglects the dynamic capabilities companies require to change operational routines when developing a service business. Moreover, existing research neglects to investigate sensing, seizing and reconfiguration capabilities in a service context	Which dynamic capabilities are necessary for service business development?
2. Managers have insufficient guidance for seeking potential patterns of change in service strategies in order to develop their service business	Service strategies are only explored at a specific time; they do not fully capture changes from one service strategy to another	Which patterns of change in service strategies can be identified?
3. Companies struggle to align their service strategy and organisational variables with their operational capabilities	Research rarely pays attention to exploring how a strategic fit may be achieved between service strategies and organisational variables	What are the appropriate alignments of service strategies and organisational variables for characterising operational capabilities?
4. It may not be possible for a company to master internally all the relevant activities required for moving from products to services which, moreover, rarely makes economic sense. Consequently, companies resort increasingly to complex business (service) networks	Business networks in the context of moving from products to service are rarely researched	What types of business networks for providing solutions are feasible? What kinds of dynamic and operational capabilities are required to form and utilise these networks?

5. Difficulties in shaping the organisational variables of operational capabilities to meet an international expansion of their service business are faced by companies	Service business development in the context of different international markets tends not to be considered by researchers	How should organisational variables (i.e. operational capabilities) be adapted for expansion into international markets?
6. Companies positioned as suppliers have difficulties in implementing the existing recommendations drawn from the experience of OEMs	Little attention is paid to the challenges of, and requirements for, service business development at the supplier level	How can suppliers develop their service business?
7. Small- and medium-sized OEMs have difficulties in implementing the existing recommendations drawn from the experience of multinational enterprises	Research remains relatively silent as to the requirements of small- and medium-sized OEMs in service business development	What do small- and medium-sized OEMs require specifically in order to develop their service businesses?

development, (2) changes in service strategy during the development of the service business, (3) alignment between service strategies and organisational variables (operational capabilities), (4) business networks supporting the service business, (5) international aspects of organisational variables (operational capabilities), (6) service business development from the supplier perspective and, finally, (7) from the perspective of small- and medium-sized OEMs. Accordingly, this book aims at improving understanding of the following principal question: how can capital goods manufacturers succeed in service business development?

The theoretical deficits and the challenges faced in business practice allow this main question to be divided into seven parts, as shown in Table 1.4. It is these seven sub-questions that will guide the reader through the forthcoming empirical section. Table 1.4 summarises the business challenges, the corresponding theoretical deficits and the central questions that must be addressed if the gaps are to be closed.

1.4 Methodology

The academic research undertaken has been based on multiple research methodologies, such as action research, focus groups, expert interviews, benchmarking projects and empirical surveys. Initially, conceptual frameworks were developed from the literature to guide the research process of each phenomenon under investigation. This ensured that the subsequent collection of data was based on a sound theoretical approach.

Altogether this book is based on data gathered from primary and secondary data sources, including around 30 case studies and various surveys carried out during the period 1997–2010. Primary sources included interviews and workshops. These were augmented by secondary sources, gained via office-based research, such as analyses of company documentation (e.g. annual reports, internet web pages and internal journals), related publications, presentations that provided complementary observations and archival data. Cases were selected mainly among Western European manufacturing companies in different industries: varying types of products and different company sizes and legal entities helped maximise the heterogeneity of the approaches used in service business development. The participating companies cover various capital goods manufacturing industries, such as machinery, equipment, measurement instruments and electronic devices with different product types. Legal entities may be strategic business units (SBU) or entire companies. Focusing on variety and diversity in these variables is especially important since the companies are subject to different environmental demands that may affect the way in which they approach the development of their service business.

The cases studied include multinational corporations (e.g. ABB, Bosch Packaging, Carl Zeiss, Ericsson Operating Systems, Heidelberger Printing Machines, Hilti, Philips Medical Systems, Rieter Textile and Voith) as well as a larger number of 'hidden champions' (e.g. GF AgieCharmilles, Bühler, Bystronic, Deutz, Dürr, Endress+Hauser, Feintool, Hunkeler, Kaeser, StarragHeckert and Zumtobel). This concept is applied to little-known companies that are world leaders in their respective fields. All these companies explore attractive growth opportunities and achieve sustainable competitive advantages. Additionally, some cases of companies based in North America were included to reach a broader and more international audience (e.g. Caterpillar, General Electric, IBM, Magna, Mettler-Toledo and Xerox).

1.5 Structure

This book is organised in the following manner. The introduction, Chapter 1, outlines the motivation for service business development and the challenges faced in business practice, the questions that are answered and the structure of the book. Chapter 2 describes the theoretical concepts of service business development and provides a summary of the relevant academic debate. Chapter 2 also provides promising theories that can be applied to study the phenomenon of service business development and the contribution it makes to value creation in manufacturing companies, i.e. by providing organisational capabilities, service strategies and, for operational capabilities, the strategic fit between service strategy and organisational variables.

Chapters 3–11 present the main findings of the empirical research undertaken. Chapter 3 focuses on the dynamic capabilities required for initiating the development of service business. The results presented in Chapter 3 suggest two different approaches for developing service business: exploitation and exploration. Chapters 4 and 5 portray the exploitation and exploration approach by means of a case study; Chapter 6 outlines the service strategies, changes in service strategy and operational capabilities underlying the exploitation approach. Chapter 7 continues the discussion of the exploitation approach, highlighting the configurations that consist of alignments between the service strategies discussed in Chapter 6 and the organisational variables of operational capabilities for achieving a strategic fit. Chapter 8 discusses service business development from a network perspective: it describes various network approaches supporting the service business development. Chapter 9 discusses service business development in an international context, and introduces two service strategies and organisational variables for operational capabilities in the context of international markets, with particular focus being placed on the booming Chinese market. The two chapters that follow outline the specifics of service business development and the organisational capabilities necessary for small and medium suppliers (Chapter 10) and for small and medium OEMs (Chapter 11).

Chapter 12 summarises the key aspects of the empirical chapters. It draws the different perspectives together and integrates them into a concluding overview for value creation through service business development in capital goods manufacturing companies. The chapter ends with a short discussion of research topics that are recommended for the future.

2 | Basic concepts of service business development

The following chapter summarises the existing literature pertaining to the development of service business in companies that manufacture capital goods. The goal here is to provide the necessary foundation for the chapters that follow. It starts by discussing the organisational capabilities and the complexity of the service business that limit the service business development. A description of service strategies suitable for manufacturing companies follows; the section ends with a description of the specific operational capabilities that must be aligned with the service strategy in order to achieve a strategic fit.

2.1 Organisational capabilities necessary for service business development

Research on organisational capabilities takes both static and a dynamic view of change. Capabilities are classified as being either operational (static) or dynamic. Service business development and the related value creation strategies require both operational and dynamic capabilities (Cepeda and Vera, 2007; Eisenhardt and Martin, 2000). A firm needs, on the one hand, operational capabilities to make a profit from the service business and, on the other hand, dynamic capabilities to change the operational capabilities and thereby develop the service business.

2.1.1 Complexity of the service business

A potential barrier for developing organisational capabilities (dynamic and operational) can arise from a misperception of the actual complexity of the service business. Managers often believe that they already manage the development, production and sales of highly complex machines and equipment successfully. The service business, in comparison, is perceived as being significantly less complex: it is argued as providing few obstacles and should be easy to establish and extend. Various parameters suggest nevertheless quite the opposite: the service business seems, in actual fact, to be more complex than the product business (see Table 2.1).

Comparing the nature of demand, for example, suggests that the product business has a favourable position. The demand for products, despite volatile investment cycles, is quite predictable and therefore easier to forecast than the service business. In more specific terms: the basic services associated with the installed base are highly unpredictable, resulting in their demand being very sporadic. It is difficult to predict product failures that lead to basic services. When it does occur, a service employee must react as quickly as possible to the customer request. This makes the management of the service resources very complex: managers have to concentrate on optimising the capacity utilisation of the service resources. This process is usually more complicated than managing product capacities.

More advanced services, such as maintenance services and business-consulting services, are more predictable than the basic services for the installed base. Managing these services could thus prove to be less complex. These kinds of advanced service, however, create the side effect of their becoming increasingly heterogeneous. Each of these services is highly customised, making it difficult to standardise the service elements and to control the cost of their delivery. Thus, in spite of having a great number of product variants, product management is confronted with a largely homogeneous product portfolio, whereas the service business requires the management of an increasingly heterogeneous portfolio.

Finally, regarding the knowledge required either to manufacture or serve products, managers have to understand that they in actual fact only manufacture the latest two or three versions of their product. In the service business, companies offer services for 10–15 generations of a product. This implies that the products to be served may be up to 25 years old and use outdated software, mechanical components and technologies. Service business therefore has to ensure that it retains the technical competencies for serving such old product generations (Cohen *et al.*, 2006).

The complexity of the service business means that, when it is being developed, a host of hurdles are met that must be surpassed. The first hurdles involve preparing the organisation for services, as well as overcoming resistance internally (within the company) and externally (from customers). These obstacles make it difficult for companies to succeed in their 'service journey' and to exploit the payoffs of the move into the service business (see Figure 2.1). Dynamic and operational

Table 2.1: *The complexity of product and service business*

Parameter	Product business	Service business
Nature of demand	More predictable: easier to forecast	Always unpredictable: sporadic
Required response	Standard: can be scheduled	As soon as possible
Portfolio	Largely homogeneous	Mostly heterogeneous
Number of product generations	Limited	10 to 15 times higher

Source: Adapted from Cohen *et al.* (2006).

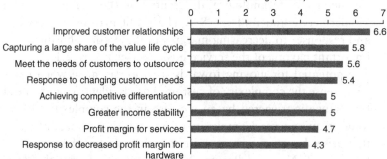

Figure 2.1: Challenges and payoffs in the service business
Source: Brown *et al.* (2009).

capabilities are key issues in dealing with the complexity of overcoming the payoffs and exploiting the benefits and payoffs of the service business.

2.1.2 Dynamic capabilities required for developing a service business

Dynamic capabilities can overcome the misperception of the complexity of the service business. They can be resolved into the elements of sensing, seizing and reconfiguring, as illustrated in Section 1.2.

Sensing the need for change towards service business development
Sensing and identifying the need for developing a service business are triggered by various factors. Section 1.1.1 outlined such triggers, which include external and internal issues, e.g. erosion of product profitability, complexity of customer needs and the installed base. These triggers can be interpreted as sensing a value opportunity and discovering service opportunities (Kindström *et al.*, 2009).

1. Managers can sense the erosion of product-based competitive advantages as being an opportunity to move towards services. The erosion of product-based competitive advantages squeezes the profitability of products (Matthyssens and Vandenbempt, 2008). It is becoming increasingly difficult to maintain technological superiority as a lasting strategy (Mathieu, 2001a). Services seem to be a potential competitive strategy that can compensate for the lack of technological differentiation (Bowen *et al.*, 1989; Vandermerwe and Rada, 1988). The profit margins of services, and responses to decreasing margins in the product business, are important payoffs of the service business (see Figure 2.1).
2. The potential for moving towards services can arise when managers sense the complexity of customer needs: identifying the need for change is triggered by an increase in the complexity of customer requirements. Complexity refers to the increasing difference that arises between customers in how they require their needs to be satisfied (Neu and Brown, 2005). Confronted with the pressure of creating more flexible companies, for example, customers apply narrower definitions to their core competencies, causing an increase in the need for outsourcing their service. Some customers

Table 2.2: *Ratio between a new order intake for products and the installed product base*

Product categories	New order intake for products/ installed product base
Civil aircraft	1/150
Tractors	1/30
Elevators	1/24
Locomotives	1/22
Automobiles	1/13

Source: Ren and Gregory (2007).

even wish to reduce the capital employed for buying capital goods: rather than owning the capital goods, they prefer to pay for using it. Under such conditions, customer demand is likely to focus on tailored service solutions, often combined with risk-sharing and performance agreements (Windahl *et al.*, 2004). Covering such increasingly complex customer needs are major determinants in improving the customer relationship: this achieved the highest rank in the payoffs in the study of service business shown in Figure 2.1. Using services to cover more complex needs of customers is also a direct response to their outsourcing needs and the change in the requirements they have of their suppliers.

3. Sensing the massive cumulative installed base of capital goods can be seen as being an attractive opportunity to yield additional service revenues. The installed base is reported to raise revenue substantially and yield attractive service revenue (Cohen *et al.*, 2006; Potts, 1988; Wise and Baumgartner, 1999). Ren and Gregory (2007) substantiate the opportunities associated with the high installed base by estimating the actual ratio between the sales of new products (or new order intake) and the installed base. This ratio indicates that, for example, companies in the civil aircraft business such as Airbus or Boeing have the opportunity of selling one new airplane whereas services can be offered to 150 airplanes already used by existing customers.

Table 2.2 illustrates other product categories, such as tractors and elevators, that possess a similar attraction in their ratio between a new order intake for products and the installed product base.

4. The high expenditure throughout the life cycle of a product makes sensing for service opportunities very attractive since the sale of a product only accounts for a small amount of the overall cost. Wise and Baumgartner (1999) give the example that the total expenditure throughout the life cycle of a locomotive is about 21 times higher than that of its purchase price. The product categories of personal computers and automotives achieve expenditures that are five times higher throughout their life cycle than their actual purchase price. Exploiting the greater value inherent in the life cycle of a product is therefore one of the highly ranked benefits of moving towards services (see Figure 2.1).

5. Services are a more stable source of revenue than products, so capital goods manufacturers sense the opportunity for compensating for the volatile product business through the more resistant and counter-cyclical revenue generated by services (Simon, 1993).

Although the five service opportunities above all appear to be quite plausible, sensing them does not happen automatically. The profit margins and stability of the incomes generated are major payoffs for services, as illustrated in Figure 2.1: understanding the economic potential of services, however, presents a major hurdle. Examining cognitive phenomena might be one way of enhancing the recognition of service opportunities (see Table 2.3).

- Managers overemphasise obvious and tangible characteristics (Kahneman *et al.*, 1982): they tend to sense the more obvious product opportunities rather than the less tangible and obvious service opportunities (Gebauer *et al.*, 2005).
- Managers may not believe in the economic potential of an extended service business because the existing cost structure of considering services as fixed, rather than variable, costs makes it difficult to estimate the profits created by services accurately (Mathieu, 2001a).
- The revenue created by one single service is not often sufficient to stimulate managers. They might simply argue that their daily business is selling equipment worth several million euros: it is quite difficult for them to feel excited about a maintenance contract worth a few thousand euros (Oliva and Kallenberg, 2003). Underestimation of the less tangible but obvious service opportunities, scepticism towards the economic potential involved and underestimation of the importance of single service revenues explain why internal resistance is still a major obstacle in moving towards services.

Table 2.3: *Cognitive phenomena limiting the rationale for developing service business*

Rationale for extending the service business	Cognitive phenomena	Difficulties in sensing the need for extending service business
Financial arguments Services are more profitable than products Potential revenue due to an attractive quantity of installed base	Overemphasis of tangible features in the business environment Disbelief in the economic potential Aversion for competing with existing customers	Preoccupation for sensing more obvious product opportunities Accurate estimation of the profit made by service (due to existing cost structures of considering services as fixed, and not variable, costs) Limitations caused by small total revenue for one single service Deliberate reallocation of resources to the product business to avoid risks inherent in providing services
Strategic arguments Comparing total offerings becomes more difficult Services have the potential of creating a resource-position barrier and thereby exclude competitors		

- Managers prefer investing resources in products, which has a less risky outcome than that of investing in services. A potential risk a company faces in developing a service business is that of becoming a competitor of their own customer. Resistance from customers is a major hurdle for moving towards services (see Figure 2.1). Customers might consider it to be a potential threat if suppliers start to demand that they take over (i.e. outsource) maintenance activities. Managers with a risk-averse behaviour would then deliberately reallocate resources from the service to the product business (Gebauer and Fleisch, 2007).

Managers should be aware of the cognitive phenomena that could limit the sensing of service opportunities vital to the development of their service business. Appropriate approaches for guiding sensing activities are downstream analysis and service need analysis, in combination with the life cycle analysis or evaluation of the service potential of the installed base.

Downstream analysis
Downstream analysis (Wise and Baumgartner, 1999) assists companies in assessing the attractiveness of moving downstream in their value chain. One evaluation criterion used helps a company establish just how attractive a move downstream in their business would be and balance it with the importance that providing such a service would have to the customer relationship. Other criteria include the ratio of the installed base to new product sales, estimates of the economic potential in the whole product life cycle in comparison to the actual product costs and differences in the margins of products and services. The assumption is that the higher the ratio, economic potential and differences between product and service margins, the more attractive the move into the service business. Criteria for assessing the importance of the customer relationship include the magnitude of the product-based differentiation and the share of the profit earned by the top 20 per cent (or top five) customers. It is assumed that a high magnitude of product-based differentiation, along with concentrating on few strategic customers, might make the move towards service less attractive (Wise and Baumgartner, 1999). The first assumption has, however, been jeopardised recently. The example of IBM in Exhibit 1.2 illustrates that companies need not delay moving into the service business because they still experience strong product differentiation. Moreover, using services for covering more complex customer needs might be an attractive opportunity, especially in a strategic partnership with few customers (see Figure 2.2).

   Managers can also utilise downstream analysis to evaluate their internal service performance: potential criteria are the amount of services charged separately, quality of the service and the proportion of the service revenue to the total revenue. Companies can assess the need for improving their service business depending on the levels of these criteria.

Life-cycle analysis based on estimating service needs
A life-cycle analysis substantiates the criteria used in downstream analysis: it estimates the economic potential in the entire life cycle of the product with respect to the actual costs of the product. As shown in Figure 2.3,

Attractiveness of going downstream in the value chain

Low   High

Criteria	Levels		
Ratio of installed base to new product sales	2:1	10:1	20:1
Economic potential in the whole product life cycle to the product costs	1:1	3:1	5:1
Difference between product and service margins	−10%	+/− 0	+10%

Importance of service to the customer

Low   High

Criteria	Levels		
Magnitude of product-based differentiation	High	Medium	Low
Market share of top five customers	10%	30%	50%
Share of total profit earned from top 20% of customers	−10%	+/− 0	+10%

Importance of improving the service business

Low   High

Criteria	Levels		
Share of services charged separately	High	Medium	Low
Service quality	Outperforming customer expectation and competitors	Matching customer expectation and competitors	Underperforming customer expectation and competitors
Proportion of service revenue to total revenue	>25%	10–25%	<10%

Figure 2.2: Downstream analysis
Source: Adapted from Wise and Baumgartner (1999).

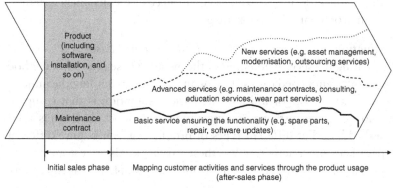

Figure 2.3: An example of a life-cycle cost analysis

Number of products (installed base)			
	Product age		
	< 2 years	2 to 6 years	> 6 years
Product group A	35	78	84
Product group B	52	198	587
Product group C	102	62	–

Service		
Service	Group B (>6 years)	
Service offerings	Group A (>6 years)	
	Description	€
Spare parts	Units sold through regular maintenance or modernisation	52,000
Modernisation	Refurbishment of the machine	12,000
Maintenance	Extended maintenance activities	25,000
Exchange of modules	Repair and maintenance costs exceed costs for a new module	16,000
...	...	...

Total amount of potential service revenues (number of products x sum of € for the service offerings) 53 million €

Figure 2.4: Excel spreadsheet for evaluating the service potential of the installed base

the customer activities are listed along the life cycle of the product and the costs and expenditure associated with these activities are estimated.

Different perspectives should be applied in order to ensure diversity in the service activities that are listed. The use of different categories of service needs, such as functional requirements, factors for ensuring customer success, problem-solving and fulfilling emotional needs, for example, can provide companies with a broad picture of the needs and activities that are related to the customer throughout the entire life cycle of the product. An alternative in the life-cycle analysis could be the application of utility layers, which involves questions for understanding the customer's productivity or needs for convenience, simplicity, environmental issues or image.

Evaluation of the service potential of the installed base
Evaluating the service potential of the installed base is another method that can be employed to assist companies in understanding the importance of service opportunities. The basic assumption is that companies do not have just one common type of product that forms their installed base but different types of products, which require different types of customer activities. It is these varying kinds of customer activities that offer other service opportunities. A simple management tool

that can assist in evaluating the service potential of the installed base is an Excel spreadsheet (see Figure 2.4) that comprises different product categories and assigns the necessary services to each category.

Seizing service opportunities
The concept of 'seizing opportunities' refers to visualising a strategic response to the service opportunities sensed. Seizing service opportunities is, therefore, considered as envisioning service strategies. Relevant service strategies and strategic responses include, for example, Davies' (2004) description of systems integration, operational services and business consulting, Mathieu's (2001a) customer services, product services and services as products, or Oliva and Kallenberg's (2003) strategies of consolidating product-related services, entering the installed base service market, expanding into relationship-based or process-centred services and taking over end-user operations. The various service strategies that can be utilised for seizing service opportunities are described in detail in Section 2.2.

A common aspect of seizing is the deeper examination of the service opportunities. It uses the service opportunities that are visualised once they have been sensed via the downstream analysis explained above, service need analysis, life-cycle analysis or evaluation of the service potential of the installed base. The literature offers three alternatives for seizing such service opportunities:

1. The service opportunity matrix (Sawhney *et al.*, 2004).
2. A matrix comprising a multi-vendor orientation of services and product/customer orientation of services (Raddats and Easingwood, 2010).
3. The emergence of service opportunities via ownership of the product and the type of service offering (Windahl and Lakemond, 2010).

(1) The service opportunity matrix
New service opportunities can be identified in the service opportunity matrix along two dimensions:

- Focus on growth (where do service opportunities appear?)
- Type of growth (how do service opportunities appear?)

The question of 'where' is typically answered by considering the primary and supplementary, or adjacent, customer activity chains. Primary customer activities have a direct link to the product offered

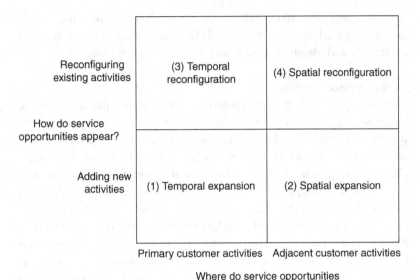

Reconfiguring existing activities	(3) Temporal reconfiguration	(4) Spatial reconfiguration
How do service opportunities appear?		
Adding new activities	(1) Temporal expansion	(2) Spatial expansion
	Primary customer activities	Adjacent customer activities

Where do service opportunities appear?

Figure 2.5: The service opportunity matrix
Source: Sawhney *et al.* (2004, p. 36).

and thus affect its functionality and availability. These primary activities can generally be divided again into pre-sales, sales and usage phases. Adjacent customer activities are not directly linked to the product and thus have no direct effect on its functionality and availability; examples of such activities include logistic and administrative customer processes. The second dimension describes how growth comes about.

The question of 'how' distinguishes service opportunities firstly by adding new activities and, secondly, by reconfiguring existing activities. Whilst growth potential can, on the one hand, be generated by extending the service offering for customer activities it can, on the other hand, be created by shifting responsibility for performing customer activities and processes to the service provider.

Merging the focus of growth with the type of growth results in the 2x2 service opportunity matrix (see Figure 2.5). The four elements of the framework are:

1. *Temporal expansion*: growth from services that add new activities to the primary activity chain of the customer.
2. *Spatial expansion*: growth from services that add new activities to the adjacent chain of the customer.

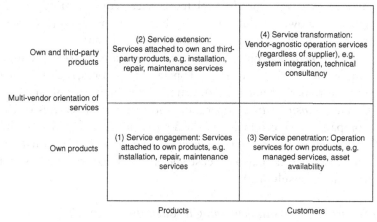

Figure 2.6: Typology of service strategies and service opportunities
Source: Raddats and Easingwood (2010, p. 1341).

3. *Temporal reconfiguration*: growth from services that change the structure and control of activities in the primary chain.
4. *Spatial reconfiguration*: growth from services that change the structure and control in an adjacent chain.

(2) Matrix comprising multi-vendor orientation of services and product/customer orientation of services
Raddats and Easingwood (2010) offer an alternative approach for visualising service opportunities in relation to service strategies that uses two dimensions. The first distinguishes between product-centric services, i.e. services are either closely linked to products (product-related services) or services in the customer's environment (operations services). The second dimension distinguishes between focusing either exclusively on the company's own products or also including the products of other companies, which may be competitive in nature. Figure 2.6 shows that the combination of these two dimensions leads to four strategic avenues that may be followed in the development of service business:

1. *Service engagement*: product-related services concentrating on the company's own products (e.g. spare parts, repair, inspection, maintenance and training).

2. *Service extension*: product-related services concentrating on the company's own products and also third-party products (e.g. spare parts, repair, inspection, maintenance and training).
3. *Service penetration*: operation services of the company's own products (e.g. service-level agreements and operational services, such as taking over customer's maintenance function and technical consultancy).
4. *Service transformation*: operation and integration services of the company's own products and third-party products (e.g. design and construction services, service-level agreements and operational services, such as taking over customer's maintenance function and technical consultancy).

(3) Service opportunities emerging through the ownership of the product and the type of service offering
Windahl and Lakemond (2010) describe opportunities emerging in the context of moving towards integrated solutions. They use the following two concepts:

• Product ownership. The installed product can be retained by the customer or transferred to the supplier.
• Type of service offering. According to Windahl and Lakemond (2010), service offering can either address the functionality of the product (product-orientated offerings) or the performance of the customer (process-orientated offerings).

The combination of these two concepts leads to four strategic avenues that can be taken when developing service business, as illustrated in Figure 2.7, namely:

1. *Maintenance offerings*: extended, product-orientated, service offering for the installed base after the product has been handed over to the customer.
2. *Operational offerings*: extended, process-orientated, service offering for the installed base after the product has been handed over to the customer.
3. *Rental offerings*: extended, product-orientated, service offering that does not involve a transfer of ownership of the product from the supplier to the customer.
4. *Performance offerings*: extended, process-orientated, service offering that guarantees the delivery of a defined performance for a particular process.

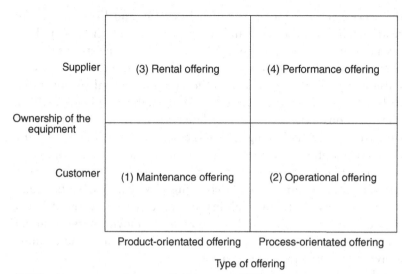

Figure 2.7: Service opportunities for moving towards integrated solutions
Source: Windahl and Lakemond (2010).

Reconfiguring to match service strategy with operational capabilities

'Reconfiguring' refers to managing the bilateral dependence between service strategy and operational capabilities to achieve a strategic fit (Teece, 2007). A strategic fit leads to coalescence, where service strategy and variables for operational capabilities are internally consistent, complementary and mutually reinforcing. Reconfiguration corresponds to the application of 'process models' for moving from a manufacturer of products towards being a provider of service. The process models most appropriate here are:

- The transition from products to services (Oliva and Kallenberg, 2003).
- Six steps for managing service networks (Cohen *et al.*, 2006).
- Overcoming the service paradox (Gebauer *et al.*, 2005).
- Four steps to selling services profitably (Reinartz and Ulaga, 2008).
- Defining strategic intent and source of competitive advantages for moving towards services (Auguste *et al.*, 2006).

Transition from products to services
The transition line from products to services consists of four phases: (1) consolidating product-related services, (2) entering

the service market for an installed base, (3a and b) expanding to relationship-based services and to process-centred services, and (4) taking over customer processes. The third phase consists of two parallel steps whereas the others represent a sequence. Each phase is initiated by specific triggers and follows a unique goal, as illustrated in Table 2.4; the goals can be achieved through a number of actions. Phase 1 (consolidating product-related services), which is triggered by customers complaining about the service performance and by competitors offering superior services, aims therefore at improving service performance. Indicators for improving service performance embrace the cost efficiency of delivering service and sales, the quality of the service, the availability of spare parts and the delivery time of the service. Potential actions refer to moving services under one roof or responsibility, evaluating existing services and defining activities for creating improvement.

Table 2.4 depicts the triggers, goals and actions of the preceding phases. The phases and their corresponding triggers, goals and actions serve as a preliminary managerial guide for companies wanting to move from selling products to providing services.

Six steps for managing a service network
Companies can succeed in setting up and identifying a service network by following the six steps given below (Cohen *et al.*, 2006). The product for which services are to be offered must first be identified. The options open are

1. only servicing their own products (i.e. the installed base);
2. servicing their own products and those of competitors (i.e. attacking the competitors' installed base); and
3. also servicing complementary products.

Servicing their own installed base is relatively easy, since companies have access to spare parts and possess the technical competencies necessary for repairing or maintaining the product, whilst offering services for complementary or competing products becomes increasingly complex. In order to cope with this complexity, managers should define ways of gaining access to the parts and competencies necessary. Furthermore, managers should describe how they intend to achieve and sustain competitive advantages for offering such services compared with manufacturers of complementary and competing products.

Table 2.4: *Transition line from products to services*

Phases	Triggers, goals and actions
1. Consolidating product-related services	*Triggers* - Customers complain about the performance of services - Competition offering services *Goals* - To improve performance of services (e.g. cost-efficiency, service quality and delivery time of service) *Actions* - Moving services under one roof or responsibility - Evaluating existing services and defining improvement activities
2. Entering the service market of an installed base	*Triggers* - Recognition of the profit potential of services - Competition offering services - Need to improve customer satisfaction *Goals* - To create revenues in the service market of the installed base *Actions* - Analysing the installed base - Creating a separate service organisation - Creating a service infrastructure to respond to service demands
3a. Expanding to relationship-based services	*Triggers* - Customers request more advanced services *Goals* - To increase the utilisation degree of the service infrastructure through more scheduled service activities *Actions* - Undertaking the operational risks of the products - Pricing the availability of the products - Exploiting cost-advantages provided by the delivery of the service
3b. Expanding to process-centred services	*Triggers* - Customers request more advanced services *Goals* - To transfer competencies in product development to the service business

Table 2.4: (*cont.*)

Phases	Triggers, goals and actions
	- Exploiting opportunities for integrating systems *Actions* - Developing consulting competencies - Setting up the networks of other suppliers, manufacturers and service providers
4. Taking over customer process	*Triggers* - Customers increasingly request to pay for performance and usage of the product instead of owning it *Goals* - To take over the responsibility for customer processes *Actions* - Developing pricing mechanisms for selling product performance. - Setting up operating knowledge

Source: Adapted from Oliva and Kallenberg (2003, p. 165).

Once the products have been defined, the next stage is the creation of a portfolio of services. Critical tasks include defining service levels or prices, e.g. determining the reaction time required by a customer to product breakdowns: prices and service processes differ significantly between a service level of one hour and 24 hours. Defining the price level of a service leads to the third step: selecting the business model for the services. This forms the foundation on which the after-sales service organisation and the design of the after-sales service supply chain are based. Monitoring the service performance continuously precedes the design of the after-sales service supply chain. Table 2.5 illustrates the six steps for managing a service network.

A process model for overcoming the service paradox
A similar model is recommended to overcome the so-called service paradox. The triggers and actions of this model can be divided into six specific phases, starting with establishing a market-orientated, and clearly defined, service development process. It continues by extending the service offerings and initiating a marketing relationship. Subsequent steps

Table 2.5: *Six steps for managing a service network*

Steps	Actions
1. Identify the products for which services are to be offered	- Assess the products and select one of the following options: own products (all or some), complementary products and competing products
2. Create a portfolio of service products	- Position service products according to response times and prices
3. Select business models to support the service products	- Use different models for different products and life-cycle stages
4. Modify after-sales organisational structures	- Provide visibility, incentives and focus for services
5. Design and manage an after-sales services supply chain	- Decide on the location of resources; prioritise resource utilisation; draw up a contingency plan
6. Monitor performance continuously	- Evaluate: benchmarking and customer feedback

Source: Cohen *et al.* (2006).

comprise defining a clear service strategy, establishing a separate service organisation and creating a service culture. All six phases are given in Table 2.6.

Four steps to selling services profitably

This provides a similar model for avoiding the service paradox and increasing the profitability of providing services (Reinartz and Ulaga, 2008). The four steps are:

1. recognising that the company is already in the service business;
2. industrialising internal service processes;
3. creating a service-orientated sales force;
4. focusing on customer processes.

The primary aim of the first step is making both the managers and the customers aware of their service value. Once they recognise the value of services they are more likely to switch from offering services for 'free' to charging for them. Companies should begin by listing all the services that are currently being offered to customers. The list can

Table 2.6: *Phases for overcoming the service paradox*

Phases for overcoming the service paradox	Actions for implement
1. Establishing a market-orientated and clearly defined process of service development	- Identifying customer needs systematically - Obtaining information regarding customer needs through wide-ranging market research and workshops with lead customers - Defining the service development process with precision - Dividing the development process into five preliminary phases: (1) identifying the market, (2) composing a service idea, (3) describing a preliminary service concept, (4) performing a pilot study and (5) introducing services to the market
2. Focusing service offers on the customer value proposition	- Expanding service offerings initially with product-related services - Continuing to expand service offerings with the addition of customer support services - Changing the focus from production efficiency to the end-user: to the efficiency of the product and its effectiveness in the customer's process - Changing the focus of customer interaction: from a transaction to a relationship
3. Initiating a marketing relationship	- Creating a fixed price that covers all of the services over an agreed period - Making service offers more 'tangible' to the end-user by pricing these services on the basis of equipment availability - Using measures such as corporate image to change the customer's perception of what is being offered: excellent services that fulfil their requirements rather than high-quality products - Establishing a continuous communication between the customer and service workers with the aid of the various communication tools (personal dialogues, newsletters, questionnaires, etc.) allows contact to be maintained - Training and empowering sales people and service technicians so that they offer services actively - Encouraging employees to gain a better understanding of the benefits a particular service can offer a customer

4. Defining a clear service strategy	- Defining how the company differentiates itself from competitors by means of service offers - Developing a service strategy with a comprehensive understanding of the market with respect to customer needs, market potential and future service trends - Building up a network of sales, technical staff and external experts, such as a market research department, that systematically collect and record current and future needs of customers - Involving all areas of the company affected by the service strategy in its development process. - Increasing acceptance of the strategy and the commitment to the relevant business components or departments - Implementing systematic and transparent procedures (strategy analysis, development, implementation and monitoring) - Considering the service strategy process as a non-linear process, i.e. a circular flow, incorporating frequent feedback loops
5. Establishing a separate service organisation	- Running a decentralised service organisation with profit-and-loss responsibility - Breaking down the goals to the level of individual employees: link goal achievement to an incentive system - Creating a dedicated sales force and service technicians for the service organisation - Investing in an information system to monitor the business operations in order to provide the new service business with financial transparency
6. Creating a service culture	- Maintaining a symbiotic relationship between manufacturing values and service-orientated values - Establishing an appropriate service awareness to overcome the typical habits inherent in the culture of product manufacturers - Changing managerial attitudes from regarding services as being optional extras to being 'value added' activities - Actively promoting the 'value added' attitude from the managerial to the employee level

then be segregated into services that are provided for free and services that customers are charged for. Managers can assess which of the former services might be transferred to being the latter. This transfer requires an estimation of the value of the customer as well as appropriate prices of the services in question.

Step two entails the industrialisation of internal service processes. The main aims are twofold: standardisation of the service processes and modularisation of the service offers. Standardisation can be achieved through typical service blueprinting; modularisation requires service packages to be defined in the form of modules that comprise the offer made to the customer. Core service modules should cover basic customer needs appropriately, and it should be possible to offer them separately. In the elevator industry, for example, such core modules would entail regular greasing and oiling of the elevator cables, as well as safety checks. Supplementary modules serve as expansions of the offering (Dörner *et al.*, 2011). Both standardisation and modularisation prevent delivery service costs from eroding the service margins (Reinartz and Ulaga, 2008).

The third step is the creation of a service-orientated sales force, which suggests that once companies ensure cost-efficient service delivery, they should proceed with training and educating their sales forces to sell services. Motivating service people to sell services also requires the reconsideration of financial incentives, e.g. profitability should be measured instead of order volume. Measuring profitability restricts the tendency of integrating services into the product price, i.e. augmenting the product by offering the service for free. Education and training should also concentrate on building competences for designing and selling customer solutions, which consists of different product and service components.

The fourth, and final, step aims at increasing focus on customers' processes. If customers are to be convinced to pay for services that have previously been provided free of charge, and high-margin services are to be sustained, managers have to ensure that the problems and requirements of the customers are addressed appropriately. These problems and requirements change continuously, so managers should gather information on the processes and structures of the customers in question. This requires the whole organisation being orientated around the customers' process rather than on the products and services alone (Reinartz and Ulaga, 2008). Table 2.7 summarises the four steps to selling services profitably.

Table 2.7: *Actions for improving service profitability*

	(1) Recognising that the company already deals with services	(2) Industrialising internal service processes	(3) Creating a service-orientated sales force	(4) Focusing on the customers' processes
Key issues	How do we currently sell services across business units and countries? What are the best practices inside our organisation? Which services can be moved from free to fee?	Which services are profit generators/drains? How can we ensure cost-efficient service processes? How can we tailor services to meet customers' needs?	Is our sales force ready to promote services along with products? Can we explain the benefits of our services to customers? Are we willing to move to longer sales cycles?	Are our offerings aligned with the goals and processes of our customers? Can we address their problems holistically? What further expertise do we need?
Key goals	To draw up a list of services we currently provide to customers To generate revenue from easily chargeable services To appoint a senior executive to oversee the development of service capabilities	To standardise service processes and control mechanisms To establish service platforms flexible enough to meet the needs of individual customers	To improve service-selling skills or organise separate sales forces To instate incentive systems promoting the sales of services To adopt tools for documenting value and communicating it to customers	To describe in detail the core concerns and operating processes of our customers To shift performance indicators from being activity-based to result-orientated instead To draw up a checklist of the capabilities necessary to compete in new service segments

Source: Adapted from Reinartz and Ulaga (2008, p. 95).

*Definition of strategic intent and source of competitive advantages
for moving towards services*
The last management approach to reconfiguring operational capabilities involves the definition of strategic intent and source of competitive
advantages (Auguste *et al.*, 2006). This approach supports companies
in formulating and implementing service strategies and involves the
management making two crucial decisions. These are:

• The primary focus of the service business, which can be either
  for supporting the product business or be a new and independent
  growth business.
• The source of competitive advantages, which can be either from
  economies of scale or economies of skills. The former results in the
  standardisation of services and high service sales volumes; the latter
  emphasises hard-to-imitate knowledge and resources, which causes
  competitors great problems.

Combining both of these crucial management decisions forms a 2x2
matrix. Confusion within the company can be avoided if, as Auguste
et al. (2006) suggest, one field in the matrix is focused on at a time.
Attention may be diluted if, for example, focus is placed on achieving
economies of scale and economies of skill simultaneously. The risk
is that a company instead does neither well enough, becoming not
sufficiently cost competitive compared to high-scale service providers and not sufficiently superior in knowledge compared to service
specialists.
     As illustrated in Table 2.8, the decision pertaining to the source of
competitive advantages and strategic objectives is preceded by various
actions regarding pricing services, sales structures, delivery processes
and organisations.
     The process models outlined above embrace the reconfiguration
of organisational variables of operational capabilities such as
corporate culture, human resource management, organisational
structure, measurement and reward systems and service development processes (Galbraith, 2002; Gebauer *et al.*, 2005; Johnstone
et al., 2008; Matthyssens and Vandenbempt, 1998; Mintzberg and
Westley, 1992; Neu and Brown, 2005; Oliva and Kallenberg, 2003;
Shah *et al.*, 2006). These operational capabilities are explained in
Chapter 3.

Table 2.8: *Actions for implementing the chosen source of competitive advantages and strategic intent*

		Strategic intent	
		Protect or enhance product	Expand independent services
Source of competitive advantages	Economies of scale	*Pricing*: groups of products and services; volume-based pricing; price level set to optimise product penetration and life-cycle profit *Sales*: single product/service sales force; sales support to sell standard add-on services *Delivery*: integrate services with hardware/software where possible; consolidate service delivery assets *Organisation*: single business unit; specialised development of service offering; measure life-cycle profits (e.g. 'attach rates') and unit delivery costs	*Pricing*: volume-based pricing for separate services; high surcharges for customisation *Sales*: separate sales force for product and services; sell mostly standard solutions to potential large customers and self-service to small customers *Delivery*: consolidate service delivery assets and standardise platforms; incorporate delivery standards into automated or employee work flow *Organisation*: independent business unit; measure sales growth and cost per unit of service delivered
	Economies of skill	*Pricing*: grouped or separate; menu-based prices to reflect customer value of solution and to optimise life-cycle profits of the product line *Sales*: single sales force with service specialists; sell integrated solutions to reduce total cost of product ownership *Delivery*: design products to be serviced; enhance productivity of skilled delivery force via knowledge management *Organisation*: single business unit; measure life-cycle profits, revenues and productivity per service delivery employee	*Pricing*: separate menu-based prices according to customer value and potential alternative for gain-sharing price models *Sales*: independent sales force; sales personnel as trusted advisers; best-practice database *Delivery*: focus on bringing best practice to each service interaction; knowledge management tools *Organisation*: independent business units; measure revenue, profits and end-to-end productivity per service delivery employee

Source: Auguste *et al.* (2006, p. 47).

2.1.3 Operational capabilities required to make the service business profitable

Service business development extends the existing set of operational capabilities through which companies earn their living by providing products, services or solutions (Fischer *et al.*, 2010). In order to be successful, companies have to evolve the capabilities necessary to develop, sell and deliver services before they can integrate these services into customer-specific solutions. The former includes establishing a service culture (Bowen *et al.*, 1989) which, in turn, lays the foundation for increasing the degree of service orientation in the management of human resources and, more specifically, in the recruitment, development and assessment/compensation of personnel (Homburg *et al.*, 2003). The necessary competence in the field of human resources includes the technical expertise to deliver repairing, inspection and maintenance services as well as to provide design and construction services. It is nevertheless imperative that technical expertise is supplemented with a customer-orientated attitude. This involves listening and communication skills, both of which are essential when, for example, adapting maintenance services to the specific operational needs of customers (Neu and Brown, 2005).

The service organisation should be managed as a separate organisational unit in order to gain momentum in service revenues and profits, promote a service culture and ensure a more service-orientated management of human resources (Oliva and Kallenberg, 2003). As a separate organisational unit, the service organisation then takes responsibility for developing, selling and delivering services. This involves developing capabilities that allow services to be innovated systematically, define service prices adequately and achieve service of a superior quality (Matthyssens and Vandenbempt, 1998). A superior quality of service is achieved through the above-mentioned technical expertise and customer-focused attitudes. Introducing new services requires evolving capabilities that allow an in-depth understanding of the operational and business needs of the customer: the specific service component to be developed can be identified and new services can be developed systematically by means of a typical stage-gate model (Schuh *et al.*, 2004).

Pricing requires not only an estimation of the cost of delivering the service (Kinkel *et al.*, 2003) but also capabilities to assume the operating risk of the capital goods. Oliva and Kallenberg (2003) argue that adequate pricing mechanisms depend on the ability of the company to gather information and monitor the customer throughout the usage of the product. The activities of monitoring and gathering information rely heavily on IT-related skills (Matthyssens and Vandenbempt, 1998). IT skills may be an integral part of remote services that collect data on status, diagnostics and usage of the capital goods in question (Allmendinger and Lombreglia, 2005). This data supports companies in assessing the failure risks and predicting the failure rates of capital goods. Additionally, the profitability of service depends on the utilisation of capacity. Once a company has set up a service organisation, the service resources become a fixed cost and the main generator of profitability is then capacity utilisation (Oliva and Kallenberg, 2003). Managing the demand and supply of service becomes a key capability of the service business.

As far as integrating these services into customer-specific solutions is concerned, companies need to develop capabilities for a comprehensive understanding of the needs of the customer. Integrating a diverse set of product and service components requires multi-skilled and cross-functional service competencies: key account management, financial knowledge, technical design expertise, communication skills and project management (Davies *et al.*, 2007). Companies should, therefore, be located in close proximity to the customer in order to understand which combination of products and services is the most suitable for their requirements (Windahl and Lakemond, 2010). Confronted with customers with heterogeneous needs (Neu and Brown, 2005), companies have to be flexible, regardless of whether they combine products and basic services to ensure the functionality of products or offer a package deal comprising design and construction services, products and maintenance services to provide total life-cycle solutions (Windahl and Lakemond, 2010).

Companies should emphasise the modularisation of service components if they are to be cost-efficient in such circumstances. Modularisation supports the units that interact with the customer in balancing the standardisation and customisation of the various elements. Whilst the customisation of service elements is a part of the responsibilities of these units, standardisation is an issue for the internal service offices. Service office units should rely on standardised business processes, pricing and guarantees for service quality and reliability; the portfolio of service elements must be constantly revised and optimised (Davies *et al.*, 2007).

2.2 Service strategies for manufacturing companies

Sensing and seizing of service opportunities are highly interrelated. The interrelation leads to service strategies for manufacturing companies. Service strategies are based on extending the breadth of services within the total offering (e.g. Davies, 2004; Gebauer, 2008; Martin and Horne, 1992; Mathieu, 2001a; Oliva and Kallenberg, 2003; Sawhney *et al.*, 2004; Vandermerwe and Rada, 1988). According to Martin and Horne (1992) and Kotler (1994), the shift in total offerings follows a specific pattern: it begins with pure goods, continues to total offerings dominated by goods and services, and ends with pure services. Other authors regard the concept of total offering as a system of product and service layers. Belz *et al.* (1997) view services as representing different layers around the core product. Gummesson (1994), using a similar concept of a core product surrounded by an outer service layer as a basis, expects services to change their role from being the layer around the product to being the centre of the layers. The literature generally agrees that extending the breadth of services can be considered as moving along the transition line from products to services in the product service continuum, with the two ends being services as the add-on and tangible goods as the add-on (Neu and Brown, 2005; Oliva and Kallenberg, 2003) (see Figure 2.8).

Service strategies represent different positions on this continuum. The following descriptions of service strategies are those most often used:

- Service strategies for moving downstream in the value chain (Wise and Baumgartner, 1999).
- Service strategies within manufacturing (Mathieu, 2001a).
- Transformation strategies for moving from manufacturing to service business (Oliva and Kallenberg, 2003).
- Moving towards high-value integrated solutions (Davies, 2004).
- Service strategies and service transition trajectories (Matthyssens and Vandenbempt, 2010).
- Five types of new service-based business concepts (Lay *et al.*, 2009).

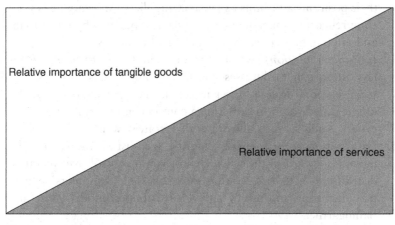

Relative importance of tangible goods

Relative importance of services

| Services as add-ons to goods | Tangible goods as add-ons to services |

Figure 2.8: The product service continuum
Source: Oliva and Kallenberg (2003) and Neu and Brown (2005, p. 4).

Service strategies for moving downstream in the value chain
Wise and Baumgartner (1999) describe a spectrum of four different
service strategies for moving downstream to the customer's end of
the manufacturing value chain. They argue that firms move downstream to capture profits throughout the entire product lifecycle of
the installed base which, in many industries, comprises a number of
products that is an order of magnitude greater than the number of
new products sold annually. Their four strategies can be explained as
follows:

1. *Embedded services* are the result of new digital technologies that
   allow traditional downstream services to be incorporated into a
   product. Such newly-configured, 'smart' products can save considerable labour costs by liberating the customer from performing
   those services. Honeywell's Airplane Information Management
   System (AIMS), for example, performs a variety of tasks that used
   to be undertaken manually thereby enabling airlines to reduce
   labour costs, reduce the turnaround time of aircraft and improve
   overall efficiency.

2. *Comprehensive services* are services that cannot be built into
   products but can be offered by manufacturing companies using

their positions and skills as product suppliers. An example is GE's comprehensive financing services business pursued by GE Capital and often in tandem with GE's product businesses.

3. *Integrated solutions* combine products and services into a seamless offering that addresses specific customer needs. Nokia's shift from a second league player in cellular equipment to a provider of integrated solutions, offering a comprehensive array of telecom products and services, illustrates this strategy well.

4. *Distribution control* entails entering the customer's business by moving forward in the value chain to gain control over lucrative distribution activities, as illustrated by Dell Computers' hybrid manufacturing and use of a direct distribution model (Wise and Baumgartner, 1999).

Service strategies within manufacturing

The investigation of manufacturing companies carried out by Mathieu (2001a) suggests a typology of service strategies (or service manoeuvres) with two dimensions that comprise avenues companies can take to extend the service business. The first dimension of service specificity describes different positions in the product service continuum where the nature of services ranges from consisting of customer service to product services and, finally, service as a product. Each position reflects a different service strategy for exploring the marketing, financial and strategic benefits of value creation through services. The second dimension of organisational intensity refers to both the strength and scope of the impact of the service strategy on the company. The levels of intensity range from tactics to strategy to culture. Figure 2.9 highlights the service strategies in manufacturing companies described by Mathieu (2001a).

The service specificity dimension:

1. *Customer service* addresses the general quality of interactions between a seller and a customer. It includes various aspects of facilitating supplementary services that are required for offering products (e.g. information, ordering, billing and payment). These services offer marketing opportunities by augmenting the product offering during the sales phase. An example here is the online service provided by Dell Computers.

2. *Product services* support the correct functioning of a product in the form of after-sale services or technical assistance, for example. Typical examples of product services include the description, documentation, transportation, training, inspection, spare parts and repair of the product. Product services require fewer assets, are often counter-cyclical and can provide higher margins than the products themselves (Oliva and Kallenberg, 2003). Caterpillar's comprehensive after-sales service is a good illustration of product services.
3. *Service as a product* embraces the services that are independent of the company's goods, i.e. a customer may partake of the company's service without consuming its goods. Examples include a car manufacturer that offers repairs for its competitors' cars and Fiat's decision to sell IT consulting services independently from its car business.

The organisational intensity dimension:

1. *Tactic* corresponds to specific actions within a company's product marketing mix that has limited impact on the organisation. Tactical service activities can be illustrated, for instance, by a toll-free number of packaged goods or an extended guarantee for household appliances.
2. *Strategy* refers to adding key competencies to a company's portfolio without changing its mission or basic values. The newly developed training service offered by GE Medical Systems, for example, which is based on a strong partnership with its clients, represents a new competency for GE and the industry as a whole.
3. *Cultural* service strategies reshape the mission of the company. They have the potential of modifying fundamental characteristics of the organisation, including the underlying belief system. Two examples are the switch made by IBM from a manufacturer of computers to being a consulting firm with IBM Global Services, and Toyota's shift from selling luxury cars to providing a luxury service package: a switch that had a great impact on the basic shared values, norms and behaviour of the companies and thereby altered their organisational cultures (see Exhibit 1.2).

Mathieu (2001a) suggests that combinations of these two dimensions (service specificity and organisational intensity) form strategic avenues that move in a direction towards services.

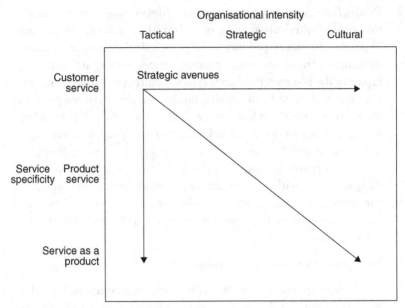

Figure 2.9: Service strategies in manufacturing companies
Source: Aadapted from Mathieu (2001a, p. 453).

*Transformation strategies for moving from
manufacturing to service*
Oliva and Kallenberg's (2003) study provides an explicit model of
the nature of the process when transforming from a purely manufacturing business to a service business. They found that recurring
patterns of actions are taken in successful transitions along the product service continuum. The transition was seen to progress through
four stages:

1. The existing, fragmented, product-related services that had trad-
    itionally developed in different parts of the organisation were
    consolidated; they were often relocated in a newly-created service
    unit.
2. The service market for the installed base was entered: it was defined
    and analysed before an infrastructure for marketing, delivering
    services and responding to local service demand was created.
3. Relationship-based services were then expanded or process-centred
    services were focused on. In the former, the way service was priced
    was changed from a mark-up for labour and parts every time a

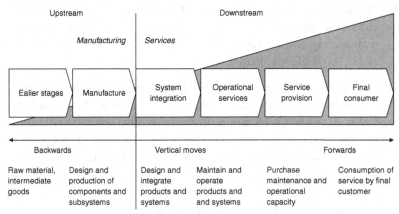

Figure 2.10: Supporting service activities in the capital goods value chain
Source: Davies (2004, p. 737).

service was provided to a fixed price that covered all services over an agreed period (the companies thus took the risk of equipment failure upon themselves). In the latter case, the focus of the customer value proposition was changed from the efficacy of the product (ensuring that it functioned correctly) to its efficiency and effectiveness within the customer's process over its complete life cycle.

4. Taking over the end-user's operation and assuming the full operating risk and responsibility for the customer's processes was the final stage in the transition, which then became a pure service organisation.

Moving towards high-value integrated solutions
Davies (2004) argues that manufacturing firms alter their total offering towards value creation via services by moving downstream in the capital goods value chain into high-value integrated solutions, as illustrated in Figure 2.10. The organisational move towards integrated solutions is made by employing one of three strategies, namely (1) systems integration, (2) operational services and (3) providing intermediary services.

1. *Systems integration* includes design services to integrate components such as product hardware, software and embedded services into a functioning system.
2. *Operational services* embrace ensuring the operation and maintenance of products, including the taking over of responsibility for the operation and maintenance of the products.

3. Providing *intermediary services* refers to business consulting services that advise customers on designing, financing, purchasing, maintaining and operating the products, as well as financing services (Davies, 2004; Kotler, 1994).

The findings of Davies' (2004) case study suggest that firms moving into the provision of integrated solutions need first to develop a core capability in systems integration. In order to offer complete solutions to meet the needs of their customers, however, companies must be able to leverage additional capabilities, including operational services, business consulting and financing.

Service strategies and service transition trajectories
Matthyssens and Vandenbempt (2010) suggest using two dimensions (degree of customisation and added customer value in the offerings) to describe four service strategies in a 2x2 matrix, and four types of transition trajectories within the service strategies through the addition of service (Figure 2.11):
Service strategies:

1. *After-sales service*: offering reactive support services.
2. *Service partner*: being a mere service company.
3. *Solution partner*: tailoring complex offerings to fit customer needs.
4. *Value partner*: providing pure integrated solutions.

Service transition trajectories:

1. *Product-focused customisation*: concentrates on the total cost of capital, technical cooperation, joint problem solving, design and engineering.
2. *Addition of standardised service*: focuses on customer orientation and optimising customer support.
3. *Customer process optimisation*: focuses on selling outsourcing solution, offering uptime and process integration.
4. *Addition of tailored service*: focus on systems integration, integral solution and guaranteed result.

Five new types of service-based, business concepts
Lay *et al.* (2009) assert that, due to the trend of manufacturers becoming service providers, these companies need to change their strategies and formulate new business concepts. The authors suggest using a

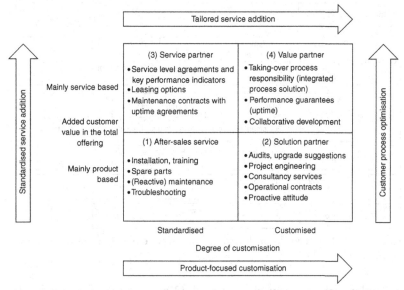

Figure 2.11: Service strategies and transition trajectories via the addition of service
Source: Adapted from Matthyssens and Vandenbempt (2010).

framework, with the following parameters, for describing new, service-based, business concepts that alter traditional supplier–buyer relationships in manufacturing industries (Figure 2.12):

- Ownership during phase of use: defines which party has the property rights to the machinery or other equipment during the term of the contract.
- Ownership after phase of use: describes who has the right of disposition after the contract expires.
- Responsibility for manufacturing personnel: refers to the allocation of the manufacturing workforce in a business concept.
- Responsibility for maintenance personnel: refers to the allocation of the maintenance workforce in a business concept.
- Location of operation: describes where the production equipment is installed.
- Number of customers: refers to the exclusivity of use of the machinery.
- Payment model: describes how suppliers and buyers exchange deliveries and payments.

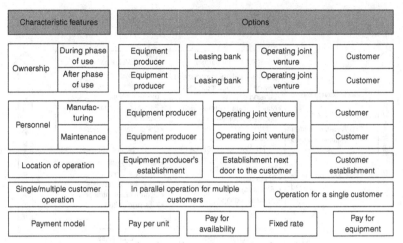

Characteristic features		Options			
Ownership	During phase of use	Equipment producer	Leasing bank	Operating joint venture	Customer
	After phase of use	Equipment producer	Leasing bank	Operating joint venture	Customer
Personnel	Manufacturing	Equipment producer		Operating joint venture	Customer
	Maintenance	Equipment producer		Operating joint venture	Customer
Location of operation		Equipment producer's establishment		Establishment next door to the customer	Customer establishment
Single/multiple customer operation		In parallel operation for multiple customers		Operation for a single customer	
Payment model		Pay per unit	Pay for availability	Fixed rate	Pay for equipment

Figure 2.12: Framework for describing new service-based business concepts
Source: Lay *et al.* (2009).

Applying the framework, Lay *et al.* (2009) describe five new kinds of service-based business concepts that have developed from the traditional business concepts found on the right side of the framework. In the traditional concepts, the producer of equipment sells machinery to customers who operate it on their own sites. Customers only pay for the equipment since their employees are responsible for both manufacturing operations and maintenance activities. The five new service-based business concepts are:

1. *Focus on new arrangements of ownership, financing and payment procedures for production equipment.* Suppliers offer their customers the right to use the equipment without having to purchase it, in contrast to the traditional model. The remuneration is paid according to the use of the machinery and is based either on per part or per use depending, naturally, on the relevant contract clauses.
2. *Focus on operational aspects of production equipment.* Operations and maintenance personnel are employed by the equipment producers instead of the customer. The personnel costs are, moreover, paid by the customer through a combination of fixed and performance-based rates.
3. *Focus on both financing and operational aspects on the customer's site.* A combination of the first and second type, with focus on both

the financing and operational aspects, the supplier retains own-ership of the equipment, operates it at the customer's plant and employs maintenance personnel, and in some cases, operating per-sonnel as well. The supplier is paid either per use or per part.

4. *Focus on both financing and operational aspects at the supplier's site.* This differs from the third type in that the equipment pro-ducer installs the production machinery either on their own shop floor or next door to the customer's facilities in a supplier park. The supplier is then able to meet specific customer requirements, such as transient demand increases, or offer additional produc-tion capacity in case of machine malfunction, etc. The equipment producer retains ownership of the equipment, operates and main-tains the equipment with its own personnel and is paid on a per part basis.

5. *Involve a third party to form an operating joint venture.* An oper-ating joint venture or a contractor assumes the risk associated with owning the production equipment by investing in, and operating, the equipment on behalf of the customer.

Although these five service strategies and five types of new, service-based, business concepts are frequently used, there are other service strategies that may be adopted. Table 2.9 provides an additional over-view of the service strategies employed, showing the main positions companies occupy during service business development.

2.3 Strategic fit between service strategy and operational capabilities

Variables of operational capabilities have to be aligned with the actual service strategy adopted in order to achieve a strategic fit. The main operational capabilities can be classified into the following categor-ies: (1) the service orientation of corporate cultures, (2) the service orientation of human resource management, (3) the service orienta-tion of organisational structures, (4) service development process and, finally, (5) information and communication technologies (ICT) as ena-blers of service orientation (e.g. Antioco *et al.*, 2008; Galbraith, 2002; Gebauer *et al.*, 2005; Johnstone *et al.*, 2008; Martin and Horne, 1992; Matthyssens and Vandenbempt, 1998; Neu and Brown, 2005; Oliva and Kallenberg, 2003).

Table 2.9: *Additional overview of service strategies*

Authors	Description of the service strategies
Chase (1981)	(1) Managing a quasi-manufacturing organisation, (2) offering mixed services or (3) pure services
Vandermerwe and Rada (1988)	(1) The company is either in a goods or services business, (2) goods and services are combined in offerings and (3) offerings are complex packages of goods, services, information, support and self-service elements
Martin and Horne (1992)	(1) Pure goods, (2) core goods with accompanying services, (3) core services with accompanying goods and (4) pure services
Gummesson (1994)	(1) The product is the core of the total offering, and services are layers around it and (2) the services are the centre of the total offering and the products are the layers
Belz et al. (1997)	(1) The product is the core with the services as the add-on and (2) total offering consisting of the product with various service layers around the product
Holmström et al. (1999)	Supplier moves the demand process upstream and advances the point from which it co-produces value onwards with the customer
Grönroos and Helle (2010)	Basis is adoption of a service logic for the entire manufacturing business, rather than separately for industrial service activities alone. By matching supplier and customer practices, and thereby aligning corresponding processes, resources and competencies, suppliers can support customers' businesses more effectively: joint productivity is promoted and the resulting gains can be shared between the business partners
Holmström et al. (2010)	Three distinct provider–customer constellations that reflect specific types of visibility (i.e. tracking, retaining and sharing the evidence on which service requirements are based) and represent optional service strategies from the perspective of the demand–supply chain: (1) collaborative service supply chain management, (2) condition-based maintenance as a service, and (3) visibility-based asset management
Hypko et al. (2010)	Increasing the importance of performance-based contracting as a service strategy in the manufacturing industry: includes financing as an essential issue and may include maintenance as well as operation

Table 2.10: *A comparison of product-orientated and service-orientated corporate cultures*

Product-orientated corporate culture	Service-orientated corporate culture
Values	*Values*
- Innovativeness and technological superiority are the major determinants for gaining competitive advantages	- Along with innovativeness and technologic superiority, customer centricity is a major determinant for gaining competitive advantages
- Service is an add-on to products	
- Service is a necessary evil to ensure product functionality	- Service is a major revenue source
- Service is a cost-driver	- Service is an opportunity to cover the business and operational needs of the customer
	- Service is a creator of profit
Behaviour	*Behaviour*
- Administrating and minimising service costs	- Managing service growth
- Having a customer service mentality	- Managing business
- Being a troubleshooter	- Being a performance enabler and a trusted adviser
	- Being flexible when developing customer-specific solutions

The service orientation of corporate culture involves two main variables, namely the corporate values of the company and the behaviour of its employees (see Table 2.10). It refers to the value of services within manufacturing companies and the degree to which employees behave in a service-orientated manner. The value of services includes financial, strategic and marketing opportunities (Oliva and Kallenberg 2003); the behaviour of employees includes the employees' understanding of their role. According to Neu and Brown (2005), the employees must behave as reliable troubleshooters, performance enablers and trusted advisers in order for the service business to expand successfully.

The service orientation of human resource management involves three variables: personnel recruitment, personnel training and personnel assessment/compensation (Homburg *et al.*, 2003). Homburg *et al.* (2003) argue that the service orientation of (1) personnel recruitment

Table 2.11: *Service orientation in human resource management*

Service orientation of human resource management	Characteristics
Personnel recruitment	- Intensive efforts are made to find talented junior staff for service-related activities (e.g. apprentice training) - Social competence and face-to-face contact with customers are considered decisive criteria for recruitment - The motivation and willingness for undertaking services of newly-recruited employees are evaluated
Personnel training	- Specific training of newly-recruited employees for interacting with customers is implemented - Focus is placed on the initial and on-the-job training of social competencies - Focus is placed on training communication skills and behavioural competencies - Means of measuring qualifications are established so that training in social competence, communication skills and behavioural competencies of employees can be undertaken
Personnel assessment/ compensation	- The service performance of both employees and managers is recorded and evaluated systematically - Outstanding service is appreciated and rewarded - An interesting career development for high-performing service employees and managers is assured - Employees and managers exhibiting a distinct service orientation are rewarded using financial and non-financial bonuses and incentives

refers to the extent to which the selection of personnel focuses on service-related aspects, (2) personnel training refers to the degree to which employees are trained for interactions with customers, and (3) personnel assessment/compensation refers to the extent to which service-related performance is evaluated and rewarded within the organisation. Table 2.11 offers a short description of the characteristics of the service orientation of personnel recruitment, personnel training and personnel assessment/compensation.

The service orientation of the corporate culture and the management of human resources both interact with the behavioural orientation of the company in an international context, which results in an ethnocentric, polycentric or geocentric approach being adopted (see Section 9.1). Ethnocentric means that personnel recruitment, training and compensation, as well as values and behaviour, are in favour of the home-country. The polycentric perspective acknowledges that subsidiaries are permitted to exercise discretion in certain areas of decision-making, values and norms in favour of the host-country (Kotler and Keller, 2005). Geocentricity, in the meanwhile, balances home-country and host-country orientation (Perlmutter, 1969).

The service orientation of the organisational structures comprises two variables. The first refers to organisational distinctiveness, which represents the degree to which the service business unit is set up as a distinct business unit, with the corresponding profit-and-loss responsibility (Oliva and Kallenberg, 2003). It concerns separating the service business from the product business: when the service organisation is integrated into that of the product, it is often argued that it functions merely as a cost centre. Separation can allow the service organisation to have its own profit-and-loss responsibility. Furthermore, distinguishing between the product and service businesses means that the amount of resources shared between product and service business are accounted for is relatively low. Integration within the service organisation is normally associated with strong intra-business collaboration between units. The service and product organisations share, therefore, an essential amount of resources. Separating the service organisation from the product organisation would, in contrast, lead to little intra-business unit collaboration and few resources would be shared with the product organisation (Neu and Brown, 2005).

The separation and integration of service and product organisations has both advantages and disadvantages. Separating product and service organisations is associated with a momentum for creating service profit and revenues. It also helps defend the service culture and thus avoid clashes between product-orientated and service-orientated values and behaviours (see Table 2.12).

The second variable covers the proximity of the service organisation to customers, i.e. the extent to which external customers are aware of the service organisation and can identify appropriate points of contact. Proximity to customers is also associated with the terms centralisation

Table 2.12: *Advantages and disadvantages of separation and integration*

	Organisational distinctiveness between product and service business	
	Integration	Separation
Advantages	- Exchange of knowledge between product and service organisations - Having just one person meet the customer has the potential of increasing the quality of the supplier–customer relationship - Little effort is required to coordinate the product and service businesses - Potential of sharing resource between the product and service businesses	- Clear financial transparency is possible between the product and service businesses - A unique service culture without clashing with the product culture can be developed - Momentum for increasing the financial contribution of the service business is created - An awareness of services can be increased in the whole organisation - Motivation to innovate new services is high - Motivation to enhance service performance across various performance measures (service costs and service quality) is high
Disadvantages	- Conflicts arise between product-orientated values and behaviour and service-orientated values and behaviour - Difficulties encountered in creating momentum for growth in service revenue and profits - Little motivation to innovate new services - Little motivation to enhance service performance beyond ensuring service delivery costs	- Transparency can lead to internal conflicts between product and service units - Two different customer interfaces can be confusing and reduce the quality of the supplier–customer relationship - Greater efforts are made to coordinate the product and service businesses - Organisational distinction makes sharing resources more difficult

Table 2.13: *Basic types of service orientation of organisational structures*

	Integration of product and service businesses	Separation of product and service businesses
Centralisation of service competencies	- Services are exported from a service cost-centre, which is incorporated in the product business	- Services are exported from a distinct service organisation (strategic business unit for services)
Decentralisation of service competencies (indirect or direct)	- Services are promoted, sold and delivered through sales agents or sales subsidiaries, that focus on the product business	- Services are promoted, sold and delivered through specific service agents or service subsidiaries that focus exclusively on the service business

and decentralisation of service competencies. The service competencies in the former are concentrated within the headquarters of the company whereas they are close to the customers in the latter. In an international context, proximity to customers is closely coupled with the mode of market entry: export, indirect or direct. When companies choose to 'export' services, proximity to the customer is relatively low. An indirect market entry via licensing and partner agreements increases customer proximity. The highest proximity to customers can be achieved by entering the foreign market directly. Table 2.13 combines both variables; it shows four basic types of service orientation of organisational structures.

Service development processes consist of two variables: market-orientation and a systematisation in the approach taken to innovation. A market-orientation, particularly the systematic identification of customer needs, is an indispensable prerequisite for developing new services (De Brentani, 2001). The services developed will then be closer to the current needs of customers and thereby more likely to ensure market success. In conjunction with such market orientation, a systematically coordinated and transparent procedure supports the development of new service products. The process by which service is developed should be defined precisely, as should the criteria on which conscious decisions are made in the development process (Cooper and Edgett, 1999). Companies should divide the development process into five preliminary phases. The needs of the market are identified first. New service ideas, based on these market needs, can then be created in the second phase. A preliminary service concept is generated in the third phase, whilst a pilot study is conducted in the fourth. The services are introduced to the market in the fifth, and final, phase.

Information and communication technologies (ICT) can be utilised as enablers for service orientation and, as such, are regarded as being important (Kowalkowski *et al.*, 2010). Enhancing the exchange of information between provider and customer, ICT provides the potential for deepening relationships between them. ICT is also a driving force in extending service offering, such as integrated solutions (Penttinen and Palmer, 2007). The internal efficiency of service processes can be enhanced by ICT such as software-based planning and the scheduling of service technicians, spare parts or condition monitoring systems. Diagnostic applications can promote more preventive services whereas ICT aims at profiling and tracking customer behaviour that could result in new service innovations. ICT adds connectivity to products and services. It allows information to be collected, e.g. about a product that is about to fail, customer processes that lack efficiency and effectiveness, or that a customer is running low on parts and consumables (Allmendinger and Lombreglia, 2005).

3 | Dynamic capabilities for service business development

This chapter discusses two distinct strategic approaches for developing a service business. A short comparison is made between the approaches, which is followed by an explanation of the specific phases of each approach. The dynamic capabilities associated with each phase are then introduced, and cover the sensing, seizing and reconfiguring activities (see Section 2.1.2).

3.1 Exploitation or exploration: two distinct approaches for service business development

There are two different approaches to service business development: (1) exploitation of service opportunities through temporary expansion of the service business along the primary customer activity chain and (2) exploration of service opportunities through spatial expansion and reconfiguration along the adjacent customer activity chain. Figure 3.1 illustrates these two approaches in relation to the service opportunity matrix.

1. *Exploitation of service opportunities*: this is the approach preferred by the majority of companies. Exploiting service opportunities along the primary customer activity chain continuously increases the share of revenue created by services. The share of service revenue of the exploiting companies can grow from about 10 per cent to 30 per cent over a period of around 15 years. Exploitation means that the business logic becomes more service-orientated incrementally through specific value-adding services (Möller, 2006). Exploiting service opportunities focuses on the efficiency of capital goods in customer processes, increasing service productivity, controlling access to the installed base, certainty of financial service revenues and profits and reducing the variance in competitors' reactions by creating a dominant design in the total

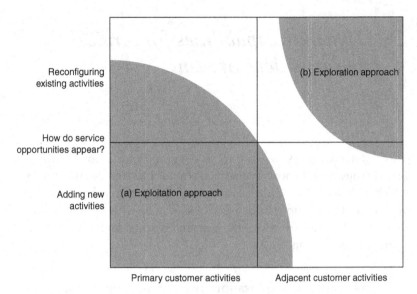

Figure 3.1: Exploitation and exploration in relation to the service opportunities

offering (O'Reilly and Tushman, 2007). Exploiting companies are driven primarily by increasingly comprehensive customer needs within the primary customer activity chain and the desire to differentiate the total offering from competitors. The primary customer activities (those linked directly to the product) are well known to the company. Managers are, therefore, in a favourable position for estimating customer needs and expectations; they can also anticipate the reactions of both customers and competitors to service offerings.

2. *Exploration of service opportunities*: exploration involves searching and discovering new service business opportunities by providing strong freedom to innovate new services. Exploring service business opportunities allows companies to embrace strategic variation (O'Reilly and Tushman, 2007). The notion of exploration suggests that companies made a radical 'jump' up to a new strategic state that focuses on services addressing the adjacent activity chain of the customer. The leap towards the new strategic state is evident in the share of service revenue. In contrast to the exploitation approach, the exploration approach increases the share of revenue attributed to services from less than 20 per cent to more

Table 3.1: *Characteristics of the exploitation and exploration approaches*

Characteristics	Approaches for service business development	
	Exploitation	Exploration
Type of organisational change	Incremental improvements of the existing strategic stage	Radical jump towards new strategic stage
Primary service opportunity addressed (customer activity chain)	Temporary expansion within the primary customer activity chain	Spatial reconfiguration within the adjacent customer activity chain
Value constellations	Value-adding to existing value constellations	Defining new value constellations
Management knowledge	Managers have deep insights into customer needs and expectations; they are able to anticipate the reactions of both customers and competitors	Managers are uncertain about actual customer needs and expectations; they find it difficult to anticipate the responses of both customers and competitors
Service-orientated performance improvements	10 per cent to 30 per cent share of the service revenue within a period of about ten years	From less than 20 per cent to more than 40 per cent share of service revenue within a few years

than 40 per cent within a few years. Exploration includes major reconfiguration of the organisational arrangement, value-creating processes, business relationships and roles of the participants, and even the whole business model. Exploration forms a new value constellation based on services, which makes the way in which companies previously competed with each other obsolete. Needless to say, exploration is not free from exploitation activities.

Managers found it useful to estimate and understand customer needs and expectations in the adjacent customer activities: they are also highly uncertain of the potential reactions of customers and competitors once their company tries to reconfigure customer activities and to provide services for adjacent customer activities. Visualising the needs of the customer and the strategic responses incurred lie beyond the traditional consideration of strategies. The key concept of the second approach is nevertheless exploration, from which the name is derived.

Table 3.1 shows both approaches and summarises their key characteristics.

3.2 Phases of the exploitation and exploration approaches

Both approaches can be divided into three basic phases (Figure 3.2):

1. *Exploitation* involves (1) integrating the basic services into the price of the product, (2) separating the service from the product business to increase the profit and revenue of the service and (3) utilising the expansion in service along the primary customer activity chain.

2. *Exploration* phases involve (1) integrating the basic services into the price of the product, (2) creating a new value constellation and (3) utilising the expansion in service along the adjacent customer activity chain. The first and last phases have elements in common with the corresponding phases of the exploitation approach. The second phase, on the other hand, shows a substantial difference: it resembles a sudden, short burst that alters the industry fundamentally.

Each phase in the exploitation and exploration approaches to the development of service business requires a specific set of dynamic capabilities.

Phases of the exploitation approach

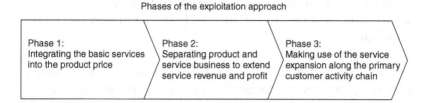

Phases of the exploration approach

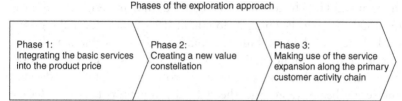

Figure 3.2: A comparison of the phases used to explore or exploit service opportunities

3.3 Dynamic capabilities required in the exploitation approach

3.3.1 Phase 1: integrating the basic services into the price of the product

The companies consider the market structure as being exogenous. Service opportunities are determined by competitor offerings and the obvious needs of the customer. Companies compare their service offerings with those of competitors to exploit value opportunities whenever new services are introduced on to the market.

The activity of sensing relies on using services to differentiate the total offering and integrating them into the price of the product. This type of total offering composes the early, and dominant, type of total offering in which the profit generated by service is embedded into the price of the product, as explained below. Adding new services to the total offering would, therefore, facilitate differentiation of the product from the service and create additional costs for the latter. Once the new service has been introduced to the market, companies reconfigure their service processes and structures to achieve minimum operational costs. The typical organisational set-up is to integrate the service business into the product organisation in the form of a cost centre (Noch, 1995). In essence, the aim of business models in the first phase of the exploitation approach is to secure cost advantages in the service infrastructure and protect the installed base, and thereby imitate the competition.

Once the service infrastructure is aligned to be cost-efficient, the only uncertainty that remains is whether or not competitors follow a similar path. Spurred on by the importance of competitor service offerings in exploitation activities, the management focuses on making rapid and timely decisions to create a dominant design to embrace the total offering. Forming a dominant design includes making tactical choices on how to bundle capital goods and services and how to charge them (Malleret, 2006). The intention is to design the total offering, the underlying revenue and profit streams. Once a dominant design begins to emerge, the choices competitors have of offering additional services, or charging for services in a different way, become much more limited.

Initially, a typical dominant design emerges that integrates basic services into the price of capital goods. This means that basic services, such as training, installation, inspection, repairs and maintenance activities, are not charged for separately but are offered 'free of charge' to the customer. Customers, on the one hand, are the driving force behind the evolution of the emerging dominant design because it reduces the risks associated with unpredictable service costs. Services, on the other hand, are regarded in times of attractive product margins in the capital goods industry as being add-ons to products for the mere purpose of facilitating sales of products. There is, however, no great need for services to contribute to the company's revenues and margins. Minimising service costs would allow service profits to be embedded in the price of the product. Generally speaking, there are only a few exceptions to this early dominant design of integrating services into the price of the product.

Seizing and reconfiguring this early dominant design and reconfiguring the internal organisation (e.g. setting up the service organisation as cost centres within the product-orientated business units) creates an unexpected side effect (Gebauer *et al.*, 2009; Oliva and Kallenberg, 2003). Regarding services from the perspective of cost advantages encourages internal processes and routines to seek beyond the obvious needs of the customer. Attention is focused on the requirements of the customer in terms of ensuring the functionality of the capital goods.

3.3.2 Phase 2: separating the product from the service business to improve the profit and revenue generated by service

Confronted with eroding margins, the early dominant design becomes obsolete. Prices are put under pressure and there is little margin remaining in which to embed service costs and profits. Thus, the sensing activities of companies begin to search for new ways of making profit from service (Reinartz and Ulaga, 2008).

Applying rapid and timely decision routines, the management focuses on services already being offered to customers. Charging separately for services that were originally included in the price of products is seen as a new profit pool. Sensing, seizing and reconfiguring activities concentrate on exploiting these profit pools. Reconfiguring their organisational structure, companies set up a separate strategic business unit for services with profit-and-loss responsibility. These service units are thus forced into selling services separately, thereby increasing the profits and revenues attributed to services (Auguste *et al.*, 2006; Oliva and Kallenberg, 2003).

Being a separate strategic business unit, the service organisation controls the sales of service as well as delivery and innovation activities. Rapid success in these activities requires that the sensing and seizing capabilities concentrate on the obvious needs of the customer and make the most of the opportunity of adding services to the customers' primary activities to charge for the services. The rationale for concentrating attention on, and gathering information and filtering processes of, the customers' primary activity chains results from the familiarity with these types of activities. Managers already have an established, cumulative knowledge of the customers' requirements for their primary activities and prefer to exploit this knowledge rather than explore new opportunities pertaining to the customers' adjacent activities (March, 1991; O'Reilly and Tushman, 2007). Managers assume that customers rely on the reputation of the product when evaluating services for customer activities related to its operation and maintenance. The risk perceived by customers when they consider purchasing a service from a capital goods manufacturer with a superior product reputation is assumed to be relatively low.

The successful launching and running of the strategic service business units requires that the internal procedures and activities change course: from administering the service costs and reacting to customer complaints to managing the service business in a professional and profitable way. Business managers are best suited to plan and execute the strategy for running the service business unit.

Separating the product from the service business is also driven by managerial awareness on potential threats. When managers formulate a deliberate strategy to sell more services and increase service revenue, the responsibilities of traditional product sales will change (Ashforth and Lee, 1990). This potential threat to the sales organisation leads to an internal resistance in formulating a service strategy and high political costs for overcoming this resistance. Managers tend to set up a separate business unit for services in order to minimise political costs and avoid resistance.

Managerial awareness of emerging threats from keeping product and service business integrated is accelerated by the risk of losing customers to more efficient core-value producers in the product or service business. Separate business units for products and services are often argued as being the optimal response to competitors that only concentrate on products or specialised providers of service.

3.3.3 Phase 3: making use of the service expansion along the primary customer activity chain

The expansion in service includes subsequent changes in the total offering. The first change included ensuring functional capability during the period in which the customer actually uses the product: services are offered to the customer in the event of any failure. The total offering includes standardised, predefined services, such as spare parts, repair, inspection, a hotline and basic training, which are priced and charged for individually as a mark-up for labour and parts. The next change led to individual maintenance service packages. The individual service packages are made more attractive to customers by pricing the services based on typical performance measures, e.g. machine availability (uptime) and yield, rather than on the costs of performing scheduled maintenance services (Oliva and Kallenberg, 2003). The final change captures R&D orientated services in the pre-sales phase, where companies design or construct the product according to the specific technical requirements of the customer. The design and construction services are charged for separately; should the customer purchase the product in question, the service price is then refunded.

As far as decision-making is concerned, pricing is the biggest issue connected to exploitation. The sales organisation for products gathers information pertaining to services that should be an integral part of the product price. Services that are charged for separately are communicated internally. The aim here is to communicate the impact of charging for service on the price of the product but not to reconsider the dominant design of the total offering, with its underlying revenue and profit streams. Difficulties are experienced in making adaptations to the dominant design, which is evident from the fact that companies are prepared to sell their products at cost-price in order to increase their market share of the installed base, thus leading to increased revenue and margin levels from their service business.

The narrowness of sensing activities is reinforced by the methods and procedures applied to examine the information. Making sense of the information is aided by the top management or central business development department articulating the intended service strategy at an early stage. Such articulated service strategies for service business development (e.g. after-sales or customer support services) form a filter that is laid over the attention of the management. It ensures that their attention is not diverted to every single service opportunity but is, instead, focused on the particular service strategies that have been articulated and are not validated and challenged by alternative strategic avenues. Deliberate service strategies are more reminiscent of the rigid planning of scenarios that only involved one scenario of how the needs of the customer and the service offerings of the competitors are expected to develop, similar to the 'planned strategy' of Mintzberg and Waters (1985).

The fact that companies consider only one scenario for developing service business means that there are very few investments options for service innovations. Once again, the only remaining uncertainty refers to whether competitors follow a similar innovation path. The prevalent route for service innovations starts with organising services for the installed base, continues with maintenance services and, finally, leads to R&D orientated services (see Section 6.1.2). The capability in the prevalent route of being able to constantly generate intelligence of the expressed needs of the customer in the primary activity chain, along with the ways in which these needs may be satisfied, is essential to the continuous creation of superior customer value (Slater and Narver, 2000).

Table 3.2: *Dynamic capabilities necessary for exploiting service opportunities*

	Phase 1: integrating basic services into the product price	Phase 2: separating product and service businesses to extend service profit and revenue	Phase 3: making use of the service expansion along the primary customer activity chain
Sensing capabilities	• Focus on identifying service opportunities to differentiate the total offering and see which can be integrated into the product price • Information-gathering routines to observe the service offerings and behaviour of competitors • Information-gathering routines to observe obvious customer needs • Fast and reliable capacity for processing information to prepare a strategic response and quick reaction to the service activities of competitors	• Sense service opportunities by combining obvious customer needs, adding services to customers' primary activities and the possibility of charging for services • Processes and routines to identify service profit opportunities from services which can be charged for • Mechanisms for gathering and filtering information for service opportunities re: customers' primary activities • Capacity to exploit existing knowledge of customer requirements in customers' primary activities • Customer sensing capability, i.e. assessing the risks of purchasing service as perceived by the customers	• Routines for gathering and processing information to constantly generate intelligence of the customer's expressed needs in the primary activity chain • Sensing capability limited to services that can be added to the core product offering (either embedded or charged for separately) but do not change the dominant design
Seizing capabilities	• Routines involving quick and timely decisions to create a dominant design of the total offering • Capacity to form a dominant design (tactical choices on the bundling and charging of goods and services)	• Routines of quick and timely decisions to adapt strategy to charge customers for services • Exploit service profit opportunities by charging for services which were previously offered for free	• Capacity to satisfy the expressed needs of the customer in the primary activity chain and to formulate strategic responses • Formulate 'planned strategies' for service business development involving a rigid planning of scenario

| Reconfiguring capabilities | • Capacity to redesign service processes and structures to achieve minimum operational costs (set up cost centre in product organisation)
• Procedures and routines to minimise service costs to achieve service profits embedded in product prices | • Capacity to commercialise services that were originally included in the product prices and communicate changes to the customer
• Being able to plan deliberate strategies and execute them to create a distinct professional service business (business manager qualities)

• Ability to turn service activities into a professional business and make it profitable (business manager qualities)
• Managerial awareness of potential threats from formulating a deliberate profit-orientated service strategy and ability to deal with threats
• Capacity to overcome internal resistance and conflicts
• Capacity and resources to set up a separate strategic business unit for services with its own profit-and-loss responsibility | • Articulate intended strategies early and clearly to direct the gathering and filtering of information and to focus management attention
• Strategic vision that articulated strategies respond to the development of the needs of the customer and the service offerings of competitors
• Routines to reconfigure assets and resources to protect the spare parts business from imitation
• Routines to maximise the ratio between manufactured and purchased parts, control the parts supply chains and optimise parts logistics
• Capacity to reconfigure technical assets to ensure remote access to the installed products for condition monitoring, service activities and use of copied parts |

The success of this path depends, in addition, on whether or not companies can reconfigure their assets and resources to protect their spare parts business. The latter is argued to be the original reason for exploiting this path: on the one hand, they remain relatively free from imitation, making it difficult for competitors or external providers of service to provide repair, inspection and maintenance services for the installed base whilst, on the other hand, separating the service and product businesses from each other means that spare parts are an important component in acting as a bridge between them. Companies therefore concentrate on protecting their spare parts business from imitation. Typical routines refer to maximising the ratio between manufactured and purchased parts, controlling the parts supply chains and optimising parts logistics. In addition, companies reconfigure their technical assets to ensure remote access to the products installed for condition monitoring and arrange potential authorised and non-authorised service activities as well as the replacement of original parts with copies. Table 3.2 summarises the dynamic capabilities for the exploitation approach.

3.4 Dynamic capabilities necessary for succeeding with exploration

3.4.1 Phase 1: integrating the basic services into the product price

In the first phase, companies employ similar sensing, seizing and reconfiguring capabilities as associated with exploitation. They form an early dominant design by integrating basic services into the product price. Key issues in the dynamic capabilities refer to the identification of service opportunities for differentiating the total offering, observing the service offerings of competitors and the needs of the customer, redesigning service processes and structures to achieve relatively low services costs, and so on: see Table 3.3 for further details.

3.4.2 Phase 2: creating a new value constellation

In contrast to exploitation, the companies consider the structure of the market as endogenous: the result of innovation and learning. Managers deliberately do not accept the service market as being static but dismantle instead the needs of both the market players and customers

(Jaworski *et al.*, 2000). They substitute the embedded theory-in-use valid for service markets with something fundamentally new through generative learning (Senge, 1990; Slater and Narver, 1995).

The sensing activities of companies are characterised by the fact that managers also emphasise the capability of creating markets and new customer value opportunities either to drive the structure of the market or shape its behaviour. Companies are also aware of the tendency observed in the primary customer activity chain that the behaviour of the customer and the competitor, along with the past competitive behaviour of the companies, most probably act as successive hurdles in reshaping the structure of the market and the development of the service business. Rather than sensing new service profit pools by charging separately for services that were initially integrated into the product price, sensing activities open up towards adjacent customer activity chains, new value constellations resulting from reconfiguring whole value chains and reach beyond the borders of the industry.

Routines supporting extensive sensing activities are the regular benchmarking and investigation of other industries, observing customers and non-customers and mapping all related activities comprehensively. In addition, investigating other industries, and transferring the key insights gained, requires companies to master analogical thinking for problem solving (Gavetti *et al.*, 2005).

The cognition of these opportunities, and the associated new value constellation, is confronted with potential biases: providing services for the adjacent customer activity chain, for example, can be far beyond the existing core competencies of the company. It is also questionable whether their positive reputation for supporting the primary activities of customers can be transferred to purchasing decisions of services supporting supplementary customer activities. Overcoming such biases requires a cognitively sophisticated and disciplined approach to decision-making. Compared to exploitation, the decisions made are less timely and rapid. The operational procedures and routines involved do not focus on establishing a dominant design whereby services are charged for separately: they attempt instead to sense, seize and reconfigure new value constellations.

The greater level of uncertainty of new value constellations results in strategies being formulated as what Mintzberg and Waters (1985) call 'umbrella' strategies, i.e. general guidelines for behaviour that define only the boundaries of the strategies. The boundaries are left open to primary, and adjacent, customer activity chains as well as potential value constellations downstream and upstream in the value chain. They even include moving away from cooperation with customers and towards being potential competitors of existing customers or suppliers, as well as entering new industries and value chains.

Awareness of the fact that one scenario inherent in such an 'umbrella' strategy for the new value constellation might cause the collapse of the exploration approach allows numerous scenarios to emerge. Discussing various scenarios is beneficial because it facilitates managerial cognition of a broad range of different business opportunities. Managers are observed to be not only more flexible throughout the strategy process but also more open to discussing new aspects of the service business. The attention and resources of management are, of course, limited; considering different scenarios may lead to bottlenecks and delays in time where implementation is concerned. The companies exploring service opportunities avoid such bottlenecks by allocating sufficient resources and applying realistic time frames. They even consider time as not being critical in the implementation of a new value constellation and have very flexible time schedules.

Internal procedures and activities require the mindset of an entrepreneur (e.g. strong managerial foresight and entrepreneurial alertness) for the successful launch of the exploration of service opportunities and not that of a business manager, as is the case with the exploitation approach. Managers with a strong entrepreneurial way of thinking thus guide exploration activities. Being entrepreneurs, the strategy is not planned and executed but emerges instead through processes of trial and error within the potential scenarios and strategic avenues.

The innate uncertainty and novelty of exploration involves dealing with many risks that have to be considered in the process of formulating the strategy. This requires specialised visioning and risk-assessing skills. Despite developing different scenarios, there is still a significant amount of risk involved in the development of service business. The remaining risks have therefore to be incorporated into the new value constellation. Pricing and estimating risks form key parts of each scenario. Although exploring new service opportunities naturally involves the serious consideration of risks, and developing different scenarios may aid them in coping with the uncertainty of exploration, managers are, nevertheless, more willing to accept higher risks. They therefore require certain competencies that would allow them to foresee the value production logic of the business after change has occurred, and to anticipate the way in which the change may influence the roles of the actors and their processes of value creation (Möller, 2006).

Reconfiguring intangible and tangible assets of a company also differs for both approaches. Besides reconfiguring internal operational capabilities to implement service strategies, exploration also involves reconfiguring the relationships with external resources such as customers, suppliers and partners in the value-creating processes.

Contradictory to the argument that separation of service and product business is important for getting momentum to extend service revenue and profitability, companies employing exploration favour the integration of service and product activities. Rather than totally separating these activities, products and services are seen as essential components of service business development both forming the basis of the solutions offered.

Therefore reconfiguring the organisational structure seemingly refers to integrating service and product activities, or even re-integrating them, as the case may be. Managers following an exploration strategy do not see the risk of losing customers to more efficient core-value producers in the product or service businesses. The threat they recognise is that they should regard their markets in terms of the product and service offerings that they sell and not in terms of customer value. Managers believe that what customers buy and value is never a product or service: it is always the utility (benefit or value) of the product or service.

3.4.3 Phase 3: utilising the service expansion along the primary customer activity chain

Once the new value constellation has been set up in Phase 2, the companies turn towards making use of the resulting service expansion and reconfiguration along the primary customer activity chain. Dynamic capabilities are required to stabilise the new value constellation: this is connected to adapting the operational capabilities to benefit from the new value constellation.

The necessary dynamic capabilities are, in addition, similar to Phase 3 of the exploitation approach. Companies may thus be able to exploit, as a side effect, the service opportunities within the primary customer activity chain by following the sequence of service extensions outlined

Table 3.3: *Dynamic capabilities necessary for exploring service opportunities*

	Phase 1: integrating basic services into the product price	Phase 2: creating a new value constellation	Phase 3: utilising the service expansion along the adjacent customer activity chain
Sensing capabilities	• Identify service opportunities to differentiate total offering and see which can be integrated into the product price • Routines for gathering information to observe service offerings and behaviour of competitors • Routines for gathering information to observe obvious needs of the customer • Fast and reliable capacity for processing information to prepare strategic response and rapid reaction to the service activities of competitors	• Emphasis on creating markets and new customer value opportunities, driving the structure of the market or shaping market behaviour • Awareness that, within primary customer activities, customer and competitor behaviour as well as the past competitive behaviour of the companies most probably act as successive hurdles for reshaping the structure of the market • Sensing activities directed towards adjacent customer activities and new value constellations beyond traditional value chain logic and industry borders • Routines and procedures including regular benchmarking and investigation of other industries, observing customers and comprehensive mapping of customer activities • Master analogical thinking for problem solving to investigate other industries and transfer key insights	• Routines for gathering and processing information to continuously generate intelligence of how to offer utility to the adjacent and primary activity chains of the customer

| Seizing capabilities | • Routines of rapid and timely decisions to create a dominant design of the total offering
• Capacity to form a dominant design (tactical choices on bundling and charging goods and services) | • Service management with strategic vision of new value opportunities, willing to take risks in exploration and empowered to drive strategy formulation
• Sophisticated and disciplined approach to decision-making under uncertainty
• Formulate and articulate 'umbrella strategies' for the new value constellation, i.e. allow strategy to emerge within behavioural boundaries via trial and error processes
• Allow various scenarios to emerge within the 'umbrella strategies' to deal with uncertainty
• High degrees of managerial flexibility and open-mindedness within strategy formulation to explore a broad range of different business opportunities
• Set up a cross-functional team for exploration and provide it with sufficient resources and flexible time frames | • Capacity to support the primary and adjacent activities of the customer and to formulate strategic responses
• Establish routines and procedures to stabilise the new value constellation
• Formulate 'planned strategies' for service business development involving more rigid planning of scenarios after stabilisation |

Table 3.3: (*cont.*)

	Phase 1: integrating basic services into the product price	Phase 2: creating a new value constellation	Phase 3: utilising the service expansion along the adjacent customer activity chain
		• Entrepreneurial mindset of managers includes visioning and risk-assessing skills to anticipate new value creation logic (managerial foresight and entrepreneurial alertness) • Risk management routines to incorporate the remaining risks into a billing model for the new business logic	• Continuously adapt operational capabilities to new value constellation • Reconfigure assets and resources to stabilise and protect the new business model
Reconfiguring capabilities	• Capacity to redesign service processes and structures to achieve minimum operational costs (set up cost centre in product organisation) • Procedures and routines to minimise service costs to achieve service profits embedded in product prices	• Reconfigure internal operational capabilities to implement service strategies • Reconfigure business relationships with external resources such as the customer, suppliers and partners in the value-creating processes • (Re-)integrate service and product activities within organisational structure • Managerial belief that the customer values utility and not the product or service	

in the exploitation approach. Key issues in the dynamic capabilities for Phase 3 refer to: stabilising the new value constellation, formulating more 'planned' strategies for the development of their service business involving more rigid planning of scenarios after stabilisation, continuously adapting operational capabilities to form new value constellation and, finally, reconfiguring assets and resources to stabilise and protect the new business model. Further details of the relevant dynamic capabilities are shown in Table 3.3.

4 | A case study: using the exploitation approach to develop a service business

SIG Pack is a typical example of a company following the exploitation approach. SIG Pack was dedicated to manufacturing packaging machines and systems. SIG Pack belonged to the Swiss Industrial Company Holding Ltd. before it was acquired by Bosch Packaging in 2004. Prior to this acquisition SIG Pack had begun to follow the exploitation approach.

4.1 Phase 1: integrating basic services into the product price

Services were initially considered to be an addition to the packaging machines and systems: they were interpreted as being an integral part of the machine and systems offerings. Services were often used to augment SIG's premium prices for packaging machines and systems during negotiation processes. Sales managers felt uncomfortable with the idea of trying to convince customers to pay for services. They preferred to provide the services free of charge instead of giving customers price discounts for the machines and systems. SIG's sales personnel were even reluctant to mention services in the negotiation phase: they thought that discussing services would imply that their packaging systems and machines could malfunction which, in turn, would erode SIG's reputation for quality.

The result was that SIG Pack did not pay much attention to after-sales services. Their service organisation was integrated into the product divisions (machines and systems), as illustrated on the left-hand side of Figure 4.1. These divisions paid insufficient attention to services and restricted their service activities to merely provide warranty services, which were integrated into the prices of packaging machines and systems. Once the warranty time of the packaging machines had passed, SIG Pack assumed that reliability was a core characteristic of their packaging machines and systems. Their service staff was, therefore, obliged to ensure the functionality of the packaging machines

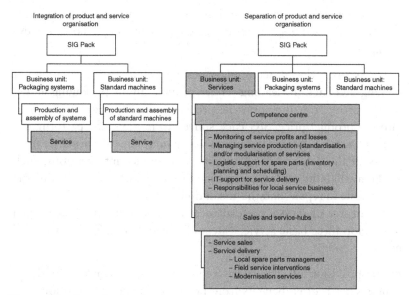

Figure 4.1: Organisational structures

and systems in order to make them function at an optimum. Some after-sales services were still offered free of charge even after the warranty period had expired. SIG Pack's service market was, needless to say, highly underdeveloped.

4.2 Phase 2: separating product and service businesses to increase the profit and revenue generated by service

Three key issues triggered SIG Pack's management team to reconsider its approach to providing services.

1. Management recognised that maintenance services were becoming increasingly important in protecting the customer's investments in packaging machines and systems. Maintenance services not only ensure the functionality of machines and systems but also improve the efficiency and effectiveness of the customer's packaging processes.
2. Maintenance services are a more stable source of revenue and can compensate for fluctuations in the revenues of both machines and systems.
3. An attractive business opportunity is offered by maintenance services. The goal was to achieve about 30 per cent of the total

revenues via services. Additional revenues generated by services were expected to compensate for the eroding margins of the packaging machines and systems.

These three triggers were integrated into a clear strategy aimed at making SIG Pack the leading service provider in the packaging industry. Departing from their previous preoccupation of integrating services into the product price, SIG Pack started to improve the performance of their services. Specific attention was paid to key performance indicators of the delivery of spare parts and service interventions, such as the availability and delivery time of spare parts, as well as to the 'mean time to repair' and the 'mean time between failures'. Once a sufficient degree of service performance was achieved, SIG Pack started to develop three basic service categories: spare parts, field service and modernisation.

- The provision of spare parts represents the most profitable business since it often benefits from being in a monopoly position. The spare parts in this case can be divided into those manufactured by SIG Pack and those purchased from suppliers. Manufactured spare parts are more profitable than those purchased: regardless of the type, customers require their rapid delivery. Slow responses from SIG Pack in providing spare parts will result in the customer being highly motivated to switch to alternative suppliers. These alternative suppliers of spare parts are not only local manufacturers that copy SIG Pack's original parts but also SIG Pack's suppliers. These suppliers sometimes bypass the equipment manufacturer and sell their spare parts directly to the customer.
- Modernisation services enhance the lifetime of the packaging machines and systems; they also provide the customer better returns on their investments. Modernisation services also involve spare parts.
- Field services embrace typical repair and inspection activities. The aim of regular inspections and repairs is to prevent failures in the packaging machines and systems. Emergency repair services are necessary when breakdowns or failures occur. Field services compete not only with third-party providers of service but also customers that perform regular repair, maintenance and inspection services themselves. Third-party providers of service include service specialists who concentrate on a few services, and sometimes even former

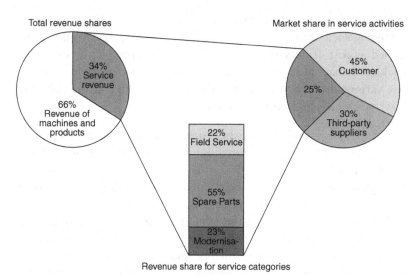

Figure 4.2: Financial indicators
Source: Hänggi (2004).

service technicians who have started their own companies in the service business. Such service specialists and service technicians are able to offer cost advantages over SIG Pack.

Together these three basic services comprise SIG Pack's value proposition of designing, manufacturing and servicing packaging machines and systems. These packaging machines and systems are of superior quality and position in the premium segment; they are also complex and highly-customised. Services embracing spare parts, modernisation and field service, for example, add to their value.

SIG Pack and/or Bosch Packaging thus follow an incremental path in increasing the contribution that services make to value. In 2006, the share of service revenue reached by Bosch Packaging was 34 per cent. This corresponds to a market share of 25 per cent of all the service activities necessary to operate packaging machines and systems. Customers remain the major competitors regarding service activities, capturing a market share of about 45 per cent. Third-party providers of service have a market share of 30 per cent. Revenues from service are divided by the three basic services: field service covers 22 per cent, spare parts around 55 per cent and modernisation the remaining 23 per cent (see Figure 4.2).

Restructuring the after-sales services was the main obstacle in achieving such attractive service revenues. Initially, service units functioned as cost centres and were attached to the product divisions for packaging machines and systems. This initial organisational structure has various disadvantages if it is to create attractive growth of both service revenues and profits, namely:

- The whole organisation experienced that insufficient focus was placed on the customer throughout the entire life cycle of the packaging systems.
- Services were perceived as being an addition to the products when they were regarded as cost centres. They were seen as having a pure cost-monitoring function rather than being a measure of the growth in service. A service cost centre would also gain little momentum in improving the service performance and quality for enhancing customer satisfaction. Only customers who are truly satisfied with the performance and quality of the services, however, are happy to pay for them.

SIG Pack decided to create a separate strategic business unit for services in order to overcome these disadvantages. This business unit covered various responsibilities, as illustrated on the right-hand side of Figure 4.1. The responsibilities include being in charge of the sales and service hubs that promote, sell and deliver services as well as supporting the functions for the actual operation of the sales and service hubs. These support functions include standardising the service processes and IT-infrastructures, managing the products for the services and managing the handover between the machine and system division and the service division.

Two main arguments provided the rationale for creating the separate strategic business unit for services:

- As a strategic business unit, the service business has its own profit-and-loss responsibility, which is based on the financial transparency of service costs and revenues. Financial transparency allows SIG Pack not only to track the profitability of services and their economic impact on the overall performance of the company but also to provide sufficient resources for developing the service business. Financial transparency, however, also has a major drawback: it assumes that the services, and not the machines and systems, create the majority of the profit. Executives from the product divisions were observed as being rather reluctant to using such transparency: the use of a 'double accounting' system is a temporary solution that may overcome this reluctance. Such an accounting system enables SIG Pack to track profitability as before, with the added bonus that the financial impact of the service business is transparent.

- Being a separated strategic business unit, the service organisation benefits from creating a dedicated service culture. SIG Pack has not previously emphasised values and behaviours when expanding the service business. It focused instead on the prototypic values and behaviours of manufacturing that support manufacturing efficiency, economies of scale and the belief that responding to the service needs of the customer is costly. A service culture is based on values and behaviours that encourage customisation and flexibility when responding to the customer's business and operational needs. Attempting to develop and retain both a manufacturing and a service culture can be viewed as a dominant culture clashing with a counterculture. The managerial challenge is not only to create a service culture but also to maintain the uneasy symbiotic relationship that exists between the dominant culture and the counterculture. In effect, managing this relationship is a means of diffusing resistance to change by balancing the manufacturing and service cultures instead of totally substituting one set of values and behaviour for another. Managing the product and service businesses in separate business units is an attractive way of creating a service culture without eroding the manufacturing culture. SIG Pack's strategic business units for services have laid the foundation for new ways of thinking about value creation and customer orientation. More specifically, the service staff developed a distinctive service mentality whereby employees were not only aware of the importance of comprehensive and high-quality after-sales services but also acted accordingly. The latter illustrates that, where field services are concerned, the service staff developed the values and behaviours required by reliable troubleshooters for enhancing the performance of the customer's packaging process. In addition, the service employees actively took on the role of problem-solver and regarded the service needs and concerns of the customer as being of great importance.

4.3 Phase 3: exploiting service expansion in the primary customer activity chain

Once the service division was in place, SIG Pack and/or Bosch expanded service offerings incrementally. Based on substantial financial returns of the three basic services (spare parts, field service and modernisation) increasingly customised service packages were assembled and the idea of offering service-level agreements was considered. Further details of Bosch and how it continued to extend its service business are illustrated in Chapter 6.

5 | A case study: using the exploration approach to develop a service business

This case study examines the exploration approach used by Hilti in the development of its service business that led to the formation of a radically new service-orientated business model. The focus of the model lies in describing the development from the perspective of the dynamic capabilities required. The structure of the case is: company background, initial situation and triggers for the development of the service business, exploring service opportunities and, finally, reconfiguration of the business logic.

5.1 Background of the company

Hilti is a leading provider of technology to the global construction industry. Hilti's products, services and system solutions address professional construction and building maintenance activities: measuring and opening (such as drilling and demolition), executing cutting and grinding work and, finally, fastening and closing after work has been completed (Figure 5.1). Hilti's strategic positioning is reflected in the corporate strategy, which is based on the customer, competency and concentration. The strategy puts the customer first and then seeks to align corporate activities with customer needs: the goal is to be the customers' best partner in fulfilling their requirements by focusing on proximity and application know-how. Competency represents Hilti's commitment to being a leader regarding innovation and quality, having direct access and relationships to the customer, as well as ensuring internationally uniform effective marketing and sales processes that benefit the customer to a maximum. Two-thirds of the employees, for example, work directly for the customer in sales organisations and in engineering. Concentration stands for the focus on products and markets where leadership positions can be achieved and sustained. Hilti's corporate strategy is thus based on three components: product leadership, market scope and operational excellence. Figure 5.2 illustrates

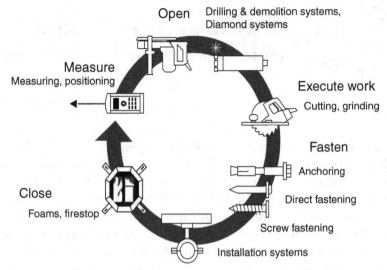

Figure 5.1: Hilti System Solutions
Source: Hilti (2004).

the business model and corporate strategy based on the customer, competency and concentration.

5.2 Initial situation and triggers for developing the service business

Hilti was highly reputed for developing, manufacturing and selling high-quality tools and offering product-related services such as maintenance and repair for a long time prior to the repeated identification of complaints by dissatisfied customers pertaining to after-market service studies, which initiated the development of a distinct after-market strategy at the end of the 1990s. Strategy development started as a typical exploitation approach to the development of the service business. As a part of strategy development Hilti's corporate development department initiated a project to evaluate the potential of extending the service business. It was based on analysing the actual need for Hilti to extend their service business and identifying the general conditions that favour the development of their service business. Identifying

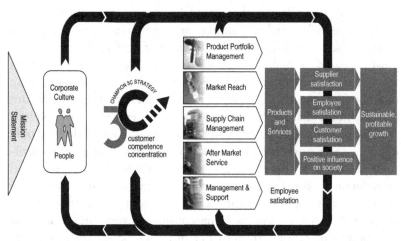

Figure 5.2: The Hilti business model and corporate strategy
Source: Hilti (2004).

these favourable conditions focused on three perspectives: company, customer and competitor. The company perspective, for example, included factors such as a high installed base, decreasing product margins, a volatile product business or bargaining power in the market. The customer perspective referred to an increasing tendency towards outsourcing, a lack of know-how, pressure to reduce costs or enhanced customer needs. The competitor perspective included the homogenisation of the market of the product in question, the degree of maturity of the industry and/or the service offered by competitors. Hilti analysed the service business in various manufacturing companies in order to take advantage of the favourable conditions of the competitive situation. The intention was to identify the distinct success factors and barriers for developing the service business in these companies and then transfer the best practices to their own business activities, if they were applicable. Furthermore, benchmarking the service potentials in various sectors, such as the aircraft, computer/printer, automobile/automobile supply industries, served to evaluate Hilti's service potential by comparison. The analysis was based on criteria that included the installed base versus new product sales ratio, the economic activity of the life cycle relative to the cost of the product or the declining ability to differentiate the product.

The major conclusion that could be drawn from analysing the service potential of various manufacturing companies within different industrial sectors was that the development of product-related services must be based on high-value products such as expensive production machinery and elevators. Hilti recognised that services supporting only the functionality of its power tools would not create a significant increase in the share of revenues attributed to services: i.e. the exploitation of product-related service opportunities provided Hilti with only a limited service potential. However, changes in the competitive environment caused by low-end entrants who benefited from lower global manufacturing costs to become sufficiently good to compete in, and erode away at, the market for high-quality tools led to the development of the service business being considered anew and a different direction being taken. Driven by one of Hilti's local market organisations, the exploration of new service opportunities resulted in a radically new service-orientated business model. The dynamic capabilities of Hilti's exploration of service opportunities follow herewith.

5.3 Exploring service opportunities and reconfiguring the business logic

5.3.1 Sensing service opportunities and threats

The recognition that Hilti Power Tools only represented B or C-classed products for customers (Dickies, 1951) drove the search for service opportunities beyond the primary customer chain of activity that is traditionally addressed. In contrast to the initial after-market development that follows exploitation, Hilti's local market organisation decided to identify and explore service opportunities not by observing competitor behaviour and obvious customer requirements in their primary activity chains but by concentrating on revealing and focusing on latent customer problems in adjacent customer activities, which was aided greatly by its direct customer access. Hilti's customers focused on the higher value A-classed products such as heavy construction machinery that are also required for construction work but, relatively speaking, did not pay much attention to Hilti products. Products such as power drills or hammers were, instead, often considered as commodities; rather, the brand name did not always matter as long as the desired function was provided. An illustration of the low emphasis placed on Hilti products is, for example, customers who reported that they had bought a large number of Hilti tools over the years but had lost track of them because nobody had paid them any attention. A consequence of Hilti products being B or C-classed is that of common neglect, causing the customer problems that include a lack of transparency over the tool fleet, high administrative costs, high fluctuating costs, old and worn-out tools being used and many thefts. All in all, B and C-product management was unproductive and inefficient. It was discovered that the latent problems of the customers' management of their tool fleet provided a promising opportunity for developing Hilti's service business.

Hilti wasted no time in looking for analogical solutions to similar problems in other industries, being ready to reconsider their existing traditional business logic. Hilti did not focus on stand-alone service solutions analysing, instead, innovative service-orientated business models in other industries that were based on selling usage rather than product or service units: Drucker's (1973) argument that customers value the utility of a product or service and not the product or service itself applied all the more to Hilti customers, who placed little emphasis on the B and C-classed products. The business models analysed included, for example, the 'black socks subscription' ('sockscription') model which guarantees the buyer a regular supply of black socks; manufacturers of coffee machines who offer leasing packages for coffee machines that include all maintenance costs; manufacturers of copying machines who transformed themselves from vendors of copiers to vendors of photocopied pages; companies that operate power plants for their customers and take over maintenance work, including all of the responsibility.

An interesting solution for Hilti was found in the automobile industry's established fleet management concept for cars (Table 5.1). This concept is characterised by there being just one agreement for many vehicles between the owner or user of the vehicles and the managing company along with a central procurement and administration system for the entire fleet that offers full transparency over the different types and sizes of vehicles, and includes additional services, such as full maintenance or leasing, as agreed upon.

5.3.2 Seizing service opportunities to formulate strategies

Foreseeing new opportunities to create value for both Hilti and their customers, Hilti's market organisation transferred the fleet management idea to customers' tool fleets (see Table 5.1). Hilti would place

Table 5.1: *Transferring the automotive fleet management concept to the construction industry*

Fleet management in the car industry	Hilti fleet management

• One agreement for many cars (multi-vendor approach)
• Central procurement and administration
• Cars cover different types and sizes
• Additional services such as leasing and financing
	• Fleet management for Hilti tools
	  - One agreement for many Hilti and competitor tools
	  - Additional services such as repair and leasing
	• No consumables, e.g. insert tools, anchors, struts, pipe-rings

Source: Hilti (2004).

all the tools required at the customer's disposal and provide the tool fleet with an 'all inclusive' service package for a fixed monthly sum. Exploring this radically new concept for the power tool industry meant dealing with great uncertainty and novelty. Implementing fleet management would overthrow the existing business logic and create new value constellations between Hilti and their customers, thereby requiring a reconfiguration of the traditional roles of supplier and buyer. Hilti would take over the customer's tool management, which involves taking over all the responsibility and risks from the customer. Although a leasing concept would shift tool ownership back to Hilti, solid financial and legal backup is necessary. A new business model would require a sophisticated risk management approach in order to develop a new invoicing model.

Certain managerial skills were required to foresee the changes in the value constellations and business logic and to assess the risks involved. Neither the development of the new business model nor the formulation of the strategy, however, occurred according to a rigid predefined plan or a great strategic vision: it emerged little by little, through a process of trial and error in different pilot projects, before being introduced widely into all of the relevant Hilti markets. The inherent risks and uncertainties of the new concept were reduced, for example, by the market organisations taking various scenarios into consideration in order to address the customers' adjacent administrative processes during the time the strategy was being formulated. One scenario included managing only Hilti tools whilst a second included the management of products from other suppliers. In the latter scenario, fleet modernisation

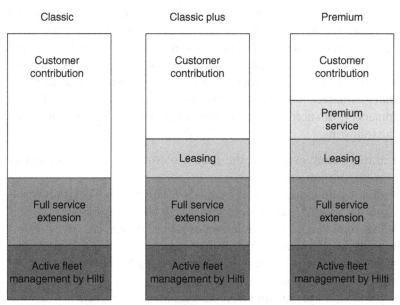

Figure 5.3: The service packages included in the new business model
Source: Hilti (2004)

activities would successively replace non-Hilti products with Hilti products as and when required. In addition, Hilti developed three service packages, each with a different scope of services, to be delivered with fleet management (Figure 5.3). The 'basic' package included active fleet management and full service for the tools being provided by Hilti; the 'medium' package included the basic package features plus leasing, whilst the 'premium' package offered additional services. Hilti thereby offered to relieve customers from the responsibilities and risks associated with customer processes. Allowing the strategy to emerge from trial-and-error processes and various scenarios was strongly favoured by the flexibility and entrepreneurial spirit of the managers in the market organisations. The open-mindedness of the top management to let the market organisations run the risk of exploring new value opportunities was backed up by the general, and deeply ingrained, culture of innovativeness that permeates the company as a whole.

Exploring various scenarios with the ulterior motive of formulating a new business model based on the management of a tool fleet was not, however, intended to replace the existing services for typical product-related problems associated with, for example, repairs and maintenance. Rather, the existing services would be integrated into the fleet management concept to form a common, field-tested and approved base. The various scenarios developed also had in common a clearly defined value proposition of the tool fleet management idea that guaranteed more productivity and less administration for the customers. More specifically, the benefits offered to the customers included the following:

- transparency over both the fleet and costs, fixed and foreseeable costs for tools and repairs;
- minimal administrative effort, modernisation of the fleet (thus ensuring an optimal fleet of tools with a high level of availability);
- low total fleet costs, a high level of tool performance;
- a high level of safety on the work site and more motivated employees;
- fixed monthly payments (thereby preserving liquidity);
- clear identification of each tool; and
- fewer shortages of equipment and enhanced flexibility.

5.3.3 Reconfiguring to explore service opportunities

The implementation of a service-orientated business model based on the fleet management concept led to a radical shift in supplier–buyer relationships and the traditional business logic. Fleet management enabled Hilti to change from selling product units to selling product usage. The major challenges for Hilti in implementing the management of a fleet, however, lay in developing from scratch the skills necessary for assessing and invoicing the risks of taking over the responsibility for customer processes, offering leasing contracts and theft insurance, as well as guaranteeing product availability and reconfiguring operational capabilities to match the new requirements, which are primarily referred to as 'adapting human resources and integrating and centralising IT processes'. Adapting human resources referred in particular to Hilti's sales force, which had to develop new skills in selling complex fleet management contracts and long-term customer relationship management rather than simply selling products, as before. Initially, Hilti trained the heads of the sales forces and selected sales staff in the belief that it would be an impossible task to educate the entire sales force in the art of selling fleet management contracts that included complicated leasing and insurance components. However, the high success and acceptance of fleet management led Hilti to reconsider and simplify the concept, thereby displaying the flexibility that allowed the entire sales force to sell fleet management contracts. As a consequence, Hilti provided all sales management personnel with greater decision-making authority in serving the new business logic. Integrating and centralising IT systems was important for the worldwide implementation of fleet management and standardised processes. Hilti's IT systems needed to be integrated and reconfigured in relevant areas and organisational divisions since fleet management included, for example, selling new products and providing service packages (such as maintenance, repairs and the replacement of spare parts) as well as leasing services, all of which are based on complex financial calculations.

Hilti considered it unnecessary, on the other hand, to modify its organisational structure widely in the course of shifting towards the new service-orientated business model. Hilti kept its local market organisations in which the sales staff henceforth sold fleet management contracts, including combined product and service packages, via the established direct sales channels to the customers instead of mere products. Product and service sales were integrated with the sales function and specialised service technicians, who were also assigned to the local market organisations, delivered services.

The main service components of the fleet management concept, e.g. maintenance, inspection, repair and training services, were already in use and did not need to be developed from scratch. The increase in productivity and decrease in administrative efforts for the customer could be achieved through operational excellence in services. The goal was to provide standardised services in a rapid and reliable manner by becoming a 'service factory' in which productivity increases through low levels of customer interaction and customisation and relatively short delivery times (Schmenner, 1986). At the same time, the use of standardised services allowed Hilti to reduce uncertainty by making fleet management planning more predictable. Being able to use existing service processes reduced Hilti's reconfiguration activities greatly.

6 | Developing service business via the exploitation approach

This chapter examines the exploitation approach in greater depth. It goes beyond the three phases explained in Section 3.3 and has three primary objectives: the first is to provide insight into the various service strategies applied by companies to exploit service opportunities. The second is to highlight the common changes in the strategies used, and the third is to provide an overview of the operational capabilities that need to be aligned with the service strategies. This overview lays the foundation for Chapter 7, which describes the configuration of operational capabilities for each service strategy in more detail.

6.1 Service strategies associated with the exploitation approach

The following paragraphs combine the traditional content perspective of the conceptualisation of service strategies and service offerings with the dynamic perspective of making changes between service strategies. By integrating both of these loosely linked static and dynamic perspectives, the objective here is to identify if, and how, companies move from one service strategy to another in order to discover the stages that are prevalent when their service business is being developed.

6.1.1 Potential service strategies

Various potential service strategies have been discussed over the past few years. In the early 1990s most companies applied either a *customer service strategy* or an *after-sales service strategy*. Since then, companies seem to have developed more sophisticated service strategies, namely *customer support services* and *development partner strategies*. Other even more advanced service strategies, developed in the last few years, refer to the *outsourcing partner strategy* or *supplementary service strategy*.

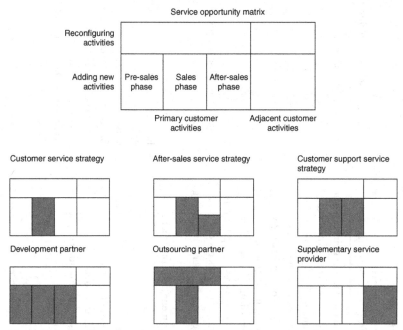

Figure 6.1: Service strategies for exploiting service opportunities

These six service strategies correspond to specific positions in the service opportunity matrix (see Figure 6.1). The customer service strategy concentrates purely on services in the sales phase; after-sales service and customer support service strategies aim at the sales and usage phase (i.e. the after-sales phase). A development partner covers the whole life cycle, starting with the pre-sales and sales phase and ending with the usage phase (after-sales phase). All of these four strategies focus on the primary activities of the customer and on adding new services to these activities. Procurement of an outsourcing partner aims at reconfiguring customer activities, whereas a supplementary service strategy is a question of exploiting opportunities in the adjacent activity chain of the customer. As illustrated in Figure 6.1, outsourcing partners concentrate on the reconfiguration of customer activities in the after-sales phase: should the customers be unwilling to outsource their activities of operating or maintaining the product, however, they add just services to the customer activity chain.

Table 6.1: *Value propositions and service offerings of service strategies*

	Value proposition	Main focus of service offering	Additional service offerings
Customer service strategy	Improving the customer relationship	Customer services, e.g. information services, sales consulting and documentation services	No additional services
After-sales service provider	Correcting product faults	Basic services for the installed base, e.g. spare parts, repairs, hotlines, inspection, installation, commissioning and training	Customer service
Customer support service provider (advanced services)	Avoiding product faults; increasing efficiency and effectiveness of the customer's processes	Advanced services, e.g. preventive maintenance, process optimisation and extensive operator training	Customer service Basic services for the installed base
Development partner	Reducing development times and costs whilst improving quality	Development and construction services	Customer service Basic services for the installed base Advanced services
Outsourcing partner	Reducing capital commitment; continuously improving the outsourced processes	Operation services for customer processes (e.g. maintenance and operator models)	Customer service Basic services for the installed base Advanced services
Supplementary service provider	Covering attractive additional customer needs far beyond the activities concerned with the product	Single services for adjacent customer activities	Customer service Basic services for the installed base Advanced services

Each service strategy possesses a unique value proposition, which ensures competitive differentiation. The value proposition is formed by a few services that dominate the service offering and some additional services (see Table 6.1).

The service strategies can be summarised in the following way:

- The *customer service strategy* (or a customer service provider) augments the product by offering customer service. It is consistent with the belief that customer service enhances both the quality of the product and its reputation by increasing the general quality of the interaction between the buyer and seller (Mathieu, 2001a).
- The *after-sales service strategy* (or *after-sales service provider*) involves offering product-related services (or basic services for the installed base) with a few customer services as add-ons to the products. Its main focus is on after-sales services that ensure the proper functioning of the product. It is similar to the notion of product services as well as entering the service market for the installed base (Mathieu, 2001a; Oliva and Kallenberg, 2003). After-sales service providers support customers during the usage of their products and ensure that product faults are remedied. They form a value proposition by providing products at attractive prices and guaranteeing the proper functioning of the product through after-sales services. After-sales service providers use an independent pricing approach that allows customers to select the after-sales services they require: prices can be compared and discounts negotiated. The service offering comprises spare and wearing parts, repairs, inspections, basic training and troubleshooting.
- The *customer support service strategy* (or *customer support service provider*) attaches great importance to maintenance services: the emphasis on basic services for the installed base is lower than for an after-sales service provider. Typical examples of such maintenance services are preventive maintenance, maintenance agreements and process-orientated optimisation. Customer support service providers thereby also concentrate on expanding the service offering to cover usage of the product. They focus moreover on services that prevent faults and breakdowns instead of merely reacting when these have occurred. Such prevention of failures and breakdowns increases the availability of the product within customer processes. Therefore, the value proposition of a customer support service provider is to avoid product faults in order to increase the efficiency and effectiveness

of customer processes. Customer support service providers succeed with this value proposition when their market consists of customers desiring outstanding product quality. Product performance and reliability remain important purchasing attributes: customers not only invest in reliable products but also increasingly demand services that improve the efficiency and effectiveness of the product in the usage phase of operating the installed base. Compared to after-sales service providers, customer support service providers are not faced with the same degree of competitive intensity regarding price levels and discounts. Providers of customer support service are still able to achieve elements of differentiation through technical superiority.

- The value proposition of *development partners* is based on providing design and construction services. The emphasis placed on maintenance services is similar to that of providers of customer support services: basic services for the installed base and operational services are of medium to low importance. A development partner tends to offer services in the phase prior to the actual acquisition of the product. Customers expect specific solutions for their operating processes. Greater specialisation of customer processes and a clearer definition of the operating processes involved are the core competencies that seem to be the driving forces of a higher demand for innovative solutions for customer processes. Development partners also report that competitive equality has been reached in the field of products and after-sales services, leading to an essentially greater competitive intensity. Sustainable competitive advantages are gained mainly by designing individual solutions for customer processes. A development partner not only develops its own products but also offers customers its development skills as a service. Such companies position themselves in the field between supporting development activity and shifting responsibility for performing individual development activities. Knowledge-intensive services, such as providing customised designs and supporting R&D tasks, allow development partners to align themselves as strategic partners of the customer. Creating customised designs or development allows specific knowledge to be transferred between the customer and development partner. This knowledge is hard to replicate and, in effect, excludes competitors from gaining access to the customer. As far as these services are concerned, the customer outsources certain activities within the development process to the development partner.

- The *outsourcing partner strategy* offers the highest level of operational (outsourcing) services. The basic services for the installed base and maintenance services are of moderate importance; R&D services are of only marginal importance. Outsourcing partners take on the responsibility of carrying out an entire customer process, which may consist of primary and/or supplementary customer activities. Assuming responsibility for an entire customer process means that a customer pays exclusively for the service rendered. An outsourcing partner combines cost leadership with service and product differentiation in order to offer attractive prices for operational services. The aim is to assume the operating risk and full responsibility for the customer's operating processes. The value proposition is simply based on reducing the capital employed by the customer and managing the corresponding risks. In contrast to providers of customer support services, outsourcing partners do not create customised service packages. Operational services are standardised and focus on efficiency, economies of scale and the belief that service customisation is costly. However, offering attractive prices for the performance of the outsourced process without sufficient quality of both product and service is insufficient: a product that fails frequently and requires troubleshooting, repairs and spare parts increases service costs which, in turn, will lead to the potential erosion of overall profitability.
- *Supplementary service providers* focus on services in supplementary customer activities that have no direct effect on the availability and functionality of the product. The value proposition has to cover a wide range of needs beyond the direct relationship to the actual product. This strategy has been observed only occasionally in companies and is, therefore, not included in the following sections. One of the rare examples of a company that has employed this strategy is Festo, a German supplier of factory and process automation. Festo established the Festo Didactic Inc., which offers an education and qualification service for automation processes. Festo Didactic is a leading company in the field of industrial training that has developed solutions for enhancing learning success over the entire spectrum of production and process automation.

These short descriptions illustrate how these service strategies differ in the characteristics of the business environment (competition and customers), competitive priorities and revenue logic. Table 6.2

Table 6.2: *Summary of the six service strategies*

Service strategies	Business environment	Competitive priorities	Business logic
Customer service strategy	- Sufficient technical functionality dominates the needs of the customer - Competitive advantages emerge from technological superiority and close customer relationships	- Costs and quality	- Refinancing R&D efforts through pure product sales - Services are offered for 'free'
After-sales service provider	- Customer expectations exceed pure technical functionality: basic services ensuring product functionality are demanded - Competitive advantages emerge from technological superiority, close customer relationships and service performance (availability of parts, mean time taken to repair, etc.)	- Reasonable product costs - Maximising time spent at the customer's site	- Refinancing R&D efforts through sales of products and services - Services are charged as labour and material costs
Customer support service provider	- Customer expectations: focus on improved efficiency and effectiveness of their operational processes	- Outstanding quality of product and service - Minimising time spent at the customer's site	- Refinancing R&D efforts through sales of products and service contracts - Service contracts are offered at a (partially) fixed price for a specific period

	- Competitive advantages emerge from superiority in the technology and quality of the product, close customer relationships and outstanding process performance (low mean time between failures)		
Development partner	- Customer seeks strategic partnerships with key suppliers - Competitive advantages emerge from the co-creation of competencies between the customer and the supplier	- Strategic partnerships with key customers - Enhancing transfer of knowledge between the customer and supplier	- Refinancing R&D efforts through sales of products and services - Service contracts are offered at a (partially) fixed price for a specific period - Design and construction services are charged separately (credit for product purchased)
Outsourcing partner	- Customer prefers to avoid owning the product and pay only for the performance of the product - Competition focuses on the costs involved in achieving the performance levels desired	- Cost leadership in operating the customer's processes	- Refinancing the product costs by paying for the actual performance
Supplementary service provider	- Customer expects outstanding services far beyond their primary activities - Competition is about identifying additional service opportunities	- Innovativeness in diverse set of customer activities	- Supplementary services are charged separately

summarises the competitive priorities of each service strategy, the business environment and the revenue logic.

Companies change their strategies over time. The next section describes these changes and explains the pattern that companies follow when they change service strategies.

6.1.2 Stages in the pattern of change

The majority of capital goods manufacturers studied changed their service strategy over time. The strategy changes that are described emerged in the three phases that characterise the exploitation approach (see Section 3.3). When service strategy is changed, four stages are seen to recur when a shift is made:

1. from a customer service strategy to an after-sales service strategy;
2. from an after-sales service strategy to customer support service strategy;
3. from a customer support service strategy to being a development partner;
4. from a customer support service strategy to being an outsourcing partner.

The first stage describes the strategic change from customer service strategy to adopting an after-sales service. Firms that rely more on customer service move towards the provision of after-sales services. Very few firms seem to adhere to the customer service strategy, suggesting that it is becoming increasingly insignificant in achieving competitive advantages.

The second involves the strategic move from being a provider of after-sales service to being a provider of customer support services (or advanced services). Again, very few after-sales service providers seem to remain with this service strategy. For example, these companies continued to move into the provision of design and construction services, thereby positioning themselves as a development partner. The emphasis of being a development partner in maintenance services suggests that this is the prevalent sequence of events.

The third stage consequently captures the strategic intent to move from being providers of customer support services to being development partners. Finally, the fourth refers to the strategic change made from providing customer support services to becoming outsourcing

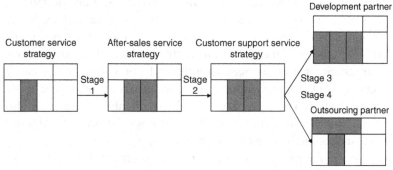

Figure 6.2: The pattern followed when service strategy is changed in relation to the service opportunities available

partners. The dominating route that is taken when moving from being providers of customer support service to adopting other service strategies, such as being a development and then an outsourcing partner, however, is less clear.

The various changes in service strategies correspond with stepwise changes in the service opportunities exploited, as illustrated in Figure 6.2.

- *Stage 1* in the pattern (*moving from a customer service strategy to an after-sales service strategy*) is triggered by an increasing understanding of the development of the service business as being a strategic option for achieving differentiation and as a source of additional competitive advantages. Furthermore, a strong recognition of the service potential of the installed bases encourages companies to make this move in strategy. Managers recognise specifically the financial potential of the service offers. The services are typically sold and promoted as service products with a clear definition of their outcome (e.g. a certain reaction time, the availability of a hotline and set service charges for repairs).
- *Stage 2* (*changing from an after-sales service strategy to a strategy embracing customer support service*) is initiated by the realisation that selling high-quality products requires a more sophisticated service approach than offering basic services. In such a situation, customers increasingly demand that failures, faults and breakdowns are prevented instead of being fixed as soon as possible. Such more advanced customer needs can only be addressed by highly

customised, preventive maintenance services. Rapidly developing information technologies enable a more sophisticated exchange of information between the customer and the service providers, thereby allowing the condition of the products to be tracked via remote monitoring services. Consequently, preventive maintenance services and the prevention of product breakdowns become more cost-effective. Therefore, the availability of information technologies is another important trigger for moving from an after-sales service strategy to a strategy of customer support service.

- *Stage 3* in the pattern (*moving from a customer support service strategy to being a development partner*) is motivated by an increasing customer demand for support in coping with rapid changes. Customers seem to rely increasingly on the R&D competencies of the manufacturing company instead of building their own technical competencies.
- *Stage 4* (*moving from a customer support service strategy to being an outsourcing partner*) is initiated when increasing competitive pressure forces customers to downsize and produce at lower costs. In such a situation, they do not consider the maintenance and/or operation of their products as being necessary core competencies believing, instead, that these become non-core activities that can be outsourced to competitors.

Table 6.3 highlights the key characteristics of the stages in the pattern followed when service strategy is changed.

The more intensive exploitation of service opportunities comes with a cost. Changing service strategy also has disadvantages: it requires investments and increases potential risks, too. For example, moving from a customer service strategy to one of after-sales service requires investing in a service infrastructure. A service infrastructure includes setting up local warehouses for spare parts and organising service centres to provide basic services for the installed base as quickly and efficiently as possible. Establishing a service infrastructure confronts the providers of after-sales service with the risks of covering its running costs, which is problematic since it is very difficult to predict product failures. A suitable way of reducing these costs is to involve partners (e.g. distributors or service specialists). Such partners could cover some of the investments costs which, in turn, would be regained through the service revenues and profits generated. In the long term, however, establishing service partners can also have a serious negative

Table 6.3: *Summary of the stages observed when service strategy is changed*

	Description	Triggers
Stage 1	• Changing the value proposition from improving the customer relationship to rectifying products faults • Extending the service offering of a customer service strategy to include after-sales services such as spare parts, repairs, inspections, hotlines, installations and commissions	• Understanding that service business development is a strategic option for creating differentiation • Recognising the service potential of the installed base • Marketing and selling services as products
Stage 2	• Changing the value proposition from rectifying product faults to avoiding faults and increasing the efficiency and effectiveness of customer processes • Extending the service offering of an after-sales service strategy to include maintenance services such as preventive maintenance, process optimisation and extensive user training	• Increasing customer demand for product efficiency and effectiveness • Realising that selling high-quality products requires a more sophisticated service approach than offering reactive after-sales services • Increasing demand for customised services
Stage 3	• Extending the value proposition of avoiding faults and increasing efficiency and effectiveness of customer processes to the pre-sales phase with reduced development times and costs whilst maintaining high quality • Extending the service offering of a customer support service strategy to include development and construction services	• Rapidly developing new technologies that enable new product and process solutions • Increasing customer demand for support to cope with rapid changes • Possessing comprehensive R&D competencies
Stage 4	• Extending the value proposition of avoiding faults and increasing efficiency and effectiveness of customer processes to reducing capital commitment and improving the outsourced processes continuously • Extending the service offering of a customer support service strategy to include outsourcing services that take over the responsibility for operating customer processes	• Growing competitive pressure that forces customers to downsize and produce at lower costs • Changing customer needs that focus on core competencies and outsource non-core activities

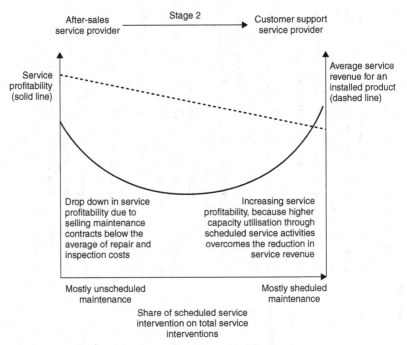

Figure 6.3: Effects of Stage 2 on service profitability and revenue

aspect: the service partners can become potential competitors once a company decides to move forward with its service strategy.

Moving from a strategy of providing after-sales service to being a provider of customer support services exposes a company to the risks that are involved when the revenue logic is changed. Instead of being paid for each service or part provided, providers of customer support services offer a fixed service fee (in the form of a contract) for a defined period of time. In order to convince customers to sign a contract, companies often reduce the cost of the actual services: the service fee for one year will be 10 to 20 per cent less than the sum of all the single parts and services. This reduction reduces the profitability in the short term so, in order to achieve a similar degree of profitability, providers of customer support services have to increase the level of the planned service intervention of the service contracts to about 40 per cent of their total capacity utilisation (see Figure 6.3).

Moving from a customer support service strategy to being a development partner brings with it a significant increase in development costs. The financial risk is the high development costs that cannot

Table 6.4: *Risks involved when changing service strategy*

Change in service strategy	Risks	Actions
Stage 1: from customer service to after-sales service	- Investments must be made to create a service infrastructure	- Involving partners to deliver the service instead of setting up own service centres
Stage 2: from after-sales service to customer support service	- Reduction in profitability due to service contracts generating less revenue	- Penetrating the installed base with service contracts to increase the rate of utilisation
Stage 3: from customer support service to development partner	- Covering of customer-specific development costs	- Charging design and construction services separately and offering to equalize them when the product is purchased
Stage 4: from customer support service to outsourcing partner	- Taking over the operational risks of the customer	- Risk pooling - Integrating risks in the pricing of performance

be covered when customers do not buy the products. The only way to avoid such a risk is by charging for the design and construction services separately. This, however, is often difficult to accomplish because customers consider such services as being a part of the sales process. Charging separately often deviates from the prevailing logic of the industry: it assumes that design and construction services form a part of the sales and pre-sales efforts of the supplier. Development partners, therefore, often charge for services but offer to equalise the service price by reducing the actual cost of the product by the same amount.

Finally, moving towards being an outsourcing partner involves taking over the customer's operational risks. The costs associated with these risks should be integrated with the price charged for the performance of the product. A supplier also has the option of setting up a risk pooling procedure in order to leverage the operational risks of one specific customer against several others.

Table 6.4 provides a summary of the stages that are taken when the strategy used is changed.

6.2 Case studies of changes in service strategy

The following four cases are typical illustrations of the four stages of change identified previously.

6.2.1 Stage 1 – Mikron changed from a customer service strategy to an after-sales service strategy

Mikron is a typical example of Stage 1: changing from a customer service strategy to an after-sales service strategy. A supplier of large volume production machinery and systems for manufacturing technology and assembly automation industries, Mikron has extended its service business from offering customer service such as advisory information services, product transport, installation and commissioning to include after-sales services for the installed base such as spare parts packages, repairs, inspections, hotlines and operator training. This development was accompanied by a definition of a distinct service strategy for the service business: previously, services were largely regarded as being free of charge add-ons to product sales rather than marketable (i.e. service) products in their own right.

The competitive challenges shifted the attention of Mikron's top management towards developing their service business as a strategic alternative in achieving differentiation. Recognising the service potential of the large installed base of machinery in the market, Mikron decided to change the focus of their service strategy away from servicing the customer in order to sell more products and towards ensuring the proper functioning of the product with after-sales services. Service business development began by Mikron marketing and selling existing services as products in their own right. This meant charging for services such as installation and commissioning that were before offered together with the product as part of the product price; it involved adapting the billing system and establishing a service controlling system. Mikron extended the breadth of services offered by developing specific after-sales services for the installed base. For example, the product development and product sales divisions combined their knowledge of product functionality and use to develop repair and technical inspection services for the installed base. Mikron focused on rapid and reliable reactions to product faults when they provided after-sales services.

6.2.2 Stage 2 – Trumpf changed from an after-sales service strategy to a customer support service strategy

Trumpf is typical of Stage 2: changing from an after-sales service strategy to a customer support service strategy. Trumpf develops and manufactures high-tech machine tools and technology for various production and medical industries. Traditionally focused on differentiation via technology and quality leadership of its products, Trumpf upgraded its service strategy from after-sales services to customer support services. This led to the combination of selling products of above-average quality with a service concept aimed at avoiding product failure and optimising customer processes.

Extending the breadth of service offering by adding process-orientated customer support services was a consequence of the demands made by customers for increased product efficiency and effectiveness. Trumpf recognised that selling highly complex and reliable products requires a more sophisticated service approach than occasionally offering the services of a help desk or a repair/spare parts service as a reaction to acute problems that occurred very rarely. Based on a good reputation for providing quality products, and to improve its position as long-term partner for its customers, Trumpf shifted its emphasis towards providing process-orientated maintenance services (such as preventive maintenance, full maintenance contracts, process optimisation and extensive advanced user training) in order to prevent product failure and increase the availability of products to its customers' processes. These services are amalgamated into customised packages according to the requirements of the customer. A customer can, for example, choose among maintenance contracts that comprise varying scopes of service offerings. Combining its product and service businesses, the change in service strategy made by Trumpf led to the formation of a unique value proposition: offering products of high quality and reliability, supplemented by outstanding preventive customer support services to avoid failures and increase the efficiency and effectiveness of the customer's processes.

6.2.3 Stage 3 – Ericsson changed from a customer support service strategy to being a development partner

Ericsson Operating Systems is a good example of Stage 3: changing from a customer support service strategy to being a development partner strategy. Ericsson is a leading supplier of telecommunications equipment and services to mobile and fixed network operators all over the world. Pursuing a worldwide differentiation strategy based on technology leadership, Ericsson has positioned itself as a service provider of high quality integrated solutions that are tailored to the requirements of individual customers. The rapidly-changing telecommunications industry forces Ericsson to be extremely committed to, and invest heavily in, R&D if it is to press emerging technological developments and satisfy increasingly demanding customers. Benefiting from its intensive R&D knowledge, Ericsson changed its service strategy from being a provider of customer support service to being a development partner.

Ericsson's service business evolved alongside the development of the telecommunications industry. This development can be seen in changes made on two different levels: the business model level of companies and the technological level. On the former level, the traditional sequential value chain is gradually being replaced by an emerging digital value network that requires the reconfiguration of the existing business models. On the latter level, rapidly developing new technologies such as broadband, multimedia and wideband are providing new solutions to old problems. The changes create the new dilemma of how a profitable business is to be maintained for both Ericsson and its customers. Confronted with this challenge, customers often do not have a precise concept or idea of the final application or installation when they plan the purchase of new equipment. Recognising the service opportunities from the challenges faced by customers, and confident in the solid base of R&D competencies possessed, Ericsson has positioned itself as a partner for developing processes and products by offering design, development and consulting services to its customers. Becoming a development partner enables customers to benefit directly from Ericsson's development competencies, thus leading simultaneously to shorter development times, lower costs and improved quality. The outcome of a successful R&D service is a specially designed and constructed product or process that is tailor-made to the individual requirements of the customer instead of a standard product in a catalogue.

Changing the service strategy from being a provider of customer support service to being a development partner, however, meant that Ericsson encountered resistance from customers: they suspected that this shift may not be the best solution to their problems but rather a solution that suits Ericsson's products. This recurring problem was dealt with by Ericsson acquiring an independent telecommunications consulting company. Although wholly owned by Ericsson, the consultancy is commercially independent, being a provider of professional consulting services that include assisting in purchases, advising on technology, business and strategy issues and business development. The acquisition of the consulting company allowed Ericsson to establish a platform for separating consulting from selling and installing systems. Combining the development of telecommunications systems with the selling of competencies in the independent consulting unit created the credibility Ericsson required to change service strategy. It could then position itself as a professional development partner for high-level integrated telecommunications solutions that included business consulting, network process design, roll-out and integration, competence development and process improvement.

6.2.4 Stage 4 – Bosch Packaging changed from a customer support service strategy to being an outsourcing partner

Bosch Packaging, a global leader of high-quality handling and packaging systems and robotics for industries such as food processing, healthcare, personal care and pharmaceutics changed its service strategy from being a provider of customer support service to being an outsourcing partner (see also Chapter 4). The change of service strategy was a step towards achieving the strategic goal of repositioning the company from being a supplier of technology towards being a provider of services and solutions, where services make a significant contribution to the total revenues and profits.

Given the large size of the installed base of handling and packaging systems, Bosch Packaging recognised the potential of providing services for the installed base at an early stage. Realising that providing services profitably cannot be approached in the same way as selling products due to their different natures, Bosch Packaging decided to focus on developing service as a real independent business additional that is equal to the product business. Services were detached successively from the product business; a separate service business unit was established as a profit centre to promote and develop the service business further. The breadth of the service offering was extended continuously to include product-orientated after-sales services and customer support services such as maintenance contracts, service-level agreements, extended warranties, parts and labour packages and process optimisation as well as services for competitor's products; a significant amount of service revenues was achieved. At this stage, Bosch Packaging was pursuing a customer support service strategy that had its focus partly on proximity to the customer and partly on selling and marketing services proactively to increase the efficiency and quality of the customer processes.

Increasing technological complexity and growing competitive pressure to downsize and produce at lower costs, however, led to changes in the needs of customers. The industrial challenges being faced required them to focus more on core competencies: the outsourcing of non-core activities such as maintenance, logistics and IT to external firms was being considered all the more. Identifying the changing needs of customers and recognising new service opportunities, Bosch Packaging decided to develop operational or outsourcing services for taking over and managing the customer's maintenance function. The value proposition for customers included reducing their capital commitment and ensuring the continuous improvement of the outsourced processes. Adding outsourcing services to the service offering, and thus becoming an outsourcing partner, meant taking over the responsibility for the customer's maintenance processes. Naturally, this meant that Bosch Packaging had to make major reorganisations that included, for example, revising the service processes so that they could provide standardised and efficient delivery of service, introducing tools for measuring the performance and improvement of service, and recruiting and training personnel. Facilitated by the full support of the top management and the organisational independence enjoyed by the service business unit, Bosch Packaging mastered the challenges that were being faced and successfully adopted the service strategy of being an outsourcing partner: it led to an increase in the number of long-term customer relationships and resulted in services contributing to 34 per cent of total revenues (Hänggi, 2004). In the future Bosch Packaging plans on including outsourcing services that offer to take over the operation of entire customer packaging lines.

6.3 Operational capabilities for service strategies

This section provides an overview of the operational capabilities that are associated with the various service strategies. Varying degrees of service orientation in their operational capabilities are necessary if companies are to make profits from service strategies.

Figure 6.4 illustrates the operational capabilities that are important for each strategy. The three operational capability categories concentrated upon are corporate culture, human resource management and organisational structures (see Section 2.3). A value of 1, or close to it, means that the service orientation of the corresponding operational capability is very important for the service strategy, whereas a value close to 0 is less important for the corresponding service strategies. The customer service strategy, for example, is characterised by low service orientation in the operational capabilities of corporate culture, human resource management and organisational structures. Managers can only implement the right operational capabilities if they understand the characteristics of the company's service strategy; more specifically, if they realise that an after-sales service strategy should focus on the implementation of service orientation in corporate values. Consequently, the service orientation of employee behaviour, personnel recruitment, personnel training and personnel assessment/compensation are of less importance. By implementing an after-sales service strategy, they do not need to make a distinction between the product and service businesses. The proximity of the service organisation to customers is of average importance for implementing an after-sales service strategy.

Managers implementing a customer support service strategy should be conscious of the service orientation of human resource management factors (i.e. personnel recruitment, training and assessment/compensation). In common with the strategy of being development partners and outsourcing partners, the customer support service strategy requires the implementation of advanced levels of service orientation in the corporate culture (corporate values and employee behaviour). The degree of distinction between the product and service businesses is also high, whereas the degree of proximity to customers is only of average importance.

The implementation of the development partner strategy is characterised by the operational capabilities reflecting the service orientation

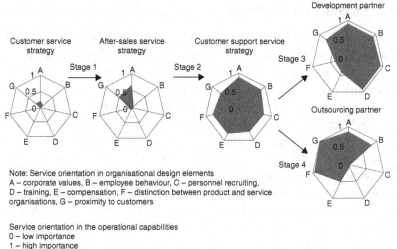

Note: Service orientation in organisational design elements
A – corporate values, B – employee behaviour, C – personnel recruiting,
D – training, E – compensation, F – distinction between product and service
organisations, G – proximity to customers

Service orientation in the operational capabilities
0 – low importance
1 – high importance

The shaded areas show the degree of service orientation in each operational
capability

Figure 6.4: Preliminary operational capabilities for each service strategy

of cultural factors (corporate values and employee behaviour) and
human resource factors (personnel recruitment and training) at a high
level. Development partners also emphasise strongly the degree of
proximity to customers, whilst the distinction between the product
and service businesses and personnel assessment/compensation are of
average importance.

Furthermore, implementing an outsourcing partner strategy requires
managerial efforts that make concise distinctions between the product
and service businesses, the proximity to customers and the service orientation of corporate values and employee behaviour. The three operational
capabilities pertaining to the service orientation of human resource
management are either of low importance (personnel recruitment and
training) or average importance (personnel assessment/compensation).

6.4 Service strategy changes as the antecedent to providing solutions

Once companies succeed with the service strategies and are able to
proceed through the various stages of service strategies, they position themselves all the more as a solution provider. Implementing

the different service strategies are therefore antecedents to providing solutions.

Exhibit 6.1: Providing solutions to manufacturing industries

In the aviation industry, General Electric and Rolls-Royce have moved from selling jet engines and maintenance service packages to selling 'power-by-the-hour' solutions. These solutions mean that the customer pays a fixed warranty and operational fee for the hours that the jet engines are actually being run. This concept forces both General Electric and Rolls-Royce to design and construct a new generation of jet engines in close collaboration with airplane manufacturers and flight operators: being a development partner ensures that the newly designed and constructed jet engines meet high standards vis-à-vis operational efficiency. It also means that both companies can either focus on taking over the entire package from the flight operators which, in turn, implies being an outsourcing partner. General Electric and Rolls-Royce can also choose to concentrate solely on the maintenance package, or even restrict themselves to delivering only basic services. Depending on collaboration with technical maintenance specialists such as Lufthansa Technik, General Electric and Rolls-Royce can be positioned as providers of either after-sales service or customer support service.

The industrial automation division of ABB offers its customers 'performance solutions', i.e. solutions that are tailored according to the individual needs of the customer. The offerings can embrace (1) simple product-related services associated with being an after-sales service provider, (2) maintenance services associated with a customer support service strategy, and (3) outsourcing the whole maintenance activities to ABB which thus becomes an outsourcing partner. Again, ABB's performance solutions are composed of implementing individual service strategies.

As illustrated in Exhibit 6.1 and Figure 6.5, a key issue of providing solutions is the combining and balancing of the service offerings associated with different service strategies. Solution providers are able to utilise innovative combinations of products and services, leading to high-value unified responses to the needs of the customer. Relying on

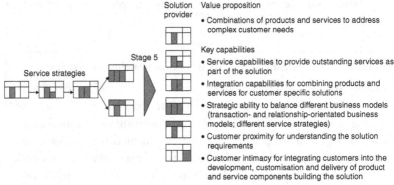

Figure 6.5: Solution providers as combination of different service strategies

the implementation of the various service strategies allows solution providers to support customers throughout the whole life cycle of the product, starting with the pre-purchase phase and ending at the product usage phase. Solution providers also cover reconfiguration as well as the extension of service support in the customer's value activities.

Solution providers include a large number of services in the overall package; since most services are customised to meet the needs of individual customers, solution providers also have to integrate products and services into customised solutions (Davies, 2004; Tuli *et al.*, 2007). Solution providers affect the services offered in the sales phase in two ways.

Firstly, performance offerings change the revenue models, thereby making financial services necessary: 'pay-for-performance' services, for example, require financial arrangements to be made so that the actual performance can be paid for. Payments for maintenance services are based on service-level agreements (SLAs) in which the benefits and/ or sacrifices of achieving/missing the targets are shared between the supplier and the customer (Hünerberg and Hüttmann, 2003).

Secondly, the increasing number of service components embraced by the solution requires the integration of services (Davies, 2004). These include customising activities that ensure that all of the product and service components interact and can be reconfigured according to the needs of the customer. Integration services such as customisation are linked closely to design and construction activities.

7 | Configurations of service strategies and operational capabilities supporting the exploitation approach

The following sections are each devoted to a configuration of operational capabilities and a specific service strategy. Adopting a certain service strategy requires increasing the service orientation in specific operational capabilities. The customer service strategy has lost the potential of providing companies with advantages of differentiation: it seems to have become obsolete in the manufacturing industry and can therefore be neglected in this chapter (see Section 6.1.2). For each of the more sophisticated service strategies (after-sales service providers, customer support service providers, development partners and outsourcing partners) enhancing the service orientation of specific operational capabilities means that companies move from having organisational structures that focus on products to those that focus on services. Whilst the former uses groups of related products as the primary basis for structuring the organisation (Homburg *et al.*, 2000b), the latter includes both product SBUs and service SBUs as the primary basis for structuring the whole organisation (Auguste *et al.*, 2006; Oliva and Kallenberg, 2003).

The characteristics of the operational capabilities pertinent to each of the service strategies are described below. These characteristics include corporate culture (corporate values and employee roles), human resource management (personnel recruitment, training, compensation, assessment and rewards), organisational structure (distinction between product and service business, collaboration between companies and proximity of the service organisation to the customer), service development process (responsibilities and processes for service development and customer involvement in the service development) and IT support for the service business (Homburg *et al.*, 2003; Neu and Brown, 2005).

Each section ends with a summary in the form of a table that serves as a checklist for implementing the service strategies. The chapter concludes with a description of the operational capabilities necessary for being a solution provider.

7.1 Operational capabilities for after-sales service providers

Providers of after-sales service modify several operational capabilities within their corporate culture, human resource management, measurement and reward system, organisational structure and service processes to support their service strategy.

7.1.1 Corporate culture

In terms of corporate culture, after-sales service providers concentrate on two elements: the value of providing after-sales services and the role of the service personnel.

Corporate values

Service employees interpret after-sales services as being an important differentiating factor in the strategy used for marketing products. They understand that services are not just an add-on to the product: they are charged for separately and represent an essential part of the total value creation. Other typical values related to services, such as innovation, customisation and the belief that flexibility and variety create profits do not necessarily develop (Bowen *et al.*, 1989). These values do not seem necessary: they are regarded as being more costly than profitable because after-sales service providers consider the appropriate value of offering after-sales services when providing a high degree of standardisation throughout the different services offered.

Roles of employees

In addition to creating service-orientated values, after-sales service providers adapt the roles of frontline service employees, requiring them not only to deliver superior after-sales service but also cope with the specific requirements of such after-sales services. The service technicians thus have two key roles to fill: being a reliable troubleshooter and delivering a standardised service. A reliable troubleshooter guarantees a rapid response in the case of breakdown or failure of a product: the problem is identified as soon as possible and then remedied. A service technician concentrates on the small range of issues that arise when delivering standardised after-sales services.

7.1.2 Human resource management

Recruiting and training personnel
Individuals recruited for after-sales services generally possess sound technical expertise. It is particularly important that they also have the ability and motivation to learn continuously, since service technicians require much training in order to develop the considerable technical expertise necessary. Providers of after-sales service are therefore required to invest heavily in training their technical experts. The training is provided by two primary means:

- *Formal classroom training* ensures that individuals have the basic technical expertise needed for the range of tasks they are expected to undertake.
- *On-the-job training* allows service technicians to learn from each other, i.e. frontline employees learn through observing and imitating more experienced co-workers.

Furthermore, after-sales service providers do their utmost to retain the technical expertise held by long-time service technicians in particular by reducing employee fluctuation.

Personnel compensation, assessment and rewards
Retaining technical expertise and reducing employee fluctuation are strongly related to the measurement and reward system used. Companies must adapt the measurement and reward system to include the performance of the newly-formed or redesigned service organisation within their existing product organisations. The cost structure of after-sales service providers typically consists more of fixed costs than of variable. Once the new service organisation is established, it becomes a fixed cost and the main driver of profitability is capacity utilisation (Oliva and Kallenberg, 2003). Consequently, the financial bonus system of service managers is based on measures relating to capacity utilisation: their financial bonuses are adapted to correspond with the individual performance of the product unit to which the service organisation belongs. This performance is measured through overall profitability, product revenue, service revenue, customer satisfaction and employee satisfaction.

7.1.3 Organisational structure

Distinguishing the products and service businesses

After-sales service providers collect the different after-sales service activities in a cost centre within the product unit. The various service activities (such as repair, inspection and management of spare parts) within the product unit are, in effect, jointly responsible for satisfying the customer's requirements of a product that functions properly. Since after-sales service providers set up the service organisation within their existing product business units, the provision of service is a clear intra-business collaboration between the service and product management functions. The human resource requirements of the service cost centre are met initially through internal resource flows from the production function. Later on, when the service cost centre is fully established, after-sales service providers continue to share resources between the after-sales service and production functions on an ongoing basis: this allows them to deal with the unpredictable demand for after-sales services, as well as to cover the peaks, in a better way and ensures a better utilisation of capacity.

Exhibit 7.1: Bucher Foodtech's service organisation and human resource management

Bucher Foodtech, a manufacturer of food presses, has established an after-sales services business to support its product business. The company recruits technicians for the service team based on their all-round technical and assembly competencies. The high level of technical expertise of the employees recruited means that further training corresponds to on-the-job training. In addition, experienced long-term employees serve as role models for the continuous training of service personnel.

Service performance is measured on the basis of the revenue and contribution that services generate, and corresponds to the success of the spare parts business. Since the service technicians represent fixed costs within the after-sales service cost centre, the level of service performance increases the more often they are utilised.

Bucher Foodtech has established a cost centre for after-sales services that is integrated in the product organisation. The integrated structure of the service business means that there is continual intra-firm collaboration between the product and service businesses in such a way that the product sales staff are responsible for selling services, whereas the product units' customer service employees are responsible for delivering them. Furthermore, such integration encourages the exchange of experiences between employees in both businesses.

Inter-firm collaboration

In contrast to the high degree of intra-firm collaboration that takes place between the service and product businesses of providers of after-sales service when they actually provide services, extensive inter-firm collaboration with their customers is unnecessary. After-sales service providers emphasise the considerable extent of their collaboration with logistics providers, as this is often required in order to serve their installed base around the world and to support their service technicians by transporting spare parts in the time allocated by the customer.

Proximity of the service organisation to the customer

The importance of this organisational structure is of medium level; it is clearly lower than for the other service strategies. After-sales service providers often rely on service agents to deliver services, aiding companies to control the costs of running a service infrastructure. In the case of a product failure, however, customers are only required to identify the correct contact points in order to gain access to service technicians, who can then remedy the problem. Thus, after-sales service providers emphasise the importance of making the contact points for customer service visible to customers, thereby increasing the transparency of the service organisation.

Exhibit 7.2: Deutz's service values and proximity of its service organisation to customers

Deutz uses a product-orientated business model that focuses on selling engines and ensuring that they function properly in the after-sales phase. In order to support the business model, Deutz set up an after-sales service business based on providing original spare parts and exchanging engines, along with a responsive customer service network for engine problems. Consequently, the company's

Exhibit 7.2: (*cont.*)

service culture reflects a typical after-sales service strategy. The overall service orientation of the corporate culture is relatively low, with the main focus placed on the machinery business. The service-orientated values embraced by the employees comprise providing reactive after-sales services to supplement the product business. True to these values, Deutz's service team focuses on their reputation of being reliable troubleshooters when the customer requires support in the event of machine failure.

Deutz increased the proximity of its service organisation to customers by assigning particular support personnel the role of 'contact person' for each engine sold. Furthermore, the support personnel had the added advantage of improving intra-firm collaboration: when a request is received related to a specific engine (which may be placed anywhere in the world since most engines are installed in mobile units), the local service technician can simply contact the corresponding support person.

7.1.4 Service development process

Responsibilities and processes for service development
Where developing service processes is concerned, providers of after-sales service place the responsibility of devising service innovations on the shoulders of the product management. They do not, however, overly emphasise service development in their daily operations: it tends instead to take the form of temporary projects. The processes for developing the service of after-sales service providers therefore embrace a rather low level of formality compared to the other service strategies. Service development usually takes a semi-structured form that can be divided into the three phases of brainstorming, development and market launch. In the first phase, new service ideas are generated during workshop sessions in which the product management, development and sales teams all participate. These workshops discuss the faults that are typical of the products and then potential service ideas designed to remedy them. The development phase involves only a basic concept being drawn up; it contains a description of the actual services and a definition of the processes to provide and market the service. A product manager who integrates the sales and development of the product

into the design of the concept manages the entire service development process.

Exhibit 7.3: The development of repair services at Mikron

Mikron sells production machines for the cost-efficient production of high volumes at attractive prices. A service business was established to support this machinery based on providing spare parts along with rapid and reliable repair and inspection services for the after-sales phase. Mikron's focus was clearly on the product business: the innovation of repair services and technical inspections was a temporary task that required a semi-structured development process within the area of product management. The development and sales of the product were integrated in an interdisciplinary project development team so that their knowledge of the functionality and use of the product could be combined in order to develop the appropriate repair and technical inspection services for the installed base.

Customer involvement in service development

There is only little involvement by customers in the service development processes of after-sales service providers. These emphasise the integration of the product sales organisations in the brainstorming phase because of their considerable knowledge of customer requirements. Customers are therefore only involved indirectly in the early process of development.

7.1.5 IT support for the service business

Providers of after-sales service do not use IT extensively in their service processes to support their services strategy. The specific use of IT in service processes is concentrated primarily on standard information and communication systems for storing customer information and on support basic services, such as documentation, hotline and the management of spare parts.

7.1.6 Checklist for implementing an after-sales service strategy

Table 7.1 provides a summary of the operational capabilities that support an after-sales service strategy.

Table 7.1: The operational capabilities required by providers of after-sales service

Operational capabilities	Characteristics
Corporate culture	
Corporate values	• Regard services as an essential part of the total creation of value
Employee roles	• Act as a reliable troubleshooter
	• Deliver a standardised service
Human resource management	
Personnel recruitment and training	• Solid technical expertise
	• Ability and motivation to learn continuously
	• Formal classroom training
	• On-the-job training
Personnel assessment/compensation	• Capacity utilisation is integrated in the financial bonus system
Organisational structure	
Organisational distinctions of the service business	• After-sales services have a cost centre within the product unit
	• Initial internal flow of resources from the production function
	• Shared resources between the service and production functions on an ongoing basis
Inter-firm collaborative structures	• Collaboration with logistics providers
Proximity of the service organisation to customers	• Medium emphasis on proximity to customers
	• Visible contact points with customer service in the event of product failures
Service development process	
Responsibilities and processes for service development	• Product units are responsible for development
	• Semi-structured process comprising three phases: idea generation, development and market launch
Involvement of customers in service development processes	• Involvement by customers concentrated to generating service ideas
IT support for the service business	
IT in service processes	• Low level of specific use of IT in service processes
	• Information and communication systems for collecting data from customers and managing basic services

7.2 Operational capabilities for customer support service providers

Providers of customer support services continue to modify operational capabilities relating to corporate culture, human resource management, organisational structure, service development processes and IT management.

7.2.1 Corporate culture

Corporate values
Providers of customer support services spend substantial amounts of time and effort in convincing service employees that customised service packages are an essential part of value creation. Being flexible, i.e. able to modify and adjust the amount of service elements that are purchased, is seen as a positive trait: it means that unexpected differences that arise between various customers can be accommodated. Consequently, managers and employees alike believe that customisation and flexibility contribute to improved differentiation which, in turn, leads to greater profits.

Employee roles
Customer support service providers also have to adapt the key roles performed by frontline employees in terms of delivering highly customised services and acting as performance enablers. Frontline staff provide unbiased recommendations to customers as to how the performance desired can be achieved by operating their products. Performance enablers develop an in-depth understanding of the individual performance requirements of customers and, more specifically, implement services to support customers in achieving the performance desired. Delivering highly customised services means that frontline employees must also be able, and willing, to assume responsibility and provide flexibility for the broad range of issues that arise when services are tailored to satisfy unique customer requirements.

7.2.2 Human resource management

Recruiting and training personnel
Customer support service providers invest in developing employees who possess the skills needed to perform specific tasks. They recruit

individuals who have solid technical expertise, behavioural competencies and an appropriate customer-orientated attitude. The technical expertise in particular includes possessing risk-assessment skills. Service technicians must assume responsibility for the operating risk of the product (e.g. costs of machine failure) if the service offering is to be priced based on performance measures such as product availability. With such a pricing mechanism, profitability depends on how accurately the service technicians assess the risks of product failure. This requires equipping the frontline staff with a new set of technical skills, which include gathering information for an accurate determination of risks. Providers of customer support services establish risk-assessment skills through IT tools (see Section 7.2.5) or learn how to predict failure rates by examining historical data (Oliva and Kallenberg, 2003). The behavioural competencies include listening and communication skills, which are essential for understanding the needs of individual customers. These skills help to convince customers that the service package offered really does fit their requirements.

These competencies are developed through mentoring programmes, on-the-job training and extensive initial training. The latter provides the service staff with fundamental technical expertise and behavioural competencies, whilst on-the-job training ensures the continuous development of these competencies. Additionally, service technicians must have both the ability and motivation to learn continuously: substantial training is necessary to develop behavioural competencies, technical expertise and a customer-orientated attitude. Service providers try to retain these competencies by making efforts to reduce employee fluctuation and invest in 'long-term' employees. Long-term employees are more likely to fulfil the role of performance enablers, as they accumulate a broad base of all the relevant competencies needed to supervise new service technicians. Furthermore, they are very cost-efficient, because they are highly experienced in customising the service offering to fulfil individual needs.

Exhibit 7.4: The service values and human resource issues of Mettler-Toledo

A manufacturer of precision instruments, Mettler-Toledo provides comprehensive quality control solutions for their own products and those of competitors. This enables the system validation procedures that are demanded in heavily regulated industries to be used. Today, Mettler-Toledo is positioned as a solution provider. When they started the transition towards services a few years ago, the service business was increasingly being seen as a factor for differentiation, i.e. being of similar importance as the product business. Consequently, Mettler-Toledo tried to establish a service culture by involving all of the company's divisions, including every single employee, in their service business: service culture is, after all, based on the conviction that providing services is everyone's responsibility. This is reflected in the compensation system that contains a variable part based on measures of service performance, such as revenue generated by services. Mettler-Toledo fosters service-orientated behaviour and commitment by emphasising a flat hierarchy and giving employees extensive authority. The roles given to the employees, therefore, resemble those of entrepreneurs with respect to providing tailored services to support customers in improving the performance of their processes.

Being encouraged to behave as entrepreneurs, with individual goals for service performance, the most important skill possessed by Mettler-Toledo's employees is that of having a distinct customer-orientated attitude. The company does not distinguish between service sales staff and service technicians: employees must, instead, be generalists with abilities that can be deployed for both selling and delivering service. In this context, personnel development focuses particularly on teamwork in cross-functional teams and teambuilding activities.

Personnel compensation, assessment and rewards

The incentive system must be modified to include the performance of the existing product division and the newly formed service division into the calculation of the financial bonus (Hill *et al.*, 1992). Thus, the incentives encourage intra-firm collaboration between the product and service business divisions (see Section 7.2.3). A total of 40 per cent of the financial bonus to which managers in both divisions are entitled is, for example, composed of the financial performance of both units and the remaining 60 per cent to that of the division to which the individual is assigned. In these cases, the performance of both units may be based on assessments made by customers regarding their total experience, and include measures such as customer satisfaction, loyalty and the repurchasing ratio. The financial performance of the product unit is based mainly on the revenue created by the product. The annual sales target, which is set jointly by the sales force and the executive managers, is influenced primarily by the evaluation of customers' investment cycles. Examples indicate that, due to intense competition in the product field, the profit goal for the operating margins of products often only equals a fraction of the corresponding goal for the operating margins of services (e.g. 2 per cent for products versus 8 per cent for services). Another financial measure of performance commonly used in service units is the service revenue generated per installed product. Revenue targets for services may, for example, be to sell services worth around €100,000 for each installed product. Both business units also use employee satisfaction as a measure of performance, which is included in the manager's financial bonus. Overall, the compensation, assessment and rewards pertaining to personnel focus strongly on committing employees and managers to entering into, and maintaining, long-term customer relationships.

Exhibit 7.5: AgieCharmilles' measurement and reward system

GF AgieCharmilles integrates regular surveys of customer satisfaction in its employee incentive system for service performance. More specifically, it uses the proportion of customers who are enthusiastic about service performance and the proportion who are not at all satisfied to calculate a 'customer satisfaction index' with the aim of increasing the proportion of enthusiastic customers who recommend services of AgieCharmilles to other companies.

7.2.3 Organisational structure

Distinguishing products from services

Providers of customer support services, in contrast to providers of after-sales services, do not establish their service organisation as a cost centre in the product unit: they create instead a new, distinct, service division that has specific and clear responsibilities for the various service offerings. Being a typical business unit, the service division assumes profit-and-loss responsibility. Making such a distinction between the product and the services can lead to separate sales and

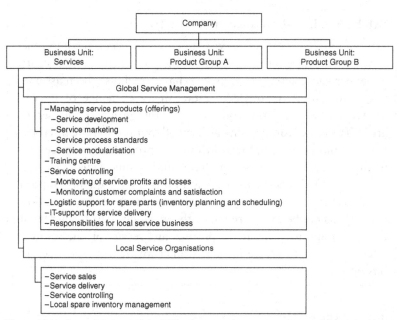

Figure 7.1: Organisation of the BU when products are separated from services

service management units in the market organisations. Rieter (manufacturer of textile machines), Wärtsilä (manufacturer of ship and power engines), Schleifring (manufacturer of grinding machines) and Philips Medical Systems (manufacturer of medical systems) are examples of companies that have established separate organisational units with associated profit-and-loss responsibilities. The common characteristics of the distinctiveness between products and services are illustrated in Figure 7.1.

Providing services is an intra-firm collaborative effort between the product and service divisions. The initial human resource requirements of the new service division are met through internal resource flows from the product units. Sharing resources between product and service divisions on an ongoing basis is not necessary. The services for preventing breakdowns achieve a very predictable demand, particularly when supported by frequently applied (remote) condition monitoring technology. This allows the service division not only to avoid bottlenecks occurring in the use of resources but also reach high average levels of capacity utilisation of their own resources.

Exhibit 7.6: Intra-firm collaboration at Trumpf

Trumpf integrates various service functions in a central competence centre for services. The employees in the service competence centre are experienced service experts who have previously been assigned to product units. In order to establish an exchange of internal knowledge and information between the product and service areas, Trumpf encourages intra-firm collaboration at the interfaces between marketing employees within the product and service sales teams and between the product R&D and technical customer service teams. The latter teams strive at improving the quality of product development by identifying weaknesses in machine generations and increasing the ease of repair of the machines. The former teams enable Trumpf to promote the product and service businesses in an integrated way to create early customer awareness of the service business.

Inter-firm collaboration

Customer support service providers emphasise the considerable extent of the collaboration they have with customers. This strategy requires the development of a shared understanding of both the market conditions and the individual needs of customers in order to optimise their operating processes. In contrast to providers of after-sales services, providers of customer support services do not consider collaborating with professional providers of logistics as being a key factor because they establish a broad range of local service organisations, including local warehouses for providing spare parts, themselves. As a consequence, scheduling the availability of spare parts and managing the inventory remains a core competence of customer support service providers, whereas logistics providers concentrate on the delivery of spare parts.

Proximity of the service organisation to the customer

The service organisation achieves a high level of customer proximity. The formation of a separate service business unit, with few hierarchical levels and clear responsibilities for the various services offered, creates transparency and increases the visibility of the service organisation to customers. More specifically, companies establish responsible contact persons for each individual maintenance contract as well as for each service category. Establishing responsibilities involves empowering the service employees with the authority necessary so that they can provide customers with support and aid, and thereby satisfy individual needs. Providers of customer support services also actively encourage communication with existing and potential customers on a regular basis.

Exhibit 7.7: Endress+Hauser's proximity to customers

Endress+Hauser places great emphasis on its service organisation being physically close to customers for several reasons. Firstly, customer-orientated market organisations are able to establish close relationships with local customers and focus on their needs. Secondly, a web-based service portal that is both user-friendly and comprehensive enables customers to access the service offerings online, and can supplement it with various electronic services. Thirdly, Endress+Hauser has defined a distinct communication strategy with three goals: to enhance the competency of the service business personnel, to make the services transparent to customers and to increase interaction with customers. This strategy includes having regular exhibitions at professional tradeshows, being visible in maintenance and service-related media directed to specific industries and, finally, ensuring a clear integration/promotion of the service business within its overall business communication strategy.

7.2.4 Service development process

Responsibilities and processes of service development
The separate service organisation is responsible for the service development process. This process is highly formal and can be divided into the following phases:

- Brainstorming phase: generating, evaluating and selecting ideas.
- Development phase: establishing a basic concept, business plan and detailed concept.
- Market launch phase: preparing for implementation in the market.

During the first phase, the service management meets the marketing and sales organisation and, quite often, selected customers. The customer's requirements are identified first of all, to ensure that the correct product specifications are being considered and to optimise product efficiency within the customer's processes. They then generate, analyse and select interesting service ideas that are based on the customer's requirements. In the next stage, a project team works with the further development of the service ideas. This team, which is composed of staff from the sales organisation and service management, is generally headed by a project manager from service management who assumes the role of a 'service champion' (Easingwood, 1986; Martin and Horne, 1992). Once the product has been successfully launched, this service champion may be appointed the product manager for the service developed.

The first step in the development process ends with the development team agreeing on a basic concept for the service innovation consisting of a description of the content of the service, the processes involved and the requirements to be fulfilled. The profit-and-loss responsibility of the service management means that the basic concept is followed by a business plan partly to determine the potential sales and costs of a particular service innovation and partly to assist the sales organisation in deciding whether or not to invest in additional service technicians. Once the business plan has been drawn up, a detailed concept for the service innovation is drafted. The results usually correspond to two to three service alternatives that can be offered to individual groups of customers. The development team then defines the competencies that are required to provide and market the services.

The development team creates a corresponding requirements profile for the service staff during market preparation phase that is used to define the measures that are necessary for developing the personnel as well as for job advertisements and recruiting new service staff.

Customer involvement in service development process

Customers may be involved directly in different phases of the service development process to ensure that it is always aligned with their requirements, which leads to relatively intense involvement by customers during the development phase. Selected customers often take part in the brainstorming phase to identify the requirements in their processes and contribute to creating ideas for service. Customers may also support the development team actively during the development phase, when the basic concept of a service innovation is being drafted; they are occasionally involved in the final phase of the detailed concept to ensure that their needs are being fulfilled.

Exhibit 7.8: The service development process used by Heidelberg

Heidelberg, a manufacturer of printing machines and systems, increased the organisational distinctiveness of its service business by rearranging its organisational structure. The market-orientated structure, which concentrated on products and services for customer segments in the market, was rearranged. It became customer-orientated and now focuses on delivering customised value to meet the individual needs of the customer. The customer-orientated structure is characterised by separate sales and service management units in each market organisation. The service managers are in close contact with the central headquarters and act as direct interfaces with customers. They have profit-and-loss responsibility in their service areas and are given wide decision-making authority to fulfil their goals.

Heidelberg increased the proximity of its service organisation to customers by focusing not only on interaction but also on true intimacy with its customers. This was achieved through its concept of total product support (which even included the removal and resale of machines) that is based on establishing a permanent network between themselves and customers via a smart monitoring service that can be integrated into the machines. Additionally, Heidelberg runs a unique academy for developing knowledge and education specific to their industry, with the focus being on individuals from the entire value chain. This academy also promotes Heidelberg's service business, which enhances proximity to customers.

Heidelberg has defined a clear, central, service development process consisting of three phases: (1) identify the requirements, (2) develop the services and (3) implement the services in the market.

Exhibit 7.8: (*cont.*)

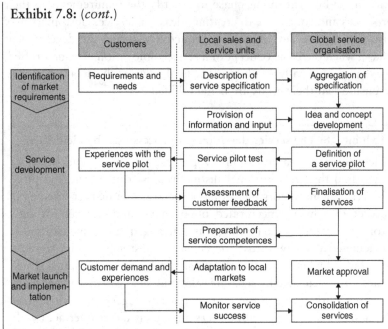

Overview of the service development process

Phase 1: identify market requirements

The requirements of the market are investigated in depth before a service is developed. Vital elements to be considered include customer satisfaction, the potential of the market, competitors and corporate strategy. A business plan is then formulated; a profile of the requirements and performance specifications are developed for the new service.

Phase 2: service development

Having a decentralised structure means that Heidelberg has to co-ordinate a large number of markets and sales and service units. Ensuring a uniform process requires procedures to be coordinated and transparent: a project-like process has been developed by Heidelberg for this purpose that defines the basic conditions, such as time, resources and goals. The company does not impose a standard but states an ideal process: it is important, nevertheless, that all areas become involved via the various process chains. The process overview for service development, given in the figure above, shows the points of contact and explains the necessity for involving the entire organisation and its customers.

Heidelberg views services as a product in their own right, developing them in the same way as it would a printing machine. The standardised process of service development has five quality gates in total (see figure below). Based on precisely defined criteria, the status of service development can be checked and evaluated at each of these gates. The development status is noted using a 'traffic light' system: as soon as all the lights are on green, the process moves forward to the next quality gate.

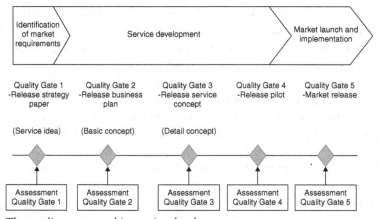

The quality gates used in service development

The development of new 'value added' services takes place according to the process model and is supported by the project management. Information pertaining to the status of the project is always available to those concerned on the company's intranet. Personnel from different countries are involved in developing services, so an extensive, user-friendly platform is necessary for the exchange of information. The data is collected by a central project management department and published on the intranet: projects are documented clearly and concisely on the service portal. Project managers are responsible for the content published on the intranet, which is updated at least once every three months. The company's intranet and general information on the projects are accessible to all Heidelberg employees.

Exhibit 7.8: (*cont.*)

Phase 3: implementation in the market

Heidelberg uses several reference models to ensure successful implementation in the market. These reduce both the time and effort required, and make initial hurdles surmountable. In addition, coordination is facilitated by the use of checklists. The process model for the provision of services is available via the service portal on their intranet.

The central development of services is complemented by decentralised development in the markets. Many services are designed autonomously, since the needs of customers vary from one market to another. Although the resulting creativity can be seen as a clear benefit, the professionalism of service development tends to suffer as the sales units often pay less consideration to costs.

Irrespective of whether development takes place within the market, it is important that the company's head office provides the market centres with an exchange platform where best practices can be presented. Heidelberg's headquarters also invite in all local market centre service managers for this purpose. When one country has developed a particularly successful service, the service manager in question is asked to present this best practice in a form which allows other countries to adopt it with a minimum of alterations.

Heidelberg has developed the concept of the remote monitoring of a machine's condition to becoming a smart maintenance service. Built-in sensors in the machines recognise, in advance, when a machine requires service and reports the information automatically online to Heidelberg's service technicians, who can then react appropriately. Worn-out parts can, for example, be replaced before the onset of machine failure or breakdown.

7.2.5 *IT support for the service business*

Unlike providers of after-sales services, providers of customer support services are characterised by the use of IT and electronic services to offer services of a higher quality, in keeping with their service strategy. The majority of companies modify their IT infrastructure to provide internet and other IT-based services. Companies focus in particular on connecting sales staff and service technicians with central customer databases via mobile IT for simplified worldwide access to data and information exchanges in order to improve adaptation of problem-solving capabilities.

In addition to standard information systems for managing customer data or spare parts, specific IT-based service processes refer especially to providing remote services, such as monitoring condition as part of maintenance contracts. Such services allow providers of customer support services to improve the time, quality and performance, as well as costs, associated with the delivery of services via technology-based remote access. For example, travel expenses can be reduced significantly when site visits are unnecessary, which, in turn, allows the service providers to use their technicians more efficiently. The tendency is that these remote services are becoming 'smart' (internet-based), i.e. they are based on built-in intelligence in the products in terms of awareness and connectivity that communicates continuously and automatically via the Internet with the service provider (Allmendinger and Lombreglia, 2005).

Exhibit 7.9: The service business of Carl Zeiss IMT

A manufacturer in the field of industrial measuring technology, Carl Zeiss IMT has completed the transformation from being a manufacturer of equipment to being a supplier of systems by expanding its service packages and becoming a full service supplier. Focusing on technical services such as maintenance, repair, installation/relocation and teleservice/diagnostics, Carl Zeiss IMT is currently meeting the increasing demand for services in the market whilst simultaneously securing growth. Its service development process is illustrated in the figure below.

Since customer satisfaction is a top priority for Carl Zeiss IMT, the company places a strong emphasis on the development of product-related services. Its development process begins with the recording of customer requests, for which explicit purpose a 'scout team' was established. The members of this team are five high-fliers, each of whom are supported by a mentor at management level. The scout team has to organise itself and develop its own solutions to the tasks it is set. Its declared goal is to ascertain, evaluate and record customer concerns so that the requirements of the market can be

Exhibit 7.9: (*cont.*)

identified at an early stage. In the next phase of the process, an analysis is carried out to determine whether existing developments can be built upon, or if a new development should be considered. The project is set up after this internal decision-making process has taken place. In the meantime, a pilot customer is actively being sought; a market investigation is also conducted. When required, Carl Zeiss IMT also works closely with universities in order to utilise the latest in scientific know-how.

Carl Zeiss' industrial measuring technology division (IMT) has set up a 'teleservice' for the remote access and diagnostics of products installed at its customers' premises. The system is networked with the customers and provides direct user support, software updates, service support and training. This teleservice enables Carl Zeiss IMT to perform preventive maintenance, assuming, of course, that the customer has already consented. Permanent monitoring by means of a leased line means that the customer can be made aware of any impending difficulties at an early stage. Intervention can then take place at the customer's end or, if necessary, external services can be commissioned. Customer processes can thereby be integrated seamlessly into those of Carl Zeiss IMT. In addition, pre-diagnosing product problems not only helps Carl Zeiss IMT to reduce the actual service delivery time on site and solve standard problems remotely, it also saves them travel expenses and time.

Other IT-supported services include a comprehensive service portal that is made available to customers, partners and internal staff in a personalised form. For customers, the portal provides free access to information that is pertinent to them (e.g. the complete history of the machine), tools for calculation and configuration, a newsletter and updates of documentation and software. In combination with a web-based database for training, customers benefit from having online access to booking and information systems for Carl Zeiss IMT's training opportunities. Carl Zeiss IMT has developed a computer-aided sales and services system (CAS) for internal purposes, which is connected to the standard enterprise resource planning system in use. The CAS system supports internal sales and service processes with information on customers: service history and current projects, installed base, service contract quotations, etc.

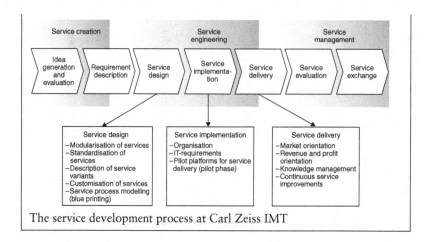

The service development process at Carl Zeiss IMT

7.2.6 Checklist for implementing a customer support service strategy

Table 7.2 provides a summary of the operational capabilities that are required to support a strategy for providing customer support services.

7.3 Operational capabilities for development partners

7.3.1 Corporate culture

Corporate values
Development partners try to convince their R&D staff to become 'superior' service providers who co-produce innovative solutions for customer processes. The R&D staff recognises increasingly that co-producing, or even co-innovating, solutions is the major new source of value creation over time, instead of believing that innovations connected to their own products are the main generators of value.

Employee roles
R&D employees are required to assume three roles: serving the customer as a trusted adviser, developing a 'learning' relationship and leading a collaborative innovation process (Neu and Brown, 2005).

1. In the role of trusted adviser, R&D employees develop an in-depth understanding of various customer processes. They collaborate

Table 7.2: *The operational capabilities required by providers of customer support service*

Operational capabilities	Characteristics
Corporate culture	
Corporate values	• Regard customisation and flexibility as enablers of value creation
Employee roles	• Deliver highly customised services
	• Act as performance enablers
Human resource management	
Personnel recruitment and training	• Solid technical expertise, excellent behavioural competencies and customer-focused attitudes
	• Risk-assessment skills
	• Initial training programme
	• On-the-job training
	• Mentoring programme
Personnel assessment/ compensation	• Incentive system encourages intra-firm collaboration
	• Performance measurement in both product and service divisions are integrated into the bonus system
Organisational structure	
Organisational distinctiveness of the service business	• Separate service division/business unit
	• Initial internal resource flow from the product units
	• No shared resources between the service and product units on an ongoing basis
Inter-firm collaborative structures	• Collaboration with customers to develop a shared understanding of market conditions
Proximity of the service organisation to the customer	• Strong emphasis placed on proximity to the customer
	• Service business unit has clear responsibilities

- Service employees are contact persons for individual maintenance contracts
- Service employees are empowered with the authority required to help customers fulfil their individual needs
- Regular and active communication with customers
- Commitment to long-term customer relationships

Service development process

Responsibilities and processes for service development

- Service organisation is responsible for the development process
- Structured process with the phases (1) idea generation, evaluation and selection, (2) development of basic concept, business plan and detailed concept, and (3) market launch
- Service manager acts as a service champion for development projects

Customer involvement during service development process

- High level of customer involvement in different development phases
- Service champion acts as direct contact to customers

IT support for the service business

IT in service processes

- High level of specific IT use in service processes
- Internet-based services and information systems (e.g. customer data, spare parts, installed base and service history)
- Remote monitoring services of machine condition

with, and provide unbiased recommendations to, customers on how to innovate new solutions for customer processes. They participate in creating and implementing innovations that improve customer processes.

2. Establishing a learning relationship with individual customers is compulsory for R&D employees. A 'learning' relationship is an ongoing connection that becomes more effective as the interaction between the supplier's personnel and the customer develops. As a consequence, the R&D staff gain an intimate knowledge of the customer's complex problems related to developing an operating process. At the same time, the customer learns about the real design and construction capabilities of the development partner, as well as their specific development capabilities. The customer discovers, in fact, whether or not the supplier's R&D staff can be trusted to provide superior design and construction services that meet the current and future challenges posed by their process (Neu and Brown, 2005).

3. The R&D staff of the development partners are required to lead a collaborative innovation process with customers if they are to effectively address the broad range of issues that arise when creating and implementing new solutions for customer processes. Therefore, the networking skills of the R&D staff are important for teaming up successfully with customers.

Exhibit 7.10: The service culture and human resource management at Bystronic Glass

Bystronic Glass uses its unique glass processing technology to develop and produce technically advanced systems and tailor-made solutions for fully automatic glass processing. The company promotes a corporate culture that is based on service-orientated values and the belief that, as providers of solutions, they should be customer-focused. The service culture is supported by central leadership that encourages all employees to view service as being a significant part of the overall business. Service employees regard themselves as being problem-solvers for customers by adapting their behaviour to deliver trusted advice to customer requests and to develop a mutual learning relationship with customers so that they can work together on innovating solutions.

Bystronic Glass bases personnel recruitment on several functional selection criteria to ensure that the service employees are able to assume the required behaviour. Service managers and engineers are recruited according to various criteria that include customer orientation, technical and engineering competencies, trustworthiness, versatility and leadership qualities. The recruitment of service technicians is based on criteria such as technical expertise, willingness to travel and versatility in terms of product and application knowledge.

The various selection criteria used by Bystronic Glass to recruit personnel also serve to identify personal development potential. The incentive system for the service staff is part of the company's financial bonus system; measures of service performance form one of the bases on which it is calculated. Measuring service performance depends on financial indicators such as service revenue and service contribution margins, time-related measures of service delivery and development service projects, and the continual measurement of customer satisfaction.

7.3.2 Human resource management

Personnel recruitment and training

Development partners invest essentially in developing and recruiting individuals with technical competencies, behavioural competencies and customer-focused attitudes. Each person they recruit to join their R&D staff is deemed able to serve the customer as a trusted adviser, develop a learning relationship and lead a collaborative innovation process primarily if they have the appropriate development expertise. Engineers are recruited at two levels: graduate engineers from technical universities and managing engineers from professional engineering consultancies or other manufacturing companies.

An intensive trainee programme ensures an initial adaptation of the skills possessed by newly-employed graduate engineers to the technical competencies specific to the company. A major part of the trainee programme consists of lessons in behavioural competencies and customer-focused attitudes. The graduate engineers learn the communication skills appropriate to the roles of being a trusted adviser, developer of a learning relationship and leader of a collaborative innovation performance. New managing engineers are usually assessed according to their technical and behavioural competence as well as their customer-focused attitudes. As is typical of R&D functions, development partners strongly concentrate on retaining the competencies they need to provide superior design and construction services. Only high employee retention ensures the effective performance of frontline employees and their developing the necessary competencies. Long-term managing engineers in particular play decisive roles in the service activities of development partners: they accumulate the broad base of expertise needed to provide outstanding design and construction services, their experience ensures outstanding service performance and they also have the advantage of becoming familiar with the skills of individual employees in the R&D function of the development partners. The close personal ties that grow between them and other engineers enhance their ability to select the best person suited to the various customer projects. In general, long-term employees are more likely to earn confidence as a trusted adviser.

Personnel compensation, assessment and rewards

Development partners modify their financial bonus systems for managers to include the performance of the new R&D team that has been established for design and construction services. The modifications encourage collaborative learning between engineers and customers. The financial performance of the new service R&D team is mainly based on the revenue and profit created via the external customer. It is usual for the head of R&D and the managing engineers of the development partners to set the annual targets jointly. Development partners, in addition, define specific product-orientated goals to guarantee the quality of internal development projects. Monitoring both sets of goals (service-orientated financial goals for external customers and quality goals for internal customers) helps development partners maintain the balance between enhancing revenue from external customers and ensuring the quality of internal development projects.

7.3.3 Organisational structure

Distinguishing between products and services

It is typical that development partners consider having a separate service R&D team as being a key success factor. Anchored organisationally within the central R&D division the service R&D team is responsible for the design and construction services achieving outstanding customer process performance. Setting up a separate service division for design and construction services is usually considered inappropriate because it would hinder the exchange of knowledge with the central R&D.

Development partners share resources on a regular basis between the service R&D team for external customers and the remaining R&D staff for internal R&D projects, which allows them to spread the knowledge created in co-producing design and construction solutions with customers in the whole R&D function. Intimate knowledge of customer applications is important to development partners for the continuous improvement of their own products: it is, however, very difficult to elucidate most of this knowledge. Whereas providers of after-sales service share resources to cope with the unpredictability of the demand for service, development partners are driven by the potential of using customer knowledge in the innovation of new products. In addition, sharing resources with the main R&D function means the service R&D team can benefit from the knowledge they obtain of the latest technological developments within the company.

Exhibit 7.11: Ericsson's acquisition of an R&D service organisation

Ericsson, contrary to most development partners that set up a special service R&D team within their central R&D division, chose to acquire an external specialised consultancy to provide technology advice and business development services as a wholly-owned, but independent, separate company. The rationale was that this approach would create more credibility for Ericsson in positioning itself as a development partner for solutions that are optimally tailored to meet customer requirements. The fear was that otherwise customers might suspect they were not being provided with the best solution for their needs but with the solution that fit best with Ericsson's standard product offering.

Inter-firm collaboration

Development partners establish inter-firm collaborative structures with customers to co-produce design and construction solutions. This includes holding regular meetings with customers, sharing IT systems and having mixed teams composed of their service R&D team and customers. Co-producing solutions leads, quite naturally, to a high degree of customisation. An important challenge in terms of inter-firm collaboration is making the knowledge created in the minds of individual experts accessible for exploitation, which is performed by using intensive knowledge management tools. These tools may include third parties, such as competency centres in technical universities, research institutes and professional engineering consultancies. Thus, in general, development partners pay considerable attention to collaborating with third parties.

Exhibit 7.12: The service organisation at Sulzer Innotec

Sulzer Innotec, the R&D unit of the Sulzer Corporation, has made substantial contributions towards creating new business opportunities for Sulzer for 60 years. The company also offers its expertise on the open market in the form of contract R&D and specialised technical services. Sulzer's decision to separate their central R&D (Sulzer Innotec) from the main company and create an independent R&D service unit for internal and external customers resulted in the central R&D division becoming a separate company. Various teams continued to perform R&D tasks within this separate company for Sulzer Innotec's parent company, while other teams started to provide R&D services for third parties using Sulzer Innotec's accumulated competencies in product development. The revenue share of external customer development projects has rapidly grown since then, and exceeds the revenue share of internal projects many times over. Consequently, Sulzer Innotec has shifted from an internal to an external customer orientation, and has greatly increased focus on proximity to, and collaboration with, external customers. In order to improve its development competencies continually, Sulzer Innotec also emphasises inter-firm collaboration and the exchange of information within a broad global network of universities and research institutes.

Proximity of the service organisation to the customer
Having a service organisation situated close to the customer's location enhances the success of development partners. This is due to

the intense degree of collaboration and interaction that is necessary between development partners and their customers in all phases of the service business: from involving the customer in the development of the service to the joint creation of design and construction solutions during the service delivery phase.

Development partners increase the transparency of their design and construction service offering for external customers by establishing visible contact points and clear responsibilities for the design and construction service business. More specifically, the engineers within the service R&D team are each responsible for individual customer projects, which facilitates the formation of long-term personal relationships with customers. Rapid decision-making responses to customer requests require that development partners empower their service R&D engineers with the necessary authority to make decisions in issues pertaining to customer projects.

7.3.4 Service development process

Responsibilities and processes of service development

Development partners anchor their service development organisationally in product R&D: design and construction service innovations require extensive technical knowledge, which is generally present only in product development and not in product or service management. The design and construction service work is usually headed by an innovation manager who reports to product development and acts as a guide through various innovation projects, thus assuming the role of a 'service champion'. The development partners place a strong emphasis on R&D so it is not surprising that service development is an important task of the R&D department that is carried out on a temporary basis in special development projects. The service development process of development partners is highly formal. It includes phases, and steps within these phases, that are similar to the strategy for customer support service providers: brainstorming (generating ideas, evaluation and selection), development (drawing up a basic concept, business plan and detailed concept) and market launch (performing a market test and implementation).

Development partners exchange experiences regularly with specific development projects to generate service ideas and create initial concepts for these ideas. The development team for a specific development project, which is headed by an innovation manager, comprises product development and product sales staff who then start working on the development project by defining a business plan. The development team then uses the business plan to produce a clear estimate of the sales expected, the invoicing concept and a specific project plan. Development partners aim at billing design and construction services separately rather than integrating them in the price of the product. Resistance from potential customers to buying products may be avoided if the development partners credit the cost of the service against that of the product if the customer is interested in developing a product after the service has been rendered. Once the business plan is established, the development team moves on to work on the details of the concept. A feature that distinguishes development partners from other service strategies is the loop that is integrated between the creation of the detailed concept and the subsequent market test, because development services have a lack of definition when beginning to create the detailed concept.

The development team then subjects the processes developed and the billing concept defined to a market test involving a selected sales organisation. The knowledge obtained from the market test can be integrated directly into the detailed concept. Defining a requirement profile for the sales organisation is unnecessary, since design and construction services are provided by the product development department rather than the sales organisation. It is the design and construction services that have the specific technical knowledge required, which is generally only present in product development. Special market preparation is therefore not deemed to be necessary.

Exhibit 7.13: Magna-Steyr's proximity to customers and development of the concept of 'total vehicle service'

Magna-Steyr, a supplier of automobile parts, was forced into becoming a development partner due to radical changes in the automotive industry caused by demands that were difficult to forecast and the increasing need for flexibility to respond quickly to market changes. Being a development partner, Magna-Steyr conjoins all the capabilities necessary to engineer, design, manufacture and assemble entire vehicles; doing so, they can support car manufacturers with customised solutions for their products and processes, which provides them with the operational flexibility they need. The degree of intimacy that exists between automobile suppliers and manufacturers means that Magna-Steyr places strong emphasis on collaboration with customers and the proximity of its service organisation to customers' sites. This is important since, in a development partnership, knowledge pertaining to optimising the development processes of vehicles, and especially with a view to subsequent series production, is created jointly with customers. The integration of Magna-Steyr with car manufacturers in the context of vehicle development projects appears to be smooth and seamless to the extent that confusion may arise, as Magna-Steyr can be assumed to be a division of the corresponding car manufacturer. Clearly, this level of proximity to the customer benefits from the close ties that are commonly found between suppliers of automobile parts and manufacturers of cars.

It was not clear when Magna-Steyr formulated its detailed concept of total vehicle development service which components should be included in the development service (e.g. assembly, electrics, drivetrain, chassis, prototyping, production planning, purchasing, marketing, quality, etc.). Detailing the concept of total vehicle service was only possible by passing through various loops, using information from the market and customer tests to adapt the concept. The loops resulted in the elements that were to be included in the total vehicle development service: strategic product planning, product definition, styling check/evaluation of appearance and a concept package comprising ergonomics, acoustics, safety and technological comparisons.

Customer involvement in the service development process
The high level of customisation of design and construction services means that development partners are dependent on integrating customers in the service development process. Customers are often involved as early as in the development phases to ensure that their requirements are met. A number of customers usually contribute to developing the detailed concept, as well as carrying out the market test. It includes holding workshops for specific customers to define the various processes required for providing a design and

construction service (internal, interactive and external processes) using, for example, the service blueprint method (Bitner *et al.*, 2008; Edvardsson and Olsson, 1996).

Exhibit 7.14: Service development at Bühler Die Casting

A manufacturer of die casting machinery, Bühler Die Casting has mastered die casting technologies and the capability for producing die casting designs that are compliant with the surrounding production environment. Using these capabilities, Bühler provides design and construction services for entire manufacturing cells around its die casting machines. The value proposition to customers is the engineering of a comprehensive solution that is tailored to meet their individual needs. Bühler provides, more specifically, integrated optimisation of the complex customer processes of designing manufacturing cells that are compliant with the die casting process, cavity filling and solidification simulations for the actual die casting procedure and achieve a high level of production. Bühler and its customers collaborate closely during the rendering of the service to co-create a customised solution that fits the customer's needs perfectly.

Service development at Bühler follows a formal process. Based on experience with the development of a manufacturing cell engineering service, Bühler considers the evaluation of the frequency of customer demand for a specific design and construction service innovation to be both an important step and a success factor during service development. Evaluating the frequency of customer demand in an early development phase allows Bühler to plan the allocation of sparse resources in a better way, as well as to initiate potential personnel recruitment or training in order to avoid bottlenecks occurring in resources. In addition, evaluation of the demand is required to calculate a sales estimate for the new service as part of the business plan. Before market launch takes place, Bühler conducts a market test of the service innovation with selected lead users: this usually results in a refinement of the detailed concept in several stages. Finally, Bühler uses a customer survey to introduce the service innovation to a broad customer base.

7.3.5 IT support for the service business

Development partners make extensive use of IT to support their service strategy: it corresponds to their strategic position of being technology and innovation leaders. However, development partners largely base their design and construction services on the extensive R&D competencies of their product business. Product-orientated R&D projects are fundamentally based on using specific IT, such as software for computer-aided design (CAD), numerical analysis, simulation, computer graphics, etc., so development partners usually adopt the same technologies for their service offering. The IT solutions used include, for example, product data management (PDM) software to track and control product-related data, two and three-dimensional standard CAD software and CAD software for designing electronics (ECAD). These R&D technologies are connected to the internal knowledge management system of the development partners to spread the knowledge they acquire within the entire R&D function.

The parties involved try to use identical or compatible IT systems during the joint creation of design and construction services to avoid interface problems and improve interaction with the customer. In addition to specific R&D technologies, development partners also use standard information systems for managing the customer's data and information related to development projects. The IT infrastructure is connected to the general ERP system and integrated into a product life-cycle management (PLM) strategy that aims at improving and enabling rapid and reliable internal and external collaboration in the design, manufacture and service of the product. The idea behind the PLM concept is to control the whole lifespan of a product or service and the information connected with it, i.e. the process of creating, handling, distributing and recording information related to a product or service (Saaksvuori and Immonen, 2008).

7.3.6 Checklist for implementing a development partner strategy

The operational capabilities relevant to a development partner strategy are summarised in Table 7.3.

Table 7.3: *The operational capabilities required by development partners*

Operational capabilities	Characteristics
Corporate culture	
Corporate values	• Provide customers with service • Recognise that the joint innovation of solutions is the main source of value creation
Employee's roles	• Act as a trusted advisor • Develop a learning relationship • Lead collaborative innovation performance
Human resource management	
Personnel recruitment and training	• Ensure a solid foundation of R&D expertise • Employ graduate engineers from technical universities • Employ managing engineers from professional engineering consultancies or other manufacturing companies • Instate trainee programmes for graduate engineers • Provide on-the-job training
Personnel assessment/ compensation	• An incentive system encourages collaborative learning between customers and engineers • Final bonus depends on the revenue generated by external customers and the quality of internal development projects
Organisational structure	
Organisational distinctiveness of the service business	• A separate service R&D team to be formed within the R&D function • An initial internal flow of resource occurs from the R&D function • An internal expert knowledge network forms between service and regular R&D staff
Inter-firm collaborative structures	• Collaboration with customers in all phases of the service business • Collaboration with universities and professional engineering consultancies

Proximity of the service organisation to the customer	• Great emphasis is placed on proximity to the customer • The service organisation has visible contact points and clear responsibilities • Responsible service engineers are contact persons for individual customer projects • Service engineers are empowered with the authority required for making rapid decisions in customer projects • Commitment to long-term strategic partnerships and relationships with customers
Service development process Responsibilities and processes for service development	• Product R&D is responsible for service development • Structured process with the phases: (1) generation of ideas, evaluation and selection, (2) development of a basic concept, business plan and detailed concept and (3) market launch • Product innovation manager acts as 'service champion' for development projects
Customer involvement during service development process	• High level of customer involvement in various development phases (e.g. generating service ideas, developing the basic and detailed concepts and market launch) • The 'service champion' acts as a contact for customers • Partnership for strategy development
IT support for the service business IT in service processes	• Intensive use of specific IT applications in service processes • Specific R&D technologies are used in product R&D (e.g. CAD, numerical analysis and simulation) • Common use of IT systems with customers for the joint creation of product and process solutions • Information systems for managing customer data and development projects

7.4 Operational capabilities for outsourcing partners

7.4.1 *Corporate culture*

Corporate values

Outsourcing partners are reported as placing considerable effort on convincing frontline staff to be 'pure service providers' that deliver the output of the operating process to the customer. Instead of believing that customised service packages or technical features are an essential part of the value creation, the frontline staff have to recognise that taking over the customer's operating processes means providing standardised services. Values focus on efficiency, economies of scale and the belief that customisation of service is costly.

Employee roles

The frontline personnel of the outsourcing partners adapt their roles to be reliable operators and intermediaries between delivering standardised and complex services. Reliable operators guarantee a defined quality of the output of operating processes; they have an in-depth understanding of the customer's requirements that makes it possible for them to fulfil them accordingly. The role of intermediary demands that the frontline staff are not only expected to provide a standardised service output but also to be confronted with a broad range of issues pertaining to delivering the outsourced services. The complex range of issues demands experience of the product's features, of operating the products and of providing services. Customers, however, are only interested in the output of the process and not in this kind of internal complexity. Therefore, the frontline staff must use their own judgment to protect customers from the complexity of the service and do their utmost to deliver a standard service.

Exhibit 7.15: The service business of Voith Railservice

Voith Railservice, the independent service division of a diversified machinery and equipment holding company, offers maintenance of rolling stock and, at the same time, incorporates responsibility for technical availability. The value proposition for a customer includes being able to concentrate on the core business, a guaranteed level of equipment availability, continual optimisation of the equipment, minimal downtime risk and improved cost structure and cash flow. Voith Railservice embodies the values of a pure service provider and, as a result of close and regular collaboration, the service mentality is passed on to the product divisions as well. The service employees of Voith Railservice are encouraged to behave as entrepreneurs. This requires assuming responsibility and making their own decisions in terms of managing the complex service projects to the satisfaction of the customers whilst focusing on the efficient delivery of service with regard to overall profitability.

The independent service organisation of Voith Railservice emphasises the importance of its proximity to customers in the form of trust-based personal relationships. It has established two structural levels for building customer relationships. At the first level, a key account manager serves as a central, single contact point for each important global customer. At the second level, service managers in the local market organisations are requested to keep close, regular contact with local customers. Furthermore, offering outsourcing services by taking over the responsibility for guaranteeing the technical availability of the customer's equipment has changed the nature of the interaction between Voith Railservice and its customers: from being an occasional encounter it has become a permanent, daily contact. This guarantees customers full transparency not only of the condition of their equipment but also of Voith Railservice's service operations. Besides the emphasis placed on personal relationships with customers during the provision of service, Voith Railservice also promotes the service business by various means: being present on the Internet, advertising in industry-related media, attending specific customer events, tradeshows, etc.

The development of Voith Railservice's business was initially based on management considerations that the original product business of the parent company cannot create sufficient sustainable growth. This resulted in a formal plan being drawn up and the strategic decision was taken to supplement the original product business. Companies specialising in industrial services were acquired and integrated into a new separate service organisation with the authority to develop the service business further. As part of the development of the service business, becoming an outsourcing partner was then triggered by customer requests for taking over

Exhibit 7.15: (*cont.*)

the full responsibility for services. After a thorough and systematic evaluation of the business opportunities involved in offering outsourcing services, the service management decided to allow the content of the outsourcing partner service strategy to be developed by a special team in a defined project environment.

This example provided by Voith Railservice highlights the typical risks associated with outsourcing services. Whereas the parent company assumed responsibility of the equipment up to the point of acceptance and handover to the customer, and focused service activities exclusively to the spare parts business, Voith Railservice, by becoming an outsourcing partner, has taken over full responsibility for the technical availability of rolling stock in the post-acceptance phase. This may lead to high penalty payments being made to the customer if the technical availability guaranteed is not achieved and the rolling stock is out of use unexpectedly.

7.4.2 Human resource management

Personnel recruitment and training

The main criterion used by outsourcing partners in their search for suitable individuals to fill the position of frontline employee is the possession of good expertise in operating processes. They try to recruit the customer's employees when taking over the operation of that particular customer's processes, and thus gain immediate access to the intimate knowledge of the operating processes. This enables them to operate the processes at the same performance level as before they took over.

Outsourcing partners do not incur great costs in the intensive training of their frontline staff in terms of advanced operational skills: they usually only have to update these former operators of customers' processes with regard to enhancing their technical experience with machines and ensuring that they have the right skills to be able to provide services. Obviously, an extensive initial training in the basic knowledge of operating processes is not necessary. On-the-job training provides the necessary training and development of technical expertise and advanced service skills. Furthermore, training in behavioural competencies and appropriate customer-focused attitudes does not seem to be important: previous employees of customers already have adequate communication skills for dealing with their former employers.

Personnel compensation, assessment and rewards
Outsourcing partners retain the previous employees of customers by using financial incentives such as higher wages (typically 5–15 per cent) and an annual bonus. In general, the measurement and reward system of outsourcing partners is similar to that of professional service organisations. They use performance measures such as customer satisfaction, employee satisfaction and business success in terms of operating margins (Heskett *et al.*, 1997). Additionally, a special incentive system encourages inter-firm collaboration between the previous product and service divisions of the main company and the new service company of outsourcing partners. The financial bonus for managers in the new service company is based on their market share in the target market, i.e. the bonus increases in direct proportion to an increase in market share. However, the financial bonus declines if the service company generates revenue beyond the target market defined. The target is influenced mainly by evaluating the importance of the customer's needs so as to reduce the initial investments.

7.4.3 Organisational structure

Distinguishing the product and service organisations
Outsourcing partners set up a separate, independent service organisation that is often a legally independent company to provide operational services. Separating the organisation from the main company diminishes internal barriers associated with taking over the operation of processes that are not related to their own products but to those of third-party companies. Therefore, integrating outsourcing services into the existing product and/or service divisions is usually not suitable for pure outsourcing partners. The initial human resource requirements at management level are met by an intra-firm collaborative effort through internal resource flows from the product and/or service divisions. At the employee level, as explained above, outsourcing partners recruit the necessary human resources mainly from customers. Outsourcing partners keep close ties between the new service company and the main company; this is relevant, for example, in terms of the replacement of spare parts within an outsourcing partnership.

Inter-firm collaboration
The inter-firm collaboration of the new service company with existing customers and banks and insurance companies is more important

than the intra-firm collaborative effort. An extensive collaboration with existing customers aids in recruiting the employees necessary. Additionally, the close collaboration clarifies the degree to which the newly-formulated strategy is aligned with the underlying needs of the customer with regard to outsourcing operating processes. Close collaboration with banks and insurance companies is important in dealing with the financial risks of operating customers' processes. As a separate service company, outsourcing partners base their business model on buying machines and charging for the costs of operating the machines. Collaborating with banks and insurance companies helps to reduce the financial risk and cover the high initial investments of outsourcing partners to make their business profitable. Otherwise, the initial investments would require operating the machines for years before making the business profitable.

Proximity of the service organisation to the customer
Outsourcing partners place their greatest emphasis on the service organisation being in close proximity of the customer. A degree of high transparency and visibility of the service organisation is obviously created when outsourcing partners take over and operate customer processes *in situ*. Taking over customer processes is generally a part of strategic outsourcing partnerships. The complex, long-term, outsourcing projects are based on extensive collaboration and interaction between outsourcing partners and their customers, which leads to high levels of customer loyalty and facilitates the formation of close personal relationships. This is important for the creation of the comprehensive mutual understanding that is necessary for operating the customer's processes at the performance levels desired. Moreover, the service business naturally requires a high level of proximity to the customer when recruiting the customer's employees for operating the customer's processes.

7.4.4 Service development process

Responsibilities and processes for service development
The entire organisation of the innovation process is similar to that of a project organisation covering both the development and execution of the service. Outsourcing services are heavily based on existing services. Outsourcing partners use existing services such as repairs, replacement

of spare parts and preventive maintenance to operate customer processes. Core elements of the innovation process are therefore not service innovations but risk management, along with intensive investigation and coordination of the cooperation and agreements of the outsourcing partnership. However, the actual development of an outsourcing service follows a relatively formal process, which can be structured into a development phase, pilot test and launch. The development phase can be subdivided into: brainstorming, launching a specific pilot scheme, drawing up a basic concept, formulating a business plan and a detailed concept. The development process of the outsourcing service also involves continuous improvement after the launch. During the brainstorming phase, ideas for outsourcing services are evaluated and selected based on risks and benefits. If the risk is justifiable in proportion to the benefit, an outsourcing project will be launched in the form of a pilot scheme specific to one customer.

Despite in-depth information regarding the services required to ensure the service parameters, there is still a certain amount of risk involved. Estimating the extent and costs of risks form a key part of the business plan: outsourcing partners quantify this remaining risk and incorporate it into their billing model when pricing the services outsourced. The detailed concept for outsourcing services contains a customer process description and an implementation plan. The outsourced service developed is then put to trial during the course of a prolonged pilot test conducted with the customer. The development process of the outsourced services does not simply end with the launch of the service at the customer in question: it also involves continual adjustment of the outsourcing services after market launch.

Customer involvement in the service development process
Service development involving outsourcing services requires intensive cooperation between the outsourcing partners and their customers. The core content of this cooperation is risk management. In order to minimise the risks of taking over responsibility for customer processes, innovation projects for the outsourced services are undertaken to create special developments with selected customers. With such customised developments, it is difficult to distinguish the actual innovation from the rendering of the outsourced service. Most customers do, in fact, expect continual improvement of the outsourced processes. Initial outsourcing projects are headed by existing customer managers.

7.4.5 IT support for the service business

Outsourcing partners make quite extensive use of IT to support their service strategy. They use standard IT systems, such as enterprise resource planning (ERP) systems, which allow them to improve communication and information flows within the firm and in their collaboration with customers. These systems facilitate the provision of standardised services for the customer processes managed, monitored and operated by the outsourcing partners. In addition, outsourcing partners use standard information systems for managing customer's data, monitoring information related to outsourcing projects and the service history, as well as IT tools to support risk management in outsourcing projects. Finally, there is a clear tendency for increased use of internet-based technologies to improve the efficiency of service processes further.

Exhibit 7.16: IT support used by ABB's maintenance management service

ABB measures the service performance of managing the entire maintenance function of its customers' production plants by monitoring and improving the OEE (Overall Equipment Effectiveness) continuously. This key performance indicator embraces availability (uptime versus planned and unplanned downtime), service efficiency (actual capacity versus designed) and yield percentage (amount of good products produced). ABB provides contractual commitment to results where such performance-based agreements are concerned: exceeding the agreed level of results leads to a bonus whereas falling short leads to a rebate.

The development of ABB's outsourcing service for the maintenance management of its customers' production plants had been focused on an agreed level of OEE: one that represented the specific expectations of the customer for the outsourced processes as well as the system for measuring the service performance. This measure could be translated into a precise profile of requirements in terms of resources and competencies that allows both ABB and the customer to co-produce the performance expected. Ongoing quality improvement of the outsourced processes was, in addition, assured through both partners setting up a joint project team to continually promote optimisation of the OEE.

ABB provides outsourcing services for managing the entire maintenance operation of its customers and guaranteeing a certain degree of availability of machinery and equipment. In this context, IT support is regarded as a basic ingredient in important service innovations. Recent examples include a software system for web-based access of data on the installed base in various information systems worldwide and a knowledge retrieval system from the data on the installed base that uses data of the product's life cycle to support knowledge-intensive service processes or mobile field service innovations. ABB's total maintenance management concept for production plants makes efficient use of an IT-based maintenance management system to support their efforts in the continual optimisation of their performance. It involves ABB employing a commercial maintenance management software program that allows standardised maintenance to be implemented systematically and speedily. Furthermore, with the rapid progress being made in information and communication technologies, ABB sees a trend towards the total connectivity of service technicians. Such service technicians are equipped with the latest mobile technologies that provide them with access to the contextual information required on the installed base whatever the time or place. Given the continuing increase in the complexity of products as a result of higher levels of integration between computerisation and software, this will inevitably lead to more efficient service processes. Service technicians will not only be part of a ubiquitous network, however: utilising the connectivity already established for remote services, ABB's products possessing built-in intelligence will be connected to the 'Internet of things' (e.g. Fleisch and Mattern, 2005; Gershenfeld *et al.*, 2004). It means that they will be able to communicate continuously over the Internet, relay information of their status and notify the service provider when a service is required automatically.

7.4.6 Checklist for implementing an outsourcing partner strategy

Table 7.4 summarises the operational capabilities that support an outsourcing partner strategy.

Table 7.4: *The operational capabilities necessary for outsourcing partners*

Operational capabilities	Characteristics
Corporate culture	
Corporate values	• Be a pure service provider
	• Concentrate on efficiency and economies of scale
	• Regard customisation of services as being costly
Employee's roles	• Be a reliable operator
	• Act as an intermediary between delivering standardised and complex services
Human resource management	
Personnel recruitment and training	• Expertise in operating processes
	• Recruit the customers' employees
	• On-the-job training
Personnel assessment/ compensation	• Financial bonus corresponds to the market share of the target market
Organisational structure	
Organisational distinctiveness of the service business	• Separate service organisation for outsourcing services, usually a legally independent service company
	• Internal flow of management resources from product and/or service divisions within the main company
	• Close ties with the main company for replacement of spare parts
Inter-firm collaborative structures	• Collaboration with customers
	• Collaboration with banks and insurance companies
Customer proximity of the service organisation	• Great emphasis is placed on proximity to the customer
	• High levels of visibility and transparency are ensured by operating customer's processes *in situ*
	• Commitment is made to long-term strategic partnerships and customer relationships

- Close personal relationships are formed with customers
- Proximity to the customer is increased by recruiting the customer's former employees
- The customer is involved in improving the process

Service development process

Responsibilities and processes for service development
- Sales or service organisation is responsible for development
- Great emphasis is placed on the development and continuous improvement of outsourcing services
- Little emphasis is placed on the development of single service innovations
- A structured development process, which includes continuous improvement after being launched
- Special developments with customers to manage risks

Customer involvement during the service development process
- Very high, and ongoing, involvement of customer during the continual development of service
- Strategic outsourcing partnership

IT support for the service business

IT in service processes
- Fairly high level of specific IT use in service processes
- Standard IT systems (ERP) for improving efficiency and effectiveness in operating the customers' processes
- Internet-based information systems for managing customer data, outsourcing projects and service history
- IT tools to support risk management

7.5 Operational capabilities for solution providers

The operational capabilities necessary for being a solution provider include having a more customer-orientated organisation and managing a process dedicated to selling solutions.

7.5.1 Achieving customer orientation

The response of solution providers that are required to address high-value customer needs is to combine products and services, as stated in Section 6.4. They combine and balance the service offerings associated with different service strategies. Logically, combining the offerings of the four service strategies (i.e. after-sales service providers, customer support service providers, development partners and outsourcing partners) requires solution providers to also have the flexibility and ability to adopt the characteristics of the operational capabilities related with each of these service strategies, as described in the four previous chapters.

In addition, the shift towards solutions will see an increase in customer proximity, a decrease in product and service-focused sales forces, an increase in customer-focused sales forces and an increase in the management of key accounts (Sheth and Sharma, 2008). The provision of solutions in particular should be considered as being a strategic, cross-functional process (Storbacka *et al.*, 2009). Solution providers tend to adopt customer-orientated organisational structures by moving from being product-focused to being service-focused, with more narrowly focused strategies, rather than making functional modifications to their operational capabilities.

In customer-orientated organisational structures, customers form the basis of the structure of the whole organisation (Homburg *et al.*, 2000b). The rationale for setting up such organisational structures emphasises the increasing importance of customer satisfaction and loyalty, which have stimulated solution providers to search for organisational ways of serving their customers in a better manner. Companies adapt their organisational concept to become customer-orientated when they move into the solution business (Galbraith, 2002 and 2005). It requires firms to move their concept away from having profit centres for products, reviews and teams for products towards having segments, teams and profit-and-loss responsibilities for customers. This leads to customer-orientated organisational units, such as global accounts, single points of contact for customers and SBUs that are structured around different customer segments rather than around products and services (Day,

2006; Homburg *et al.*, 2000b). These customer-orientated organisational units have very flexible resources in terms of assessing product and service units (Galbraith, 2002). Bosch Packaging, Mettler-Toledo and Ericsson Operation Systems are examples of companies that have established more customer-orientated organisational units.

Exhibit 7.17: The customer-focused organisational structures of Bosch Packaging

Bosch Packaging is an example of a company with the typical customer-focused organisational structures of a solution provider. Bosch Packaging is structured in two separate ways: into three SBUs that are responsible for machines, systems and services and into two SBUs that focus on customers in the pharmaceutical and chocolate and confectionery industries (see figure below). On a general level, the three SBUs make Bosch Packaging an outsourcing partner (see Section 6.2.4), whereas the two additional SBUs can be interpreted as providing solutions for these specific industries. The needs of the customers in these two industries differ fundamentally and require different competencies. The packaging process in the pharmaceutical industry is rather stable because pharmaceutical products have long life cycles, whereas that in the chocolate industry changes rapidly and often due to the large number of new confectionery products being introduced. Recognising that only sales and frontline people with specific competencies in either of the two industries will be successful, Bosch set up one customer-focused SBU for each industry.

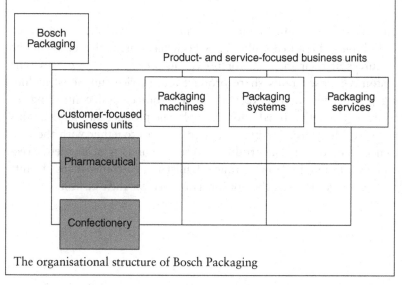

The organisational structure of Bosch Packaging

Exhibit 7.18: The customer-focused organisational structures of Mettler-Toledo

Similarly, Mettler-Toledo changed its organisation from being a structure based on different types of precision measurement instruments and services and now comprises customer-focused business units that concentrate on different measurement applications, such as industrial, laboratory and retail (see figure below). The customer-focused business units are integrated into the appropriate market organisation, such as EMEA, North America or Asia, which possess all the service competencies necessary to sell and deliver services. These market organisations also have all the competencies required for combining products and services into tailor-made solutions.

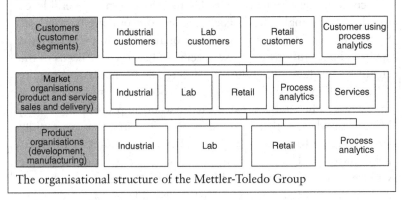

The organisational structure of the Mettler-Toledo Group

The customer-orientated business units in the two cases illustrated in Exhibit 7.17 and Exhibit 7.18 both have great flexibility in the resources at their disposal for providing products and services. The customer-focused units share product and service functions, including pricing, marketing, R&D, human resources and controlling. In the case of Mettler-Toledo, for example, the product and service units negotiate the prices for products and services together with the customer-focused unit. The product and service units typically define recommendations of the price range, whilst the customer-focused units are flexible in defining the appropriate price for their customers. As a result, companies that set up a customer-focused organisational structure must be able to track the profitability of products and services as well as individual customers or groups thereof.

Exhibit 7.19: The key account management used by solution providers

Ericsson Operating Systems illustrates a specific application of solution providers that set up key account-focused units. The distinguishing feature of these units is that, historically, their prices have differed enormously in various countries; it is from these differences that globally dispersed customers are increasingly trying to benefit. The increasing tendency of purchasing companies to emphasise synergies across countries in their procurement operations makes having uncoordinated prices geographically risky for Ericsson. Multinational customers often place order requests to multiple sales regions/countries. Sales regions/countries then send uncoordinated proposals and quotes to the multinational customers, which leads to competition between their own sales subsidiaries and, ultimately, unnecessary price reductions.

The rational response to avoid internal price competition lies in setting up a key account management system. Firms assign key account managers to be the single point of contact for major accounts, selling the entire range of products and services produced by the firm.

Ericsson Operating Systems has consequently established key account managers for global accounts such as Telefonica, Vodafone, Deutsche Telekom and Orange (see figure below). The key account management teams serve as single contact points for these global customers and offer the products and services of all three product and service SBUs (i.e. network infrastructure, professional services and multimedia solutions). Whilst Ericsson's capacities were presented previously as those of a development partner (see Section 6.2.3), the key account managers established by Ericsson Operating Systems for its major customers are a typical feature of solution providers.

Exhibit 7.19: (*cont.*)

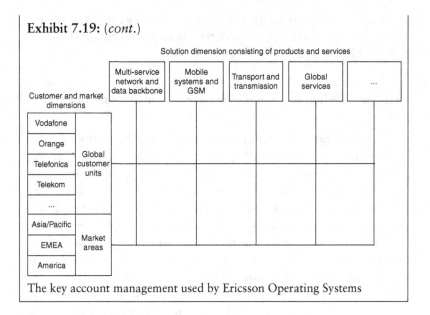

The key account management used by Ericsson Operating Systems

7.5.2 *The process for selling solutions*

Managing the process for selling solutions is a complex exercise (Tuli *et al.*, 2007). The whole process goes beyond the actual sales phase, covering three highly interconnected and iterative phases: creating, selling and delivering a solution. Literature suggests a fourth phase, that of developing a solution, which involves combining the insight of customers with the resources of the provider in order to create a solution portfolio (Storbacka, 2011). However, when companies succeed with the individual service strategies (i.e. after-sales service provider, customer support service provider, development partner and outsourcing partner), they then possess significant insights into the customer's needs.

Thus, solution providers initiate their processes for selling solutions by creating opportunities based on the demand they have identified. Selling solutions is about converting opportunities into orders. Delivering solutions aims at securing the customer's participation in the value creation process, i.e. managing the customer's value contribution to the solution.

Throughout these three phases of selling companies have to balance two key issues: commercialisation and industrialisation (Storbacka, 2011).

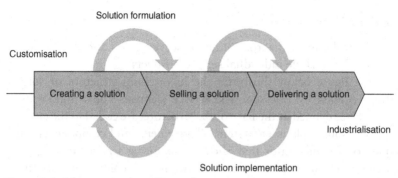

Figure 7.2: The process for selling solutions

- *Commercialisation* refers to exploiting and exploring the financial opportunities of providing solutions.
- *Industrialisation* ensures that solution providers decrease the costs of the solution continuously, as illustrated in Figure 7.2. Industrialisation benefits from the concept of 'economies of repetition' (Davies and Brady, 2000), i.e. establishing routines and learning processes to provide an increasing number of similar solutions more efficiently and effectively.

Exhibit 7.20: The service packages offered by Ericsson Operating Systems

Ericsson Operating Systems applied the following approach when industrialising its service portfolio. The business unit for global services structured the service portfolio into four levels. The first level includes areas such as GSM (Global System for Mobile Communications), WCDMA (Wideband Code Division Multiple Access) and HSPA (High-Speed Packet Access). These can revert to being specific service portfolios, e.g. network launches, professional services, managed services, consulting and education, systems integration and customer support services. These services are divided further into service packages and service products.

Although the portfolio is structured in the form of different packages, customers remain free to pick and choose, so the potential for individual and customised solutions is high. The service packages do not merely contain services from one service area or concept:

Exhibit 7.20: (*cont.*)

they can be formed across different service areas and can be customised to include individual service products.

The figure below illustrates the hierarchical structure of solutions offered by Ericsson. The service elements and components,
which are defined at the base of the structure, are coded in the enterprise resource planning system. The elements and components are
part of a configurator that allows configuring services to be used
easily, according to the customer's needs. The configurator is supplemented by specific rules that adapt the services to the customer's
situation.

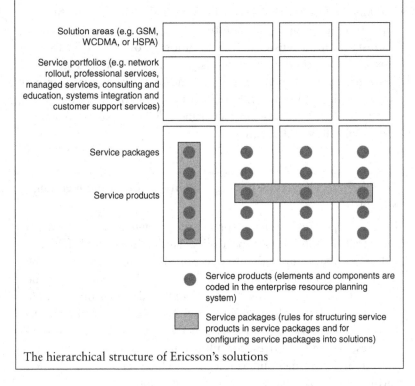

The hierarchical structure of Ericsson's solutions

8 | *Network perspective*

Manufacturers of capital goods may not be able to master all the activities and capabilities relevant to implementing service strategies internally, as described in Section 1.2, as this is rarely economically viable. Consequently, they are resorting all the more to forming complex business networks that are now replacing the traditional, vertically-integrated, relationships between suppliers and customers. Davies (2004) describes the increasing importance of using business networks as moving from being a 'system seller' to a 'system integrator'.

- *System sellers* follow a single vendor approach. They focus on the internal development of capabilities.
- *System integrators* follow a multi-vendor approach. They integrate capabilities that have been developed externally with those developed internally. The external development of capabilities means that system integrators have to rely on a business network in order to design, offer and deliver different services.

The primary goal of this chapter is to introduce types of business networks supporting service business development. Each type of business network is then characterised further by the capabilities necessary for its formation and operation. The perspective taken here is that of the original equipment manufacturing (OEM).

8.1 Dimensions of business networks

The business networks necessary for moving towards services and solutions can be described through two dimensions (see Figure 8.1). The first dimension characterises business networks as being either 'horizontal' or 'vertical': these notions describe the structure of the network (Möller *et al.*, 2005). This dimension deepens understanding of the inter-company collaborations necessary to succeed with different service strategies. The second dimension covers the scope of products and services. Both dimensions can be explained as follows:

- Upstream and downstream activities related to a company's product and service components reflect the vertical dimension of the value chain. Components upstream in the value chain include sources of supply, such as sub-components of products and services (i.e. sub-modules, assembly of sub-modules, logistic services to guarantee assembly and manufacturing activities). Components downstream in the value chain refer to the provision of products and services to the customer in order to install, maintain, operate or finance the equipment (Davies, 2004). The extension of service components in the total offering begins with basic services for the installed base, such as spare parts, inspections, repairs, maintenance and modernisation services. Further service components comprise operational services, where customers outsource their operational or maintenance services. Moreover, such outsourcing and operational services lead to additional performance guarantees being a component of the solution (Windahl and Lakemond, 2010). Performance guarantees change the revenue models and make financial services necessary: pay-per-performance, for example, requires financial arrangements being made so that the actual performance can be paid for (Hünerberg and Hüttmann, 2003). Further service components encompass consulting services and addressing business needs, as well as providing design and constructions services, in order to fulfil the customer's technical needs (Davies *et al.*, 2007). This dimension is related to the service strategies discussed earlier. The total offering can either include after-sales services, customer-support services, outsourcing services, design and construction services or just solutions. These total offerings are close to the service strategies.
- The notion 'horizontal' suggests additional product and service components that reach beyond the existing product and service value chain of the company, e.g. integrating third-party products and services into the solutions. It means that the total offering of a supplier can include products that are either offered by competitors or complement their own products. The inclusion of such third-party products into the total offering does not necessarily enhance the breadth of services, but rather extends services to include those from competing products and/or supplement products from other vendors (Raddats and Easingwood, 2010).

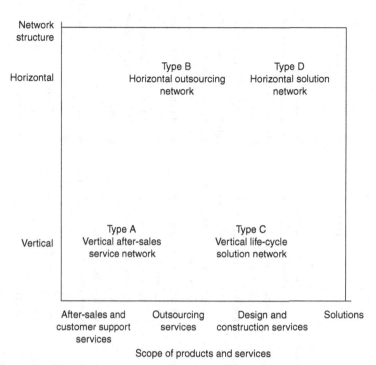

Figure 8.1: The dimensions of the four types of business networks

8.2 Types of business networks

Our work with manufacturing companies has yielded at least four types of business networks, namely:

A. vertical after-sales (or customer-support) service networks;
B. horizontal outsourcing service networks;
C. vertical life-cycle solution networks;
D. horizontal solution networks.

Although the business networks are classified here as being horizontal and vertical, it is very seldom that are they purely so. Horizontal networks, for example, can also contain vertically positioned suppliers; vertical networks can include the value activities of competitors or auxiliary actors. The vertical–horizontal terminology is used here to indicate the dominant orientation within the network. The concepts, such as after-sales service, outsourcing service, life-cycle solutions, describe the service strategy. All four types of business networks are

Table 8.1: *Description of the business networks*

(A) Vertical after-sales (or customer-support) service networks	(B) Horizontal outsourcing service networks	(C) Vertical life-cycle solution networks	(D) Horizontal solution networks
- Network concentrates on one single value chain (vertical dimension) - Network activities focus on the usage of original equipment (after-sales services) - OEM is the focal firm (grey cell) of the vertical after-sales service network - OEM offers services for maintaining the installed base in order to increase the operational efficiency of the installed base - OEM services include spare parts, inspection, repair, maintenance services - Logistic service providers support the spare parts delivery processes	- Network covers multiple value chains (horizontal dimension), or in other words, diverse set of original equipments - Network activities focus on outsourcing the operation and maintenance of a diverse set of original equipment - Outsourcing specialists are the focal firm (grey cell) of the horizontal outsourcing service network - OEMs are restricted to deliver spare parts and knowledge-intensive services for solving complex product failures - Outsourcing specialist offers intermediate service starting with inspecting, repair, maintenance until operational processes offer services	- Network concentrates on multiple value chains (horizontal dimension) - Network activities cover the whole life cycle of the equipment starting from the design phase and ending at the usage phase across diverse set of original equipment (solutions) - OEM is the focal firm (grey cell) of the horizontal solution network - OEM offers services supporting the whole life cycle of the product as well as the integration of products and services into customer-specific solutions	- Network concentrates on one single value chain (vertical dimension) - Network activities cover the whole life cycle of the equipment starting from the design phase and ending at the usage phase for one single set of original equipment (solutions) - OEM is the focal firm of the vertical life-cycle solution network - OEM offers services supporting the whole life cycle of the product as well as the integration of products and services into customer-specific solutions

- Suppliers positioned upstream in the value chain ensure the spare parts deliveries

- Outsourcing specialist aims at operational efficiency of the installed base and often takes over responsibilities for maintaining the installed base
- Logistic service providers support the spare parts delivery processes along OEMs, 1st tier, 2nd tier supplier and so on
- IT-service providers offer remote services to monitor the condition and usage of the installed base
- Bank and insurance companies support pay-per-performance arrangements associated with the provision of outsourcing services
- OEMs and suppliers positioned upstream in the value chain ensure the spare parts deliveries

- Logistic service providers support the spare parts delivery processes along OEMs, 1st tier, 2nd tier supplier and so on
- IT-service providers offer remote services to monitor the condition and usage of the installed base
- Suppliers positioned upstream in the value chain ensure the spare parts deliveries
- Engineering specialists contribute to designing the life-cycle solutions

- Logistic service providers support the spare parts delivery processes along OEMs, 1st tier, 2nd tier supplier and so on
- IT-service providers offer remote services to monitor the condition and usage of the installed base
- Suppliers positioned upstream in the value chain ensure the spare parts deliveries
- Engineering specialists contribute to designing the life-cycle solutions

networks that have not evolved organically: they have been developed intentionally and therefore require a specific set of capabilities each (Möller *et al.*, 2005).Table 8.1 provides an overview of the four types of business networks.

8.3 Vertical after-sales service networks

8.3.1 Network characteristics

Figure 8.2 illustrates the vertical after-sales service network (see also Exhibit 8.1). 'Vertical' refers to the fact that the actors cover upstream and downstream activities in one specific value chain; 'after-sales (or customer-support) services' refers to the value activities being concentrated on the usage of the product.

Exhibit 8.1: The vertical service network operated by GF AgieCharmilles

A typical illustration is the value chain of GF AgieCharmilles, a Swiss manufacturer of mould-making machines. GF AgieCharmilles has changed its service strategy from providing after-sales service to providing customer-support services, offering highly sophisticated products and services (i.e. spare parts, repairs, inspection and maintenance services) that support product usage. About 27 per cent of the revenue of GF AgieCharmilles is generated by the service business. Services are offered for their own installed base only. In order to protect service profit and revenue pool, GF AgieCharmilles moved into the service business to avoid being bypassed by suppliers. In addition, GF AgieCharmilles set up a dense service network of subsidiaries and service agents to protect the installed base from other service specialists. In Europe, for example, they operate sales and service subsidiaries in the main markets of Germany, Switzerland, Italy, France and the United Kingdom, and with service agents in minor markets such as Spain, the Scandinavian countries and Eastern Europe. In Asia, sales and service subsidiaries have been set up in Japan, South Korea, China (including Beijing, Shanghai and Shenzhen/Hong Kong) and Singapore. This dense network of service subsidiaries makes it difficult for third-party service providers to enter the service market of their installed base.

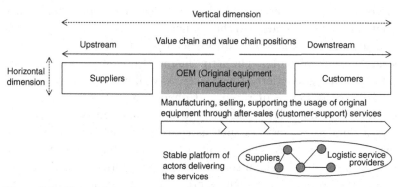

Figure 8.2: Illustration of an after-sales (customer-support) service network

In general, the network includes the OEM, logistic service providers and upstream suppliers of spare parts; the OEM emerges as the focal company in the network. The vertical after-sales service network consists of one layer, which covers all of the specified value activities distinctly. This network forms a relatively stable business system. The actors producing and delivering the after-sales services are usually known and they carry out predefined value activities. The value proposition of the whole network concentrates on the after-sales phase and/or usage of the product: the value activities performed by each actor enhance the usage of the product. OEMs offer services that include the delivery of spare parts and repair, inspection and maintenance services. By storing and transporting spare parts, logistic service providers support the OEMs and suppliers in the delivery of spare parts. In the case of small- and medium-sized OEMs (see Chapter 11), the value network may also include distributors and external service partners. Small- and medium-sized companies do not reach the critical mass required to establish sale subsidiaries in various markets: they favour instead external service partners as distributors, specialising in selling, installing and maintaining the products.

8.3.2 Capabilities

Managing a service organisation in general, and enhancing technical competences and service-orientated attitudes in particular, are illustrations of operational capabilities through which OEMs utilise a vertical after-sales service network. The dynamic capabilities of sensing, seizing and reconfiguring allow OEMs to form a vertical after-sales service network deliberately. Sensing opportunities are related to the exploitation of the financial potential of product usage, and seizing the exploitation of financial potential in specific service strategies and offerings. The term 'financial potential' refers to the attractive margins offered by services, as well as to services that are an additional source of revenue (Cohen *et al.*, 2006). In order to exploit these financial potentials, the OEM develops service strategies around basic services such as spare parts delivery, repair and maintenance services. The benefits of these strategies are not free: they require the development of complementarities with the competences of other actors such as providers of logistics, suppliers of spare parts and the reconfiguration of internal capabilities. The latter is necessary if a service organisation is to be managed in combination with a manufacturing organisation (Oliva and Kallenberg, 2003). OEMs develop service delivery capabilities within the service organisation by enhancing technical competencies and establishing service-orientated attitudes.

Competence complementarities with other actors lead to further operational and dynamic capabilities. Operational capabilities include forecasting the demand and supply of service interventions between customers and the OEM as well as the planning and coordination of the supply of spare parts between suppliers, the OEM and logistics providers. Forecasting the demand and supply of service interventions extends the range of management activities in the existing customer relationship.

Developing such operational capabilities at the network level requires dynamic capabilities that aim at visioning, mobilising and orchestrating the value creation activities of the suppliers, logistics providers and customers. In the case of suppliers, this entails motivating them to rely on the OEM for coordinating and taking responsibility of the spare parts business instead of selling and distributing the spare parts to customers directly. Furthermore, the OEM must encourage logistics providers not only to store spare parts close to the customer but also improve their service levels continuously. The OEM needs to motivate customers to create a collaborative learning relationship in which their service personnel acquire knowledge as they interact with customers' maintenance departments. Service personnel thus learn about the operational needs of the customer and, simultaneously, gain intimate knowledge as to how the service delivery processes (i.e. spare parts, repair, inspections and maintenance) should be linked with the customer's operational processes.

8.4 Horizontal outsourcing service networks

8.4.1 Network characteristics

A horizontal outsourcing service network is illustrated in Figure 8.3. The notion 'horizontal' implies that the actors cover different value chains. It is an outsourcing specialist that comprises the focal company in a horizontal outsourcing service network. These companies focus on outsourcing services for various types of original equipment. Outsourcing specialists break the dyadic relationship that existed between an OEM and its customers. They specialise in taking over responsibility for the customer's operational and maintenance services. Typical illustrations here are the value chains of automation, infrastructure and paper processing equipment, in which specialised service providers such as Bilfinger Berger, Voith Industrial Services AG, and Wisag Industrial Services took over complete responsibility for all of the services supporting usage of their products. These outsourcing specialists are directly engaged in upstream activities relative to the OEMs, the component suppliers, as shown in Figure 8.3. The value proposition of the whole network is to run the customers' maintenance and operational processes in a more cost-efficient way than the customers themselves can run them.

Contrary to Type A, the structure of horizontal outsourcing service networks consists of two layers. The outsourcing specialist mobilises, in the first layer, various actors to form a stable platform of value activities and competencies and, in the second layer, selects the necessary actors from the platform to address the customer's needs. The outsourcing specialist provides the outsourcing services and orchestrates the value activities of the actors selected. Whereas the first layer is a relatively stable system that serves as a prerequisite for providing services, the second layer can be reconfigured dynamically, according to the outsourcing needs of the customers.

In this kind of network, i.e. Type B, customers favour a reciprocal dependency with an outsourcing specialist when the operational

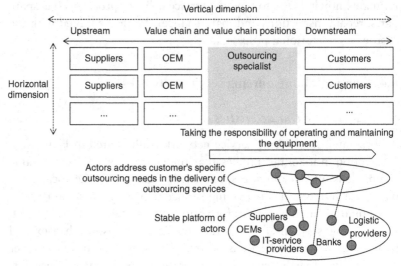

Figure 8.3: Illustration of a horizontal outsourcing network

and maintenance processes that are outsourced are not core processes (Windahl and Lakemond, 2010). OEMs are restricted to offering basic services only, such as deliveries of spare parts, warranty services and knowledge-intensive services (e.g. solving complex product failures). All other activities, such as inspection, repair, maintenance, modernisation and process optimisation, are outsourced to the outsourcing specialist. Outsourcing specialists thereby increase the operational efficiency of the installed base.

As in Type A networks, providers of logistics support the outsourcing specialist in storing and handling spare parts. OEMs and suppliers positioned upstream in the value chain ensure the deliveries of spare parts and participate in return and repair activities. Outsourcing specialists also mobilise providers of IT service in offering platforms for remote monitoring services that, in turn, enable the outsourcing specialist to monitor the usage and actual conditions of the products installed.

8.4.2 Capabilities

A horizontal outsourcing service network may be formed as an alternative to a vertical after-sales service network. The focal companies in both of these networks (OEMs and outsourcing specialists) compete in accessing and exploiting service opportunities throughout the life of the product. Sensing opportunities in Type B, however, are focused on exploiting economies of scale (Auguste *et al.*, 2006) and the customer's need to outsource their operational processes instead of exploiting the financial potential of services.

Seizing the outsourcing needs sensed is not limited to one specific type of equipment: it embraces the whole breadth of operational and maintenance processes that are not core processes for the customers. For that reason, seizing outsourcing opportunities should acknowledge the client and other OEMs as being potential competitors (Mathieu, 2001a). According to the proposed value proposition, seizing specifically takes higher cost-efficiencies into consideration rather than costs achieved by customers or OEMs. Outsourcing specialists benefit quite logically from larger economies of scale, as they offer outsourcing services that cover not only various brands of equipment but also the product range within a particular brand. OEMs, on the contrary, maintain only their own product brands. Thus, outsourcing specialists may gain a significant learning advantage by specialising in one specific service (e.g. outsourcing services of complex technical equipment). Moreover, the customer's coordinating costs are reduced significantly when they need to rely on only one outsourcing partner for a whole range of equipment rather than on different OEMs that specialise in their own equipment alone.

Reconfiguring existing operational capabilities precedes the process of seizing the outsourcing needs sensed previously. The reconfiguration process depends on the specific origin of the outsourcing specialists: this can originate either from OEMs looking to broaden their service offerings beyond their own product category (Raddats and Easingwood, 2010) or from customers setting up their own maintenance departments as separate strategic business units.

Exhibit 8.2: Acquisition activities at Voith Industrial Services

Voith Industrial Services provides a good illustration of an OEM that broadened its service offerings beyond its original product categories of (1) machines for the papermaking process (provided by Voith Paper) and (2) turbines and generators for power stations (provided by Voith Hydro). As an outsourcing specialist, Voith Industrial Services seized a cost advantage by achieving greater

Exhibit 8.2: (*cont.*)

economies of scale (e.g. by acquiring various technical service specialists between 2000 and 2010) (see figure below).

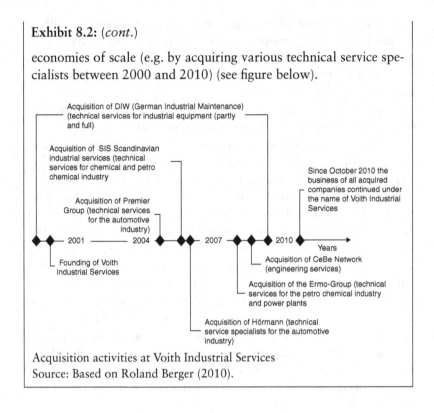

Acquisition activities at Voith Industrial Services
Source: Based on Roland Berger (2010).

An illustration of an outsourcing specialist that transitioned from having solely internal maintenance competencies to providing services to external customers is Lufthansa Technik. Lufthansa Technik moved from being an internal maintenance provider to the flight operator Lufthansa to being one of the leading independent providers of maintenance, repair, overhaul and modification services in the civil aviation industry as a whole. Lufthansa Technik gains competitive advantages by developing a collaborative learning relationship with flight operators and manufacturers of airplanes and air engines since it has an intimate knowledge of the operational and business needs of each of these network actors.

Outsourcing specialists utilise the business network by building operational competencies, such as the technical skills necessary for providing service, the behavioural skills for performing the frontline roles necessary to be a performance enabler, and fostering customer-focused attitudes in order to understand the customer's outsourcing needs. These skills are all part of managing a pure service organisation that offers outsourcing services.

Offering outsourcing services for multiple equipment categories entails competition among the OEMs moving into the service business, as mentioned above. Convincing other OEMs to concentrate on the basic services for their own installed base and knowledge-intensive services (and, in effect, demobilising the OEMs) is therefore central to the dynamic capabilities. Through intensive partnering, outsourcing specialists convince OEMs to focus solely on the provision of spare parts, warranty services and knowledge-intensive services to solve very complex product failures. Logistics services ensure deliveries of spare parts to the customer. Furthermore, outsourcing specialists motivate providers of IT services to monitor the usage conditions of the equipment, which then allows them to optimise the capacity utilisation of their service staff. Furthermore, outsourcing specialists offer performance guarantees and pay-per-performance approaches. Collaboration with banks and insurance companies is also necessary so that such payments can, in fact, be made.

Outsourcing specialists aim at achieving strong economies of scale by specialising in one specific service category. Achieving these economies of scale encourages outsourcing specialists to be very active in mergers and acquisitions. Merging with, and acquiring, other companies are insufficient in themselves: it is the competence for integrating the newly-acquired company that develops the core competency of the specialist. Exhibits 8.2, 8.3 and 8.4 illustrate the acquisition activities at Voith Industrial Services, Bilfinger Berger and Bosch Packaging.

Exhibit 8.3: Bilfinger Berger's mergers and acquisitions

The Bilfinger Berger Group is an illustration of a pure outsourcing specialist without any product business of its own. The Group, which engages in a range of activities, is composed of the business segments: Industrial Services, Power Services, Building and Facility Services and, finally, Construction and Concessions. In order to achieve economies of scale, the Bilfinger Berger Group also invested significantly in the acquisition of other service specialists (see figure below).

Exhibit 8.3: *(cont.)*

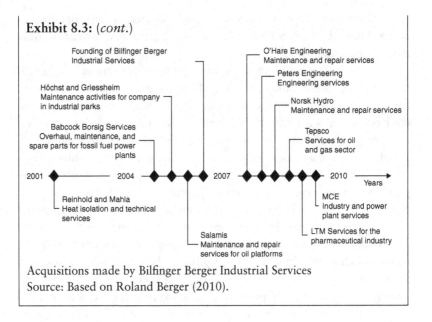

Acquisitions made by Bilfinger Berger Industrial Services
Source: Based on Roland Berger (2010).

Exhibit 8.4: Acquisitions made by Bosch Packaging

Bosch Packaging Technology was founded in 1974. The division is constantly being developed through organic growth and acquisitions. The first wave of acquisitions in the mid 1990s concentrated on market expansion, e.g. acquiring TL Systems in Minneapolis (USA) and Togum/Comeck in Germany, whereas the second wave was driven by a desire to increase the market share of the installed base. A higher market share of the installed base of packaging machines and systems now drives the economies of scales of providing service. The Robert Bosch Packaging Technology Division was founded in 2002 and extended in several stages: acquisitions include Moeller & Devicon, Tevopharm and the SIG Group in 2004. Furthermore, Bosch Packaging acquired the Dresdener Pharmatec GmbH and Schoeller-Bleckmann Medizintechnik in 2007 and Paal Packaging Machines in 2011. Under the Bosch brand, the company offers all of the line components for their filling and packaging processes from one source. The relationship between customer applications (pharmaceutical and confectionery industries) and focus on products and service (packaging machines, systems and services) delivers important synergies for developing customer-focused innovations.

8.5 Vertical life-cycle solution networks

8.5.1 Network characteristics

Figure 8.4 depicts the business network pertaining to vertical life-cycle solutions, denoted here as Type C. Again, the vertical concept suggests that activities are concentrated within one specific value chain. Type C, in contrast to Type A, is not restricted to the phase of product usage since network activities cover the whole life cycle of the equipment, starting with the development, design and construction phases and ending with the product usage. In common with Type A, the OEM is the focal company of this type of network. A typical illustration of a Type C network is Alfa Laval, which designs, manufactures and maintains water-recycling systems. Such OEMs offer services supporting the whole life cycle of water-recycling systems as well as the integration of products and services into customer-specific solutions.

It is interesting to note that this network differed in the structure of the layers throughout the life cycle of the product. In the design phase, the network consists of two layers. The OEM mobilises engineering specialists in the first of these layers to form a stable platform of value activities and competencies, as in Type B networks. In the second layer, the OEM selects the necessary engineering specialists from the platform to address the customer's individual design and constructing needs. Then, in the after-sales phase, the network is similar to that in Type A in that it consists of only one layer that covers all of the value activities specified.

As in Types A and B, providers of logistics support the delivery processes of spare parts and providers of IT services offer remote services for monitoring the condition and usage of the installed base. These are complemented by auxiliary service providers, which include engineering specialists that can offer first-hand technical knowledge.

8.5.2 Capabilities

The formation of a vertical life-cycle solution network is triggered by dynamic capabilities such as sensing opportunities for exploiting a customer's technical and business needs along the whole life cycle of the product, and seizing the chance to exploit the opportunities in terms of service strategy and offering. Seizing refers to achieving a

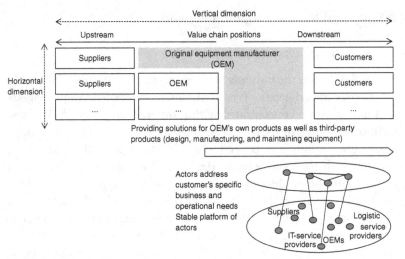

Figure 8.4: Vertical life-cycle service network

value proposition for outstanding performance throughout the whole life cycle of the product. This value proposition ranges from designing customer processes around the equipment to providing the service support for its use. The reconfiguration of capabilities aims at supplementing manufacturing with service capabilities, as in the case of vertical after-sales service networks. Such sensing, seizing and reconfiguring activities are managed by OEMs, who apply these dynamic capabilities by visioning and mobilising engineering specialists to form a stable platform. They also orchestrate these engineering specialists in taking an active role in creating life-cycle solutions and in participating in solving the customer's needs for process design and construction. Thus, OEMs start the process of orchestrating engineering specialists and suppliers in the provision of life-cycle solutions.

The operational capabilities necessary for utilising vertical life-cycle solution networks are similar to those of vertical after-sales service networks. They also include the technical competencies necessary for providing service. In addition, OEMs organise behavioural competencies for performing frontline roles, e.g. acting as trusted advisers for life-cycle solutions and developing customer-focused attitudes for understanding the customer's operational and business needs, as well as technical design requirements, throughout the life cycle of the product. These capabilities are, as with Type A, a part of managing a service organisation that supplies all of the services required in the life cycle of the product.

8.6 Horizontal solution networks

8.6.1 Network characteristics

Figure 8.5 depicts the fourth kind of business network, Type D, known as horizontal solution networks. As with Type B, the horizontal concept suggests that activities are concentrated on multiple value chains. In contrast with Types A and B, but similar to Type C, the horizontal solutions in Type D start as early as in the development phase. OEMs represent the focal company of the network, as in Types A and C. A typical illustration of this type of network is Alstom Transportation, a company that covers the design, manufacture and maintenance of transportation equipment in general, and of trains in particular. In addition, Alstom's solutions capture services for competitors' rolling stock (i.e. locomotives, railroad cars, coaches and wagons) and signalling track infrastructure.

Horizontal solution networks include a wide range of providers of auxiliary services and products which, in turn, contributes specific knowledge to the solution. Together with suppliers in the various value chains, providers of auxiliary services and products form a new value system along with the OEMs in question. The network structure here is not purely horizontal, as it also consists of a considerable number of vertical elements that may include, for example, strategic partnerships and alliances with experts possessing knowledge of the local market. Alstom formed a strategic partnership with Transmashholding (TMH), the main manufacturer of rail rolling stock in Russia. TMH has, hardly surprisingly, superior technological expertise regarding the specific needs of Russian railways. Both companies are currently engaged in developing a new generation of rolling stock (i.e. electric locomotives and double-decker passenger cars, especially for medium distances) specifically tailored to the needs of the Russian market.

Horizontal solution networks, interestingly enough, consist of two layers. In the first, the focal company mobilises various actors to form a stable platform of competencies contributing to a solution. In the second layer, it selects and orchestrates the actors necessary from the platform to address the customer's business and operational needs comprehensively. The first layer is a relatively stable system that serves as a prerequisite for providing solutions, whereas the second layer can be reconfigured dynamically according to the needs of the customer.

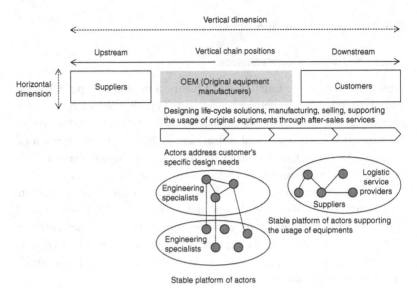

Figure 8.5: Horizontal solution network

8.6.2 *Capabilities*

Sensing and exploring new opportunities for creating value through-out the whole value network triggers the formation of a horizontal solution network. Once companies sense these opportunities they start to seize them in value-creating strategies, reconfiguring their capability base towards forming multi-dimensional value networks. Reconfiguration is accomplished by visioning and mobilising the con-tribution that actors can make to the strategies of value creation (e.g. providers of auxiliary services, suppliers, engineering specialists and customers). Once the network actors are mobilised, the focal company orchestrates their contribution: in order to do so, the focal company must have the relational capabilities necessary to form solid strategic partnerships with external actors. The focal point of a horizontal solu-tion network is, therefore, an orchestrator who coordinates the contri-butions made by the network partners towards providing a solution.

Operational capabilities incorporate technical competencies, behav-ioural competencies and having customer-orientated attitudes, all of which are imperative in networks of Types B and C. Moreover, the focal company develops attitudes and skills for performing the front-line roles that allow it to act as a trusted adviser that provides custom-ers with high-value solutions.

9 International aspects of service business development

This chapter examines in depth the exploitation approach in an international (global) context. It has two primary objectives. The first is to provide insight into global approaches to the development of service business (see Section 9.1); the second is to highlight the key issues of service business development in the Chinese market (see Section 9.2).

9.1 Global approaches to service business development

9.1.1 International service offerings

Service offerings differ in the degree of interactions between customers and service employees (Vandermerwe and Chadwick, 1989) and knowledge intensity. Basic services for the installed base and maintenance services require relatively little customer interaction, whilst the opposite applies to services such as business consulting, R&D orientated services and outsourcing services. Furthermore, the level of knowledge required by the different services within each service category differs: e.g. repair services can be divided into basic and more complex repair services. In business practice, differences in knowledge intensity refer to the first, second and third levels of service. As illustrated in Figure 9.1, delivering first-level services requires only basic service skills, whereas the third level entails specialised service skills such as behavioural competencies, technical expertise and customer-focused attitudes (Neu and Brown, 2005). The specific skills required for delivering second-level services is positioned between the basic skills of the first level and the sophisticated skills of the third. The left-hand side of Figure 9.1 depicts the main service categories and service levels, showing the various combinations of service categories and levels.

The services depicted require direct interactions with customers, so manufacturing companies must either send service employees from their headquarters to the various international locations of their customers or enter the actual international market. Entry into the market can be direct or indirect. Indirect entry occurs when the organisation providing the service is only partly owned by the manufacturing company; direct entry occurs when the manufacturing firm establishes its own organisational infrastructure for providing services in an international market (Grönroos, 1999).

It is arguable that extending the service offering will interact with the global (organisational) approach. Although services such as the delivery of spare parts, installations and basic training might fit into an ethnocentrically centralised global approach in which service activities are concentrated in the home country, maintenance services probably require a polycentric and decentralised organisation. In the latter case, local service organizations are established to respond to requests of adaptation. A global organisation embraces five highly interrelated elements:

1. *Domestic and foreign elements*: the first element pertains to the structure of global organisations. Generally speaking, these consist of domestic and foreign elements. The former refers to the central headquarters of the company; the latter include the organisation of the market at the regional or country level (Fouraker and Stopford, 1968). The terms 'central organisation' and 'market organisation' are used here to distinguish the domestic and local elements in global organisations.

2. *Organisational distinctiveness* (see Chapter 7): the second element refers to organisational distinctiveness, namely the degree to which the service business unit is established as a distinct entity, with the corresponding profit-and-loss responsibility (Oliva and Kallenberg, 2003). As highlighted in Chapter 7, whether organisational distinctiveness is beneficial to manufacturing companies depends on the actual service strategy employed.

3. *Customer proximity*: the third element embraces the proximity of the service organisation to the customer. Customer proximity also depends on the actual service strategy used. Proximity to customers refers either to centralised or decentralised service units (see Table 2.13).

4. *Organisational functions* supporting the service business: the fourth element covers organisational functions, i.e. the activities that a company must undertake in order to create, deliver and sell services (Gibson *et al.*, 2006).

Knowledge intensity

Service offering	First-level support	Second-level support	Third-level support
Customer service	• Information service • Electronic orders • Product demonstration/trial period • Customer magazine	• Cost-benefit analysis • Benefit visualisation • Just-in-time delivery • Help desk	
Basic services for the installed base	• Basic repair • Monthly inspections • Spare parts services	• Installation • Technical training for troubleshooting • On-site diagnosis	• Repair service for complex components • Annual inspection services
Maintenance services	• Cleaning services • Waste disposal	• Technical training for maintenance • Preventive maintenance services • Processing optimisation • Product and software upgrades	• Full-service contract • Preventive maintenance • Full-maintenance contracts • Annual maintenance activities • Service-level agreements • Process-optimisation through continuous maintenance
R&D orientated services		• Viability studies/problem analysis • Construction (design) services	• Technical consulting and advice • R&D support • Process-orientated design • Business consulting in product and process development

Organisational elements	Characteristics
Global structure	• Domestic elements • Foreign elements
Organisational distinction	• Separation of product and service businesses
Proximity to customers	• Centralised service unit • Decentralised service unit (close to customers)
Organisational functions	• Sales • Delivery • Development • Controlling • Planning • Marketing • Pricing
Behavioural orientation	• Ethnocentric • Polycentric • Geocentric

Figure 9.1: Service offerings and organisational elements

5. *Behavioural orientation*: the fifth element encompasses behavioural
    orientations and distinguishes between ethnocentric, polycentric and
    geocentric approaches. Cultural aspects, human resource management
    and decision processes can be classified into ethnocentric (home-coun-
    try orientated), polycentric (host-country orientated) and geocentric
    (world-orientated) approaches (Perlmutter, 1969). Ethnocentrism
    is the tendency to regard global organisation from a home-country
    perspective: the underlying belief is that the values and norms of the
    home-country headquarters are superior to those of local organisa-
    tions. The polycentric perspective acknowledges that subsidiaries are
    moving towards maturity and are, therefore, permitted to exercise
    discretion in certain areas of decision-making and the setting of values
    and norms (Kotler and Keller, 2005). Geocentricity balances integra-
    tion and differentiation between cultural and structural dimensions.
    The geocentric approach is one in which headquarters and subsidiar-
    ies are regarded as being 'partners' (Perlmutter, 1969).

Combining these five elements with the service offerings results in the
following four approaches to providing global service (see Table 9.1
for an overview):

1. the integrated and ethnocentric global service approach;
2. the integrated and polycentric global service approach;
3. the separated and polycentric global service approach;
4. the separated and geocentric global service approach.

9.1.2 The integrated and ethnocentric approach

The first organisational approach is typical for smaller companies (see
Chapter 11): these are usually more specialised and it allows them to
benefit from scope and scale effects in spite of limited resources. The
integrated and ethnocentric approach, shown in Figure 9.2, is suitable for use in the after-sales service strategy. At the central level, the
companies have integrated the service department as a cost centre into
the product organisation. The central product organisation is a relatively autonomous unit in which the management have control of the
following functions: marketing, sales, services, manufacturing, R&D,
accounting/finance and human resources. Locally, these companies
work with sales agents or subsidiaries that sell products and provide

Table 9.1: *Overview of the four approaches used to provide global service*

(1) Integrated and ethnocentric approach	(2) Integrated and polycentric approach	(3) Separated and polycentric approach	(4) Separated and geocentric approach
- The service organisation is a cost centre in the business unit for products	- The service organisation is a cost centre in the business unit for products	- The service organisation is an independent business unit with its own profit-and-loss responsibility	- A collaborative approach between the central business units (products and services) and the market organisations
- The central product organisation controls marketing, sales, services, manufacturing, R&D, accounting/finance and HR	- Market organisations are relatively independent in controlling product sales, provision of customer service, basic services for the installed base, few maintenance services and HR	- The business unit for services controls service development, spare parts logistics and service support functions	- Regional functions enhance functions involving collaboration (e.g. regional warehouses and service hubs for second-level support)
- Market organisations (sales agent or subsidiaries) sell products and provide customer service to augment the product during its sales phase	- Market organisations set up local warehouses for delivering spare parts	- Single market organisations are responsible for the product and service business, but the cost and revenue structures make clear distinctions between the product and service business	- Market organisations concentrate on selling preventive services and service contracts
- The central service organisation provides basic services for the installed base and advanced technical support	- The third-level support remains in the central organisation	- Market organisations provide first and second-level support (customer service, basic services and maintenance services). The separated central service organisation takes over the responsibility for providing third-level support	- Service hubs facilitate flows of information and promote the exchange of experiences between the different market organisations
- Services are included in the price of the product	- Key positions are filled by local sales and service employees	- Services are charged for separately, thereby ensuring their profitability	- Service hubs decide on the degree to which the standardisation of services is transferable within the market organisations
- Market organisation has a low level of authority in making decisions	- The central service organisation has a relatively low level of authority and competency in making decisions	- The central service organisation has a relatively low level of authority in making decisions	- Companies develop the best employees everywhere in the world for key positions in the global service network
	- Services are included in the price of the product		- In a few large markets, the market organisation consists of one legal entity for services and one for products

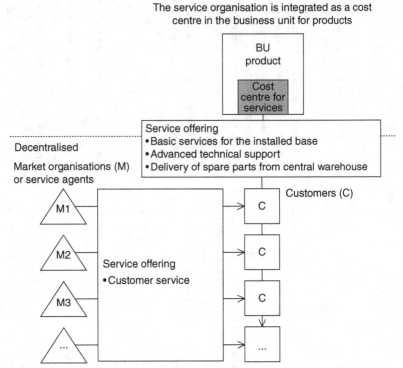

Figure 9.2: The integrated and ethnocentric global service approach

customer service to augment the product during its sales phase. The sales agents or subsidiaries also sell basic services for the installed base that are then provided by the central service department. Spare parts, for example, are delivered directly from the central warehouse; service technicians from the central service department go to the customer and provide repair services or install spare parts.

Services do not contribute fundamentally to the total revenue and profit. The behaviour of the sales agents and subsidiaries is driven by the central product organisation and can be described as being ethnocentric. This means that the structure and competencies are kept rather simple within the market organisations; only the central product organisation includes a broad range of competencies and a decision-making authority that is low down in the market organisation. Product prices and basic services are predefined from the central sales function; the market organisation has only the authority to decide on how much customer service should be provided to augment the product offering. Sales managers in the market organisation are recruited and developed in the home country (e.g. expatriates), leading to the situation that they identify themselves with the central behaviour rather than the local culture. The flow of communication between the central product organisation and the local market organisation can be described as being one-way. The central organisation communicates with the local organisation regarding orders, product prices, forecasts of product sales and advice for including basic services for the installed base in the product price.

The main drawbacks of the integrated and ethnocentric global service structure are the lack of sensitivity of the service expectations held by local customers, high travel costs for delivering the service and insufficient considerations of extending the breadth of the service offering. Thus, an integrated and ethnocentric global service structure limits the financial results attributable to services. Companies should maintain this organisational form only if their customers expect basic services and are willing to cover travel costs.

9.1.3 The integrated and polycentric approach

The second approach is an integrated and polycentric global service approach (see Figure 9.3). It is beneficial for companies following an after-sales service strategy or partly following a customer-support service strategy. It encompasses the situation where the service culture and behaviour can be described as being polycentric. The market organisations are a relatively independent unit in which the local sales managers have control of product sales, the provision of customer service, basic services for the installed base, a few maintenance services and human resources. It leads to a situation where most market organisations train local sales and service employees for key positions.

The central organisation of the integrated and polycentric global service approach is similar to the first approach but has a relatively low level of authority and decision-making competencies. The final prices of products and charges for services are decided within the market organisations. The central organisation can only determine the transfer prices from the central to the market organisation: it does not control how the market organisation sets the price paid by the customer. The central organisation simply discusses, and agrees on, goals with the market organisation and defines key performance indicators. Since the central organisation is still product-orientated and the services remain as a cost centre within the product organisation, the key performance indicators concentrate on the business surrounding the actual products (e.g. market share, overall profitability, number of products sold and revenue generated).

The different market organisations share little in the way of information and experiences regarding sales arguments, customer expectations and services. Compared to the first organisational approach, the second one does not only concentrate on customer service and basic services for the installed base but also includes a few maintenance services. Some of the services are still included in the price of the product and not charged for separately. Services are used to make comparing different product offers more difficult, thus avoiding direct price competition. The extended service offering is valuable for retaining existing customers, but the financial contribution is still quite low in terms of the share of service revenue to total revenue, or share of service profit to total profit. The market organisation provides most services directly to customers. It has the technical competencies to provide the first and second levels of service support for the installed base. Local service employees are recruited to serve as reliable providers of service that includes repair, inspection and maintenance. Market organisations even set up local warehouses for delivering spare parts. The third level of support, associated with high-level and in-depth technical skills, remains within the central organisation and usually belongs to the R&D function.

Weighing up the advantages against the disadvantages, the integrated and polycentric global service approach offers a rapid and inexpensive way of responding to local needs for servicing the installed base. Nevertheless, if the installed base has traditionally been served from a central location, the companies have exceptional rational motives for locating service centres within their market organisations. A company without localised services will be placed under enormous competitive pressure from both customers and competitors. Such pressure from customers means that they challenge the efforts made by the companies by enhancing their own service capabilities and repairing, maintaining and/or inspecting the installed base themselves. The integrated and polycentric global service approach can, however, be highly competitive and successful. Manufacturing companies can still make attractive margins from their products without necessarily having to place much emphasis on achieving high levels of revenue and profits from services. Exhibit 9.1 illustrates Bystronic's integrated and polycentric global service apporach.

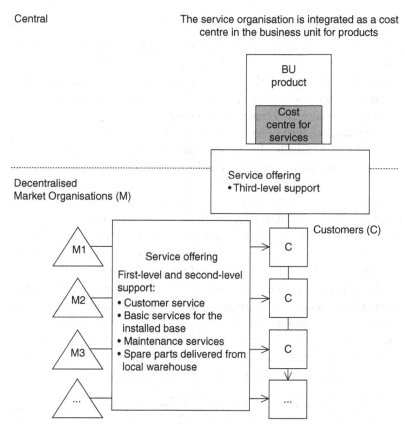

Central — The service organisation is integrated as a cost centre in the business unit for products

BU product

Cost centre for services

Service offering
• Third-level support

Decentralised
Market Organisations (M)

Customers (C)

M1

M2

M3

...

Service offering

First-level and second-level support:
• Customer service
• Basic services for the installed base
• Maintenance services
• Spare parts delivered from local warehouse

C

C

C

...

Figure 9.3: The integrated and polycentric global service approach

Exhibit 9.1: The global service approach used by Bystronic

Bystronic Glass is a typical illustration of a company with an integrated and polycentric service structure. At the global (central) level, Bystronic integrated its service business with its product organisation. In addition, sales and service subsidiaries were established in the three main market areas: (1) North and South America, (2) Europe, Middle East and Africa, and (3) Asia Pacific. These local service units can be divided further into sales and service subsidiaries and local service centres. The third-level support activities Bystronic attached to its global service support centre included: document services and database information support, extended training support, extended troubleshooting by highly qualified engineers, technology and process support, project support, stocking spares of the parts replaced most often,

Exhibit 9.1: *(cont.)*

repairing and manufacturing spare parts and, finally, sales support. Second-level support activities were attached to the sales and service subsidiaries located in the market areas, and included hotline support, preventive service programmes, basic training programmes, onsite troubleshooting, keeping replacement parts in stock in case of an emergency, handling orders for spare parts and handling commissions and start-ups. Finally, the service centres offered first-level support, which included providing language help to make contact locally, basic help via telephone, local engineering support and handling orders for spare parts. Bystronic considered this global approach as being a starting point for developing its service business. Over the last few years, Bystronic has begun to implement various activities for separating the product and service businesses in order to create momentum for service sales and revenues. In addition, Bystronic has turned its management approach to human resources from being dominated by expatriates being sent to international markets towards being more polycentric. This means that Bystronic relies increasingly on local service managers and engineers for delivering service. Bystronic has since moved towards using a geocentric approach, when it allowed suitable managers from Singapore to help set up the business in China.

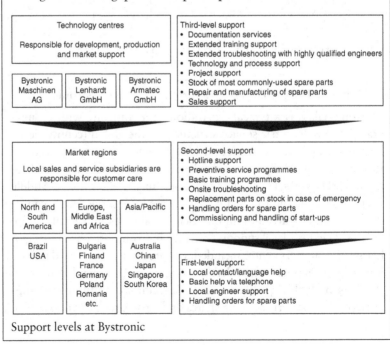

Support levels at Bystronic

9.1.4 The separated and polycentric approach

The third global service approach has a polycentric orientation and is, in addition, characterised by a separation of the product and service organisations at the central level (see Figure 9.4). The separated and polycentric approach is suitable for providers of customer-support services. Companies set up independent business units with their own profit-and-loss responsibility (see Section 7.2.3). The business unit for products has control of the following product-related functions: marketing and sales for products, manufacturing, R&D, accounting/finance and human resources. The business unit for services controls service development, spare parts logistics and service support functions.

Single market organisations that are still responsible for the product and service businesses remain in each country despite their being separated at the central level. However, the cost and revenue structure distinguishes clearly between the product and service businesses. The cost transparency between the product and service businesses enables the profitability and revenue of the products or services to be reported to the central business units separately. The delivery of service is organised similarly to that of the integrated and polycentric global service approach. The market organisation usually provides first-level and second-level support; the distinct and separate central service organisation takes over the responsibility of providing third-level support. This third-level support is a collaborative effort between the central service organisation and the R&D function.

Furthermore, the enhanced transparency of costs and revenues for products and services within the market organisations tends to limit services from being included in the product price. The result is that services are usually charged separately, thus facilitating their profitability. Maintenance services and basic services for the installed base are not included in product prices and are charged separately. It is only customer service that remains integrated in the product price to achieve a product price premium (Reinartz and Ulaga, 2008).

The behavioural orientations are similar to the integrated and polycentric global approach. A main characteristic is that the market organisation enjoys a high level of independence but has a relatively low level of decision-making authority in the central service organisation. Communication between the central business unit for services and local service centres, as well as between the local service centres of different market organisations, is limited. Furthermore, local people are trained to become service technicians and managers.

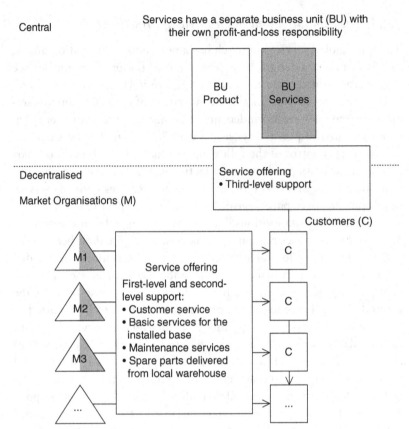

Figure 9.4: The separated and polycentric global service approach

The main disadvantage of the separated and polycentric global approach lies in the lack of communication and inadequate flow of information. There are often cases in global service structures where different market organisations develop services simultaneously. Companies simply fail to maximise potential synergies because market organisations are unable to fully enhance the sharing of service experiences, leading to the fact that they all struggle with the same problems. The lack of communication and poor flows of information also hinder services from becoming standardised. Difficulties are experienced in balancing the transferability of services across market organisations with the customisation of services for one specific market organisation.

The main advantage of the separated and polycentric global service structure is its ability to place more emphasis on the financial outcomes of an extended service offering. Thus, the separated and polycentric global approach can be highly competitive and successful when both the revenues and margins of products are under pressure and require compensation via attractive revenues and margins generated by services. The success of this approach may, however, be limited by low synergies and limited efficiency.

9.1.5 The separated and geocentric approach

The separated and geocentric global service structure is more complex, and shows stronger interdependencies between the central and local organisations, than the three approaches presented above. The aim here is to enhance the product and service businesses and to control service costs through collaboration between the central business units (products and services) and the market organisations (see Figure 9.5). The separated and geocentric approach is suitable for development partners and outsourcing partners. Furthermore, this approach lays the foundation for becoming a solution provider.

Manufacturing companies can choose to install regional functions in order to enhance the collaborative approach: e.g. instead of having local warehouses in each market organisation, regional warehouses are established (e.g. in North America, Europe and Asia). This reduces the working capital costs of the market organisation, but rapid delivery times are still achieved by using express services. The higher logistics costs for express services are of no great importance to customers, since they are balanced by the high availability of the spare parts that the regional warehouses are expected to store. These warehouses belong to service hubs that support the market organisations directly. The service hubs take over the provision of second-level support for medium-sized companies that have relatively small market organisations and few requests for this service support. The service hubs represent specialised service centres possessing advanced technical skills. The inclusion of specific service skills to the service hub increases the rate of capacity utilisation. It means that the local service organisation can cope with the predictable service demands, whereas the regional service organisation handles the service demands that are less predictable.

After a service hub has been set up, separating the product from the service business seems to be a reasonably smooth process. The hub acts as an intermediate controlling level for the services and parts operations where the distinct service business unit takes over full responsibility for the service and the logistics supply chain of spare parts from the supplier right up to the customer. The increasing strain placed on costs results from regulatory and governmental pressure for open market competition: the situation whereby customers are 'locked in' as a result of proprietary after-sales models is increasingly being viewed as monopolistic.

The separated and geocentric approach allows companies to discover that, by servicing competitor and/or supplementary products, they can build long-term relationships with customers with the potential of converting them to using their own product portfolio in the future. The service hub, with its integrated service and parts operation, is a suitable antecedent to attacking the installed base of competitors, i.e. using a strategy of service extension (Raddats and Easingwood, 2010). Furthermore, the market organisations place more emphasis on selling preventive services and service contracts. Planned preventive service interventions and service contracts reduce the variability and unpredictability of the demand put on the service capacity, leading to higher average capacity utilisation. Established service organisations typically have fixed costs, so capacity utilisation becomes the main driver of profitability (Oliva and Kallenberg, 2003). The separated and geocentric service approach improves capacity utilisation by combining advanced service skills in the service hub and placing more emphasis on preventive services and service contracts, which leads to services with high levels of profitability. The great emphasis placed on preventive services and service contracts changes the core service offering from basic services for the installed base to maintenance services.

Impelling the flow of information allows the service hub to spread best practices in selling and delivering services throughout the global service network. Based on the experiences of best practices, the hubs can make explicit decisions regarding the degree of standardisation of the service offer in order to balance the transferability of services across market organisations against customisation for individual customers. The separated and geocentric service approach enables manufacturing companies to be effective close to the customer and also gives them the opportunity of providing a global service programme. The

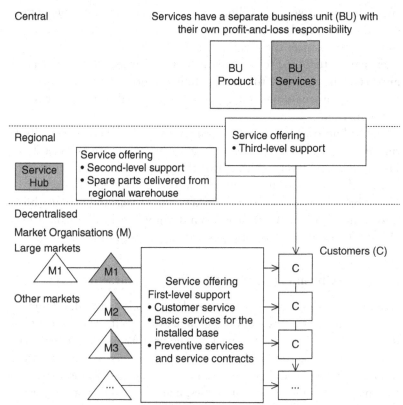

Figure 9.5: The separated and geocentric global service approach

separated and geocentric organisation overcomes the disadvantages associated with having a polycentric behavioural orientation whilst keeping great emphasis on the financial benefits of an extended service business. Additionally, it offers an interesting synergy potential and triggers service profitability by incorporating second-level support in the service hub and focusing on maintenance services.

The separated and geocentric approach also enforces the separation of product and service businesses at the level of the market organisation. The separation takes place in huge markets and leads to two different local legal entities: the first is responsible for selling products and the second for selling services. Such a separation of the local organisation is also possible in the separated and polycentric global service approach, but managers often argue that splitting the local organisation into two legal entities involves setting up two administrative, controlling and financial functions. This entails considerable initial and operational costs that the service organisation has to finance: these cannot, however, be covered by the monetary gains attributed to the separated and polycentric global service approach. In contrast, the service hub promotes cost and resource efficiency, thus enabling companies to set up two distinct legal entities in the market.

Depending on the size and maturity of the market, however, setting up two legal entities (services and products) and offering both first and second-level services through the local organisations are not always the best options. There might also be combined alternatives (i.e. hybrids) where, in specific markets, the service and product businesses still belong to the same legal entity, or where local organisations either offer only first-level services or first and second-level services.

9.2 Service business development in the Chinese market

The sections above present the global approach to the development of service business; this section highlights the specific requirements of developing it in the Chinese market. The priority of the Chinese market is increasing dramatically where the capital goods manufacturing industry is concerned. The Chinese market is currently among the top five markets for European companies, being the major market for the EU itself; within the next five years, it will be among the top five markets for most European companies.

Doing business in China is not easy: companies not only face strong competition both locally and internationally but also have to cope with cultural differences as well as being challenged by the availability and education of Chinese workers and managers.

Companies applying service strategies also tend to have inadequate guidelines for extending their service business in China. The difficulties involved in extending service businesses in China result in the share of the total revenue attributable to services being significantly lower than in other international markets. Our small survey conducted in 2006 suggests that European subsidiaries achieve 23.2 per cent (n = 32) of their total revenue through services but only 10.3 per cent (n = 23) is created through services in the Chinese subsidiaries (see Figure 9.6).

The difference in the share of service revenue might, of course, be attributed to the lower labour costs in China. These, in turn, affect the

Service revenue in percentage of
total revenue

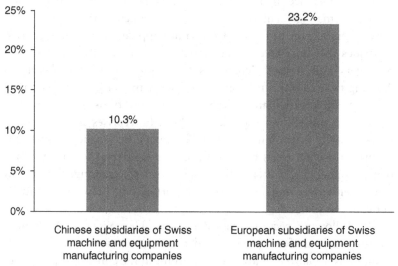

Figure 9.6: Service revenues achieved in China and Europe

price of labour-intensive services such as repair, inspection, installation and maintenance. However, the disparity in labour costs offers only a partial explanation. Also, there are two main challenges that must be faced when setting up a successful service business in China, namely:

- Cultural characteristics, such as 'face' (*miànzi* and *requin*), 'relations' (*guānxi*) and 'politeness' (*lǐmào*), etc., specifically limit the service orientation of *human resource management*.
- The use of unsophisticated *logistic* concepts means that companies face difficulties in protecting their profits generated by the sale of *spare parts*.

Recommendations for managing human resources and spare parts logistics in China are linked to the various global organisational structures for the service business (see Section 9.1). These can, in general, be applied to all four global organisational structures: integrated ethnocentric, integrated polycentric, separated polycentric and separated geocentric organisational structures. Their importance, nevertheless, increases as companies progress from using one approach to the next.

9.2.1 Human resource management in China

When local service organisations are being formed, the way in which personnel management is undertaken is frequently the decisive factor in their success or failure. Companies applying the various service strategies in China face the challenge of recruiting the right service managers and service technicians for a multitude of applications. Although China trains millions of engineers annually, the actual number of possible candidates suitable for such positions is very small in relation to this (Bitzer and Abele, 2004). Enterprises must therefore invest heavily in training. These investments are frequently not economical for enterprises because Chinese people tend to change companies immediately after completing expensive training: fluctuation rates in employee mobility are often reported to be between 10 and 20 per cent per year.

The following sections consider particular concepts of Chinese culture, such as 'face' (*miànzi* and *requin*), 'relations' (*guānxi*) and 'politeness' (*lǐmào*) that are also important in the context of personnel management and are keys to understanding the challenges that are being faced in China.

Personnel recruitment

The first critical stage is finding and selecting suitable applicants for the positions of service managers and service technicians. Service managers are required to lead a team of service technicians, maintain customer relations, sell services actively, plan capacities and coordinate fault resolution. Service technicians concentrate on the commissioning of machines, securing rapid and good quality repairs, carrying out maintenance work and doing inspections.

In contrast to the intra-firm collaboration observed between product and service businesses, the experience of companies has shown that internal employees from existing production locations have seldom managed to develop themselves further for the service area (see Section 7.1.3). The main reason for this is the physical distances that are involved when undertaking service work.

Chinese production employees are not motivated to sever their social relations and travel regularly. Service workers and managers have to be recruited from external sources, with expatriates being responsible for the recruitment process. The selection of suitable employees takes place through holding interviews. When conducting these job interviews, however, expatriates frequently make several mistakes. They actively lead the conversation and try to clarify the technical requirements for the applicants. Personnel management in China has only a supportive function, and such a distribution of roles fails. Since an expatriate can neither query qualifications obtained from Chinese universities, colleges or vocational schools directly, nor requirements such as the ability to work as part of a team, readiness to learn and motivation, it is advisable that the Chinese personnel managers have the main role when interviews are being held. Allocating the personnel managers an active role in a job interview does not mean that a clear recommendation will be formulated afterwards. The Chinese managers then only present the applicant's positive points: this avoids a potential conflict being caused should they recommend a candidate who is not the actual preference of the expatriates. In order to integrate the valuable opinion of the Chinese personnel management correctly into the selection process, it is recommended that expatriates likewise emphasise all of the applicant's positive sides, avoid mentioning negative aspects clearly and favour no one in particular. If expatriates stress more positive sides of one applicant than of another, or accentuate individual negative sides, the Chinese personnel manager will understand this as being a preference of the expatriates, even if he/she would decide differently. Maintaining harmony between expatriates and personnel managers is more important than the selection of the right applicant. This potential lack of integration of personnel managers leads to unsuitable appointments being made within the service organisation.

The following procedure is recommended for filling positions with the Chinese personnel managers being properly integrated. Listening closely to the remarks of the personnel manager is crucial following a job interview. Naturally, the expatriate is expected to formulate a first recommendation: this, as suggested above, should be done in a neutral way. The Chinese personnel manager will then repeat the remarks and, finally, expand on them. Expatriates must pay attention here to the details of the recommendations. It is important they understand that while a simple 'yes' in Western European culture is regarded as a clear affirmative, this same 'yes' in China is actually the opposite, being a denial that the applicant has the required expertise. Acceptance is only made if the applicant can describe, in detail, what the expertise consists of and how it was acquired. Sensitised for such contexts, the expatriates will be more successful in interpreting the opinions of Chinese personnel managers and be able to incorporate them into their own decision-making processes. Placement errors can thereby be avoided.

These recommendations are limited to the selection of service managers. In the further recruitment of service technicians, expatriates should not intervene actively across individual hierarchic levels. Many expatriates find it difficult to delegate staff responsibility for service technicians to service managers: there is a tendency for them to control the service organisation and to make its success exclusively dependent on their own decisions. Instead of investing resources in control and making their own decisions regarding personnel, expatriates should train the service managers in personnel management and recruitment, and make suitable tools available to them, e.g. the 'tandem' concept. This concept involves the applicant working alongside different experienced service technicians and the service manager who has been appointed their supervisor on service jobs. Subsequently each service technician makes a recommendation regarding the employment of the applicant in question. This procedure tests both the expertise and the ability of a future service technician to work in a team.

Personnel development

Once recruitments have been made, expatriates must then formulate a concept for the continuous development of the service managers and workers in question. The error that is frequently made is that they simply transfer existing training concepts to China. These inevitably fail due to differences in learning and cultural characteristics. One important difference is the kind of training documents used. Chinese characters embody symbols and pictures: e.g. whereas a short text-based description of how a machine is to be installed is sufficient in Western cultures, a more graphic description is suitable in China. Expatriates require intensive support from central functions in the production of such documents.

The training of Chinese employees is, in general, mainly theoretical and seldom takes place in small groups. Whilst expatriates must ensure that some of the training is kept theoretical and held in larger groups, they should also organise the training concept towards becoming increasingly practical and held in small groups (Thomas and Schenk, 2001). Typical examples of practical (i.e. action-orientated) training are the common execution of installations, maintenance and inspections with a small group of service technicians and the holding of employee discussions with service managers. It should be ensured, however, that there are no hierarchical or age related differences when working in small groups. The results of observing such small groups show that subordinate or younger employees do not involve themselves actively and adopt the opinion of the superior or oldest employee.

Another recommendation refers to the use of appraisal interviews in the personnel development process. When small groups present results, emphasising possible errors should be avoided. A loss of face (*requin*) is caused for each participant when this is required of the group. Expatriates must save face for a small group by stressing positive aspects and good results. Differences in results between different small groups can be achieved through the intensity of the description of the positive results.

Working with concrete role profiles is recommended as a foundation on which the continuous development of service managers and employees should be based. These role profiles describe the skills and goals that are necessary for each position. Compared with the descriptions of roles in Western Europe (e.g. service technicians at Level 1, 2 or 3) they are substantially more detailed. Figure 9.7 illustrates an example of possible role profiles.

Retaining and rewarding personnel

The art of retaining Chinese service employees and managers is based essentially on three pillars:

1. A *balanced remuneration system* that consists of monetary and non-monetary incentives. Monetary incentives are divided into a basic wage (80 per cent) and a result-based wage (20 per cent). The high demand for well-trained employees means that basic wages have an annual rate of increase of between 8 and 20 per cent: when qualifications remain the same, it is between 8 and 12 per cent. A higher rate of increase in the basic wage results from additional qualifications. A portion of this increase is credited to a specific 'training account' to prevent employees from changing companies shortly after successfully obtaining a qualification. The money in this training account is disbursed when the employees have worked for the company for at least another two years after completion of the training. The use

Role profiles of service managers

- Selling maintenance contracts and spare parts actively
- Retaining and extending customer relationships
- Planning capacity for service technicians
- Organising further studies for service technicians
- Leading different types of maintenance specialists
- Customer-orientated behaviour

- Coordinating troubleshooting activities
- Retaining customers
- Charging for troubleshooting activities according to warranty time
- Organising further studies for service technicians
- Ensuring the functionality of machines
- Leading teams of reliable troubleshooters

- Leading small teams of installation specialists
- Monitoring installation activities
- Handing over machines and equipment to customers
- Training customers in operating machines and equipment
- Recruiting new service technicians

Role profiles of service technicians

Inspection and maintenance activities of standard machines	Inspection and maintenance activities of standard machines	Inspection and maintenance activities of complex machines
Simple troubleshooting of standard machines	Complex troubleshooting of different standard machines	Complex troubleshooting of complex machines
Installation of single standard machines	Installation of different standard machines	Installation of complex machines

Product knowledge

Service competencies

Figure 9.7: Role profiles of service technicians and managers

of training accounts depends on the employment contract with the Chinese employees. The result-based salary is based on how well each employee achieves the objectives that have been set and is not subject to a direct rate of increase. The result-based salary can be increased by making adjustments to the objectives.

2. *Shares are a very good instrument for retaining employees.* A large proportion of the shares of Chinese companies, such as Lenovo and Haier, belong to the employees.

3. *Personal relations within a group.* In Western cultures, employees identify themselves strongly with the entire company and its culture, and less so with their immediate supervisor. The opposite is true in China, where personal relationships between co-workers and supervisors enable employee migration to be kept at a low level. Cultural attributes, such as loss of face, understanding harmony and group affiliation, mean that the likelihood of Chinese people ending a personal relationship is considerably lower than their terminating a relationship with a company. It is of the utmost importance that expatriates invite the families of Chinese colleagues to their homes. They must also invest time in common leisure activities (e.g. karaoke and dinners). This is the only way in which they can develop a personal relationship with their employees in the medium term.

Table 9.2 summarises the main aspects of human resource management in China. It is in the form of instructions, showing the procedure by which expatriates can build up a service organisation in China through the purposeful management of staff.

9.2.2 Spare parts logistics for the Chinese market

Alongside the management of human resources, the logistics of spare parts is an important success factor in service businesses located in China. Succeeding with service strategies, such as being providers of after-sales service and customer support service, requires sophisticated logistics concepts. China currently has two supply chain worlds: one focuses on exports and the other on the domestic market. The export supply chain enjoys a reasonable logistics infrastructure, low-cost production and streamlined logistics networks. Supported by world-class companies such as UPS, FedEx and DHL the coastal free-trade zones have efficient and simple supply chains, enjoy high quality logistics services and have solid logistic skills.

Table 9.2: *Human resource management in China*

Recruiting personnel	Developing personnel	Retaining and rewarding personnel
• Integrate a Chinese HR function in the selection of service managers and technicians • Ensure adequate interpretation is made of the feedback from the Chinese HR function • Describe the role profiles of service managers and service technicians • Educate service managers in the selection of service technicians • Apply the 'tandem' concept	• Take small steps for continuous development • Use the role descriptions to guide development • Concentrate on practical learning • Work in small groups • Do not use criticism in discussions between service managers and service technicians • Educate service managers in using appraisal interviews	• Establish personal relationships between service managers and service technicians • Define budgets for establishing personal relationships • Use shares as an incentive • Find a balance between non-monetary and monetary incentives • Award an annual increase in basic wages too, and not only for attaining further qualifications

The logistics of spare parts that are focused on the domestic market, on the other hand, are confronted with the difficulties of reaching the Chinese end-customers, and include underdeveloped transportation infrastructures, the insufficient skills of logistics providers, underdeveloped IT interfaces and protectionist customs regulations. The domestic supply chain comprises domestic players supplying small to mid-size companies and is rather fragmented. This has led to complaints of high inventory costs and long delivery times for spare parts, and is aggravated by the bureaucratic restrictions surrounding the legal importation, selling and servicing of spare parts (Hong *et al.*, 2006; Jiang, 2002).

The challenge of today could nevertheless well be the business opportunity of tomorrow for manufacturers of capital goods. Constraints can become opportunities: innovative solutions for spare parts logistics can be created specifically for the Chinese market. The combination of a relatively immature market with the shortening of delivery and response times, along with reductions in inventory and warehousing costs, should allow sustainable competitive advantages to be gained. The use of China as a logistics hub for solving challenges that arise in spare parts logistics should also benefit the Asian market in general.

Current concepts of spare parts logistics
There are two basic approaches to the logistics of providing the Chinese and, in a broader sense, the Asian markets with spare parts:

1. *Exporting directly from Europe*: spare parts are exported directly from Europe to the Asian subsidiaries whenever the customer requests them. The parts are delivered directly from the subsidiary to the customer: storing spare parts locally, with planning and control of inventory, is unnecessary. The direct export of spare parts corresponds to an integrated and ethnocentric global approach to service business (see Section 9.1.2).
2. *Stocking in local warehouses of Asian subsidiaries*: local warehouses are set up in Asian subsidiaries. Replenished from the central warehouse, a local warehouse delivers spare parts directly to the customer. This logistics approach is complemented by the direct export of spare parts if the part is not available locally. A local warehouse is responsible for inventory planning and control. Local warehouses in Asian subsidiaries correspond more to integrated and polycentric, as well as to separated and polycentric, global approaches to service business (see Sections 9.1.3 and 9.1.4).

Table 9.3 summarises both approaches: it highlights their advantages and disadvantages and illustrates the logistics activities involved.

Changing the logistics concepts for supplying spare parts
Despite the advantages of both logistics concepts, companies do not regard either of them as being an adequate way of fulfilling their logistics challenges, internal requirements or customers' expectations. The concepts were seen instead as being a starting point (See Exhibit 9.2). It was assumed that an intensive elaboration of alternative solutions in close collaboration with logistics providers, together with academic input, could lead to an alternative, and more sophisticated, solution. The logistics solution implemented, which embraced interrelated key issues that arise directly from the idiosyncrasies of the Chinese market, involved:

Table 9.3: *Advantages and disadvantages of current logistics concepts for spare parts*

	(1) Direct export of spare parts from Europe to customers in China (Asia)	(2) Providing spare parts from local warehouses, and warehouses replenished from Europe, to customers in China (Asia)
Description	• Companies run a central warehouse carrying spare parts in Europe and have no local warehouses in China and other Asian markets • Inventory planning and control are conducted by the central warehouse based on state-of-the-art methods • Parts are exported and delivered directly to the Chinese customers from the central European warehouse	• Companies have a central warehouse and also run decentralised (local) warehouses in different regions of China and in various Asian markets • Inventory planning and control are the responsibility of local warehouses that use relatively unsophisticated methods • Parts are delivered from the local warehouse to the customer if they are available locally • Parts are exported from the central warehouse if they are not available locally
Advantages	• Low inventory and working capital costs • Low operating costs for the central warehouse in Europe • High availability of spare parts at the central warehouse	• Short delivery times for parts that are available locally • High customer satisfaction due to short delivery times • Low logistics costs: bulk replenishment from Europe is more cost-efficient than single express deliveries
Disadvantages	• High logistics costs due to express transport mode • Long delivery times caused by customs clearance delays • Low customer satisfaction due to long delivery times	• High inventory and working capital costs • High costs for operating and maintaining a network of local warehouses • Limited availability of spare parts held by the local warehouses

- establishing one regional warehouse for Asia, including China, that provides spare parts to various Asian countries;
- combining bonded and non-bonded warehouse options;
- organising post-customs clearance for outbound processes;
- incorporating temporary borrowing into the outbound and return processes of the spare parts;
- defining the roles and activities in the logistics concept.

Establishing one regional warehouse for Asia, including China, that provides spare parts to various Asian countries

A regional warehouse was expected to reduce fixed costs and achieve an availability of spare parts of up to 90 per cent in contrast to the existing decentralised warehouses, which had low degrees of availability and high depreciation costs due to the lack of planning skills. This entails 90 per cent of all spare parts being delivered from the regional warehouse directly to the customer, with only 10 per cent of the parts being delivered directly to the final customer from the global European warehouse. The delivery time would, of course, be longer than for deliveries from local warehouses in each country. The total delivery time could, nevertheless, be shorter than exporting spare parts directly from Europe to customers in China: the level of availability in local warehouses is between 30 and 60 per cent, which is actually relatively low. An initial estimation of the expected delivery time from regional warehouses established in Shanghai, Beijing, Hong Kong and Singapore is between 24 and 48 hours.

The estimated delivery times reveal that the most time-consuming element is the customs clearance procedures necessary to import parts, a fact that is of the utmost importance. Although China is the major market, with the highest expectations of growth, Chinese customers are regarded as being the most demanding in terms of service levels and delivery times.

Combining bonded and non-bonded warehouse options

Companies can establish a combined non-bonded/bonded warehouse to overcome this constraint. The non-bonded warehouse would serve the Chinese market without any time delays caused by customs clearance processes since all of the parts in stock would already be declared: the additional bonded warehouse facility would deliver parts to other Asian markets. Using a combined non-bonded/bonded warehouse infrastructure, however, requires that the necessary logistics planning and coordination actually function. Using the non-bonded warehouse would also mean that the parts in stock have already been declared and that import duty and VAT (value-added taxes) have been integrated into the value of the parts: the capital cost would thus be 27 per cent higher.

Organising post-customs clearance for outbound processes
A non-bonded/bonded warehouse in China enables companies to take the post-customs clearance option. This offers clear additional advantages, the main one being that all of the spare parts can be stored in the bonded warehouse. Such a bonded warehouse is able to serve all of the other Asian markets in less than two days, and most Chinese provinces within two days as well. Parts delivered to China would not have to be declared before being delivered to the domestic Chinese customer: this option means that the part is delivered first and declared afterwards. The bonded stock remains under the responsibility of the European service organisation since it has not yet been declared. The value of the stock is calculated based on the cost of manufacturing the parts and not on the transfer price. As spare parts generate the most profit for companies, the difference between the manufacturing costs and the transfer price are, on average, 50 per cent. This stock value could be reduced significantly, which would lead to lower working capital costs.

Incorporating temporary borrowing into the outbound and return processes of the spare parts
A non-bonded/bonded warehouse in China would also enable companies to employ an additional outbound process option called 'temporary borrowing', which is a specific outbound process that is linked to the post-customs clearance procedure. Temporary borrowing offers the opportunity of supplying more than one spare part to the customer if it is not possible to specify the part that needs replacing: service technicians can, for example, order five spare parts to diagnose and repair a machine. The variety of parts means that the service technicians have a better chance of repairing the failure without any delays. The parts that are used for the diagnosis and repair but are not installed in the machine may, however, be returned to the bonded warehouse. Customs clearance will not be necessary, since the parts are only borrowed temporarily from the bonded stock. Only if the parts are not returned within two weeks will customs clearance be required. Temporary borrowing also enables the company to send the used parts from a bonded warehouse

to Europe for quality inspection (e.g. a package is opened and the parts used for diagnosis and testing only). The only type of parts that may not be returned through the temporary borrowing system to the bonded stock is the item that is the cause of the machine failure. Should these items be considered as being repairable, they are stored in a small non-bonded stock attached to the bonded warehouse. On reaching a minimum value, the repairable parts can be declared and re-exported to Europe. No export duty or taxes need to be paid if each specific repairable part is returned to China through the repair and return system.

Defining the roles and activities in the logistics concept
Finally, companies should define the following roles of the logistics concept. The global spare parts centre in Europe remains responsible for defining the strategic guidelines pertaining to their spare parts business in Asia. It plans inventory levels and monitors key performance indicators (e.g. availability, inventory levels and volume). The regional warehouse is responsible for the implementation of the strategic guidelines and shares logistics know-how with the Asian sales companies; it also monitors customer satisfaction in terms of delivery times and service levels. Responsibilities also include the selection of logistics partners for running the warehouses and local deliveries, as well as the management of the return process of repairable parts. Local sales companies remain responsible for diagnosing machine breakdowns and ordering spare parts from the regional warehouse.

Exhibit 9.2: The spare parts logistics concept used by GF AgieCharmilles

GF AgieCharmilles reorganised its spare parts logistics. Initially, an integrated polycentric global approach to the service business was employed. It involved setting up a network of Asian subsidiaries to run local warehouses and service centres. These covered Japan, South Korea, China (including Beijing, Shanghai and Hong Kong), Taiwan and Singapore: the latter covered several regions such as Australia, India and Malaysia. The various local warehouses, which functioned as non-bonded warehouses, did not have sufficient experience of inventory planning and control. This led to the availability of parts being low and the depreciation of costs being high. This low local availability of parts meant that GF AgieCharmilles

---

Exhibit 9.2: (*cont.*)

also had to rely on the direct export of parts from Switzerland. Customs clearance procedures made the delivery times of these direct exports quite long: the expectations of customers could not therefore be met and they became dissatisfied.

GF AgieCharmilles then decided to establish a combined non-bonded and bonded regional warehouse in Shanghai. This warehouse replaced the various local warehouses attached to the subsidiary companies. Most of the parts were stocked in the bonded warehouse facility, allowing them to stock parts according to their manufacturing costs instead of sales prices. For spare parts, this is an average reduction of 50 per cent of the capital costs. In addition, the parts stocked in the bonded warehouse are not declared. The value of the parts does not include the VAT and duty fee of 27 per cent, which also reduces the capital costs. The bonded warehouse facility is managed by the European service organisation.

The delivery of parts from the warehouse to China follows the post-customs clearance procedure and uses the option of temporary borrowing. The post-customs clearance procedure allows parts to be delivered directly to the end customer within 24 or 48 hours: customs clearance is done after delivery has been made. Temporary borrowing allows the return of unused parts, or parts used only for testing, without any complications arising. Parts destined for other Asian countries are delivered from the bonded warehouse facility directly to the customers from these Asian countries.

The non-bonded warehouse facility is only used for parts exceeding the temporary borrowing option (i.e. not returned to the warehouse within two weeks) and for broken parts being returned by the customer. The latter are either discarded or sent back to Europe for repair.

The investment made in the new organisation and delivery processes of the spare parts business in Asia paid off rather quickly. In addition, customer satisfaction pertaining to the delivery times of spare parts increased significantly. The improved degree of satisfaction enhanced customer loyalty, which, in turn, had a positive impact on the new machines and sales of services in general.

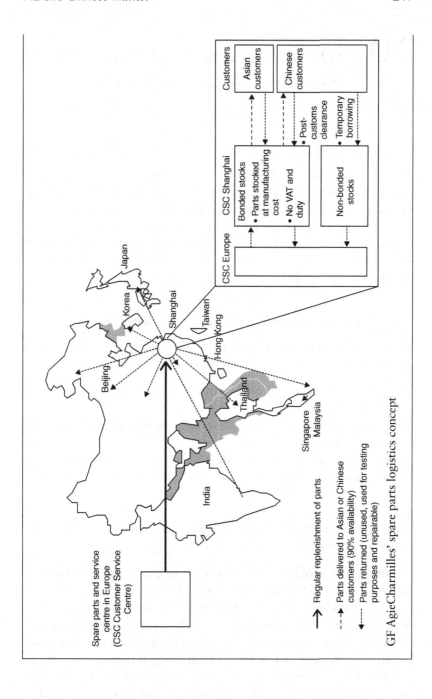

GF AgieCharmilles' spare parts logistics concept

10 | Service business development for small and medium suppliers

This chapter takes the previous discussion of the exploitation and exploration approaches pertaining to the development of service business and applies them to small and medium suppliers. The primary goal is to provide insight into how such suppliers can apply these approaches pragmatically. Following the structure of the previous chapters, the dynamic and operational capabilities necessary for developing service business are discussed herewith.

10.1 Approaches for service business development

At the supplier level, there are three approaches that may be pursued (see Table 10.1), namely:

1. Enhancing the relational value of existing supplier–buyer relationships.
2. Applying financial value-seeking behaviour to existing and new supplier–buyer relationships.
3. Taking a radical leap towards a new value constellation downstream in the value chain.

10.1.1 Enhancing the relational value of existing supplier–buyer relationships

The enhancement of relational value of existing supplier–buyer relationships is the most dominant approach used in service business development. The strategic intention is that of exploiting service opportunities in order to improve the supplier–buyer relationship (Ulaga and Eggert, 2006). The business logic with existing customers in the next value-added step changes incrementally from being transaction-orientated to being relationship-orientated. These changes rely on the fact that more intensive co-producing relational competencies are expected to be generated between suppliers and buyers. This approach embarks on paths of value addition (Matthyssens and Vandenbempt, 2008; Möller, 2006); the co-produced competencies act as a resource barrier that wards off competitors. The service offering is extended to include logistic services, design and construction services as well as services supporting product sales. The service offerings and co-produced competencies confirm the existing value constellation in providing reliable products and services at reasonable prices.

Enhancing the relational value of existing supplier–buyer relationships experiences less direct competition as far as price is concerned, which enhances profitability. The services support suppliers in differentiating their offering, creating sustainable competitive advantages and allowing a price premium of about 5–10 per cent over their competitors. However, the price premium for services surrounding the product offering does not really change the perception held by customers: they still recognise suppliers as being product-orientated, with services being offered as add-ons in the supplier–buyer relationship. The resource position is not an integral part of the service competence but originates instead from the relational competence.

The service offering integrates the resources of suppliers and customers; it affects the logistic and design processes as well as the sales processes inherent in the supplier–buyer relationships (Wouters, 2004). As customers do not pay for services, companies find it difficult to quantify the value enhancements that the services generate. They merely argue that services are used to enhance the general quality of the supplier–buyer relationship. Enhancing the relational value to existing supplier–buyer relationships thus substantiates the existing value constellation of providing reliable products and services as add-ons to products at reasonable prices.

10.1.2 Financial value-seeking behaviour in existing and new supplier–buyer relationships

A second approach that may be used is financial value-seeking behaviour in existing and new supplier–buyer relationships: it is, however, used less frequently than the first approach, i.e. enhancing the relational value. It does not follow the path of value addition but aims, instead, at enhancing financial opportunities. The business logic changes incrementally from being transaction-orientated to products to being transaction-orientated to both products and services with existing customers in the next value-added step, along with new customers in adjacent value-added steps. Products and service offerings are separated: the result is an increase in the revenue that is generated.

Separating the prices of products from those of services has three side effects:

1. Few existing customers reconsider their demand for services when confronted with separate service prices. They may decide not to use the services, thus reducing the internal costs and resources of the supplier, who can then redirect resources to customers who are willing to pay for services and appreciate their real value.
2. The price of current products can be reduced. This opens up new, if more price-sensitive, customer segments which, although they are less profitable than existing customers, have an important stabilising effect on otherwise volatile demands. They help the supplier make more efficient use of their capacity and thereby reduce costs.
3. Selling and charging for service separately attracts new service-only customers. This approach seeks beyond the existing customer base and has the potential of reaching new customers. Logistics and repair services may be offered to other suppliers of components or sub-modules. Design services are offered to engineering companies seeking out design and manufacturing competencies.

These three results of charging for services do not change the value constellation. This approach enhances the existing value constellation in providing reliable products and services at reasonable prices. The services could create, on average, around 15 per cent of the supplier's total revenue and achieve a margin leverage of two when compared to product revenue.

10.1.3 Taking a radical leap towards a new value constellation downstream in the value chain

The first two approaches involve suppliers adapting the exploitation approach (Chapter 6) whereas the third approach is close to the exploration of service opportunities (Chapter 4). Suppliers that apply this third approach embark initially on the path of value-addition but subsequently leave it. Their energies are redirected towards strategic opportunities for exploring untested service markets downstream or upstream in the value chain.

Exhibit 10.1: The radical leap taken by Fraisa towards a new value constellation downstream in the value chain

Fraisa, a manufacturer of precision cutting tools with about 500 employees, rendered the previous form of competition obsolete. Originally they produced precision cutting tools that were then sold via distributors to manufacturers of machine tools. Fraisa soon learnt that the handling and application costs associated with the precision cutting tools of machine tool users exceeded the existing costs of the actual cutting tools. Handling activities (storing, ordering, administering and controlling) did not, of course, constitute a part of the service offering of the machine tool manufacturer (i.e. provision of spare parts and repairing or maintaining the machine tools). It did, however, represent an attractive market opportunity for Fraisa, who responded to the attractive market potential by setting up a tool care concept. A new value constellation was thus formed, based on achieving attractive total costs for handling the tools through the value propositions that followed. The new concept reduced costs and the amount of capital tied up, since payment was made only for the tools that were actually used. Customers could outsource ordering, administration, service and maintenance activities for precision cutting tools, leading to a greater concentration on core competences and reduced costs. This new value constellation broke with the former value constellation in that it provided highly reliable precision cutting tools at reasonable prices. It allowed the company to open up a new market downstream in the value chain.

A new value constellation initiates the undertaking of integrated solutions that involve competencies beyond the competence base of the supplier. The supplier is, therefore, concerned with forming a new value network (including new business partners such as logistic providers, OEMs, customers and IT service providers) in which the co-production of competencies within the value network acts as a resource barrier towards competitors.

Table 10.1: *The three approaches used by suppliers to develop their service business*

	Enhancing the relational value of existing supplier–buyer relationships	Financial value-seeking behaviour in existing and new supplier–buyer relationships	Taking a radical leap towards a new value constellation downstream in the value chain
Strategic intention	• Exploiting service opportunities in supplier–buyer relationships	• Exploiting service opportunities for additional service revenues and profits	• Exploring untested service markets
Business logic	• Changing incrementally from being transaction-orientated to being relationship-orientated	• Changing incrementally from being transaction-orientated to products to being transaction-orientated to both products and service • New customers in adjacent value-added steps	• Forming a radically new value network
Competitive advantages	• Co-produced relational-competencies	• Co-produced service-competencies	• Competencies co-produced within the value network
Financial indicators	• Services create a price premium of 5–10 per cent for products	• Services generate approx. 15 per cent of the total revenue • Services achieve a margin leverage of two compared to product revenue	• Services create additional revenues and generate approx. 25 per cent of the total revenue • Service revenue achieves margin leverage of three compared to product revenue

10.2 Co-evolvement of organisational capabilities

The following three sections describe the co-evolvement of the dynamic and operational capabilities required in the approaches to service business development used by small and medium suppliers (summarised in Table 10.2 and Table 10.3).

10.2.1 Capabilities for enhancing the relational value of existing supplier–buyer relationships

Dynamic capabilities

The sensing activities of suppliers focus on marketing benefits. Sensing is dominated by the assumption that services improve supplier–buyer relationships. Seizing marketing opportunities balances the additional service costs and the price premium.

Sensing and seizing are, nevertheless, rather limited in that they appear reactively and are constrained to the supplier in question. Suppliers lack a strategic focus; they admit to having an opportunistic attitude of seeking rapid and incremental improvements in the perceived customer value. Furthermore, sensing and seizing efforts appear reactively only when customers experience a decline in business. Customers are, therefore, often perceived as being highly price sensitive, employing every possible means of negotiating additional services at fixed product prices (when services are an integral part of product prices). Suppliers, as a result, do not see any financial benefits arising from the provision of new services. This internal recognition is self-reinforcing because customers consider these services as add-ons that should be offered for 'free'. The suppliers' service expenses can nonetheless be used as additional leverage in subsequent negotiations when customers place new orders. Sensing and seizing concentrate only on marketing opportunities.

Furthermore, other network actors, such as supplementary downstream or upstream business partners, are not involved in the sensing activities of suppliers. Seizing the marketing opportunities to provide a strategic response is integrated only with the suppliers' distributors. This means that suppliers mobilise their distributors, requiring them to formulate and implement services in the sales phase (e.g. product consulting, information services, etc.) in order to augment their product offerings.

Reconfiguring takes place mainly in the context of corporate culture and human resources. Suppliers reconfigure their strong technical and product-orientated approaches to more service-orientated behaviour. Their human resources undergo changes in personnel development and compensation: the latter refers to reconfigurations observed in internal accounting and measurement systems.

Operational capabilities

Reconfiguration initiates a modification of operational capabilities. In the context of behaviour being a part of corporate culture, suppliers develop new ways of improving the general quality of a supplier–buyer relationship. Individual roles change: a reliable supplier becomes a trusted adviser who fulfils the customer's service needs. Individuals learn to employ a 'whatever it takes' philosophy to satisfy the needs of the customer. An increase in the service-orientation of human resources supports behavioural changes. Suppliers also enhance their recruiting and training procedures. Individuals are taught new ways of listening and communicating with customers in order to understand the nature of the customer's expectations at an earlier stage.

The focus of current personnel training used by suppliers is on technical skills directed towards behavioural competencies, recognising that the provision of services includes a high degree of uncertainty. Unexpected challenges that can be very diverse in nature may appear whilst personnel are providing design services: they have to be willing to address unexpected issues as soon as they arise (Neu and Brown, 2005). On-the-job training aims at developing such competencies and attitudes continuously, whereas personnel evaluation and rewards ensure that they are retained. Outstanding performance in solving customer problems is highly appreciated: individuals are compensated and rewarded for employing the 'whatever it takes' philosophy.

Suppliers change the procedures that are integral parts of the key account and accounting systems. The initial accounting systems track product profitability but not individual customers: costs are allocated initially to product categories for functional activities rather than to customers. No measurement system synthesises sales into specific key account customers that demand both products and services, making it impossible to track the profitability of the 5–10 per cent price premium. Suppliers are thereby required to recalculate activity-based profitability as and when necessary. The recalculated profitability indicators supplement the reward system and balance the non-financial evaluation of solving the problems encountered by customers.

Table 10.2 and Table 10.3 illustrate that the co-evolvement of the relatively few dynamic and operational capabilities in this approach is relatively minor when compared to the other two approaches presented in the sections below.

10.2.2 Financial value-seeking behaviour in existing and new supplier–buyer relationships

Dynamic capabilities

In the case of financial value-seeking behaviour in existing and new supplier–buyer relationships, suppliers sense not just the marketing benefits and opportunities to enhance the general quality of the supplier–buyer relationship but focus rather on potential financial opportunities. They develop corporate values away from considering services as being add-ons to products towards seeing services themselves as potential sources of revenue and profit. Sensing the financial opportunities that emerge through analysing the potential service needs of new customers, they are then converted into new business opportunities that are seized in three different stages. Firstly, the suppliers define the value associated with the new services by assessing how the customer perceives their own service needs. The customer's perceptions are then translated in the second stage into value-based prices for each service. The third stage involves the financial benefits that are sensed being verified by assessing whether or not new or existing customers demand, and are willing to pay for, the services in question. These three issues extend previous service innovation processes. Suppliers then integrate assessments of the financial benefits into the service innovation process.

Suppliers are aware that general acceptance within the industry in question is necessary if they are to create a situation in which services are to be charged for separately. They cannot mobilise other suppliers into sensing and seizing new pricing policies so, in order to achieve customer acceptance, they no longer use reactive behaviour to seek out new value-adding activities when customers reduce their orders. The most efficient approach is to encourage acceptance of the new business logic of selling services separately when customers run at peak capacity. Customers that are fully occupied with development projects are much more eager to outsource design and production and/or assembly activities. Timing is instrumental: driven by targets, outsourcing decisions are often made when the customer is in a relatively weak negotiating position. This creates a situation in which charging for design services is more likely to gain acceptance in the industry.

Suppliers sense and seize financial opportunities continuously but, before financial benefits can be transformed into new services, companies must assess whether customers can cope with running at peak capacity. This assessment supports suppliers in investing their limited resources in services with the highest potential of creating new financial benefits.

Operational capabilities

Financial value-seeking behaviour in existing and new supplier–buyer relationships avoids reconfiguring customer-focused attitudes towards a 'whatever it takes' philosophy. They aim more at a 'what is paid for and valued' philosophy and establish behavioural roles compatible with those of a reliable service provider.

The operational capabilities of human resources are concentrated on developing recruitment processes and on the training of listening and communication skills. Individuals learn the nature of the customers' expectations of the services more quickly as well as how to convince them to pay for the services. As far as personnel assessment is concerned, suppliers increasingly reward outstanding financial performance and the 'what is paid for and valued' philosophy in the form of service revenues and profits. In order to support the system of rewards and the continuous development of the corporate values and behaviours mentioned above, suppliers should set up clearly visible service teams for specific services and give them profit/loss responsibility.

Suppliers should also modify their accounting system so that they can monitor the profitability and revenue generated by each service. Costs should be allocated not only to product categories and functional activities (such as marketing and manufacturing) but also to services. Such a modified accounting system synthesises sales and costs to a specific product and set of services: it allows the profitability of each product, service and key account to be traced. When service revenue and profitability are measured directly, services can be charged for separately. Exhibit 10.2 illustrates how Escatec implemented financial value-seeking behaviour to boost its service business.

Exhibit 10.2: Escatec's financial value-seeking behaviour in existing buyer and new supplier–buyer relationships

Escatec, a manufacturer of electronic boards, deliberately implemented a financial value-seeking behaviour in its existing and new supplier–buyer relationships. The company decided that it should be able to achieve a significant share of revenue through additional services within the next seven years. Driven by meeting this target, Escatec started to analyse existing service offerings. These covered the following service categories:

- Design services for hardware and software: feasibility studies, descriptions of performance and functional specifications.
- Construction services: electronic and mechanical construction, computer-aided design.
- Transformation services for moving from design to production: design to order, target costing services, product accreditation.
- Fast prototyping services.
- Production services: manufacture of electronic boards, supply chain management, life-cycle management, test and measurement services.

Each of these services was analysed further according to their existing value contribution. It resulted in Escatec changing its management behaviour from doing 'whatever it takes' to keep the customer happy to emphasising 'what is paid for and valued' by the customer. This analysis of the existing services in combination with an in-depth understanding of the customers' service needs thus aided Escatec in verifying, on the one hand, the financial benefits sensed and, on the other hand, in assessing the willingness of the customer to demand, and pay for, services.

Escatec proceeded by taking the following steps:

- Mapping existing services that had been offered for 'free' but could be easily charged for in the future.
- Appointing a project team to oversee the development of new services and service capabilities.
- Instating an incentive system for promoting the sales of services.
- Creating tools for documenting value and communicating them to customers.

Exhibit 10.2: (*cont.*)

- Drawing up a checklist of unique selling propositions for competing with the new, and newly-charged for, services.
- Balancing the customisation of the services required to meet customers' needs with a standardisation of the service processes and elements.

The result was that Escatec instated two dedicated service teams. The first team was responsible for promoting, selling and delivering design services that were previously offered for 'free'. The second team was responsible for promoting, selling and delivering repair services. These repair services were new service innovations that were not previously offered by Escatec; they created 15–20 per cent of Escatec's revenue within a period of a few years. This revenue share was, in addition, seen as achieving the highest operating margin.

10.2.3 Taking a radical leap towards a new value constellation downstream in the value chain

Dynamic capabilities

Suppliers aiming at taking a radical leap initiate their sensing activities by developing managerial cognition of the strategic opportunities downstream in the value chain, the total cost considerations of customers, the new value constellations beyond their own industry and, finally, the existing value network boundaries. Managers should consider the market structure as being endogenous as a result of innovation and learning. They should deliberately not accept the service market and their position in the value chain as being given but, instead, emphasise the separation of market players, value chain positions and customer needs (Jaworski *et al.*, 2000). The theory used for service markets is open for substitution by something fundamentally new through generative learning (Slater and Narver, 1995).

Suppliers are not limited by their size when they sense for opportunities in creating markets and new customer value propositions. Whilst managers attempt to shape the behaviour of the market, they are also aware of the fact that their size, their position in the value chain, the behaviour of both the customer and competitors and their past competitive behaviour may act as potential hurdles in reshaping the market structure, value constellations and the development of their service business.

Procedures relevant to extensive sensing are investigated in other industries: customers and non-customers are observed and all related activities are mapped comprehensively. For example, the concept of tool care means that fixing and assembly materials (such as screws, screw accessories, dowels and plugs) are transferred to the comprehensive logistics service that deals with low-value, high-volume parts, thereby forming a new value constellation (see Exhibit 10.3). This new value constellation shows the cutting tool manufacturer in question that the handling costs of the customer exceed the purchasing costs of the products. Handling activities (storing, ordering, administering and controlling) are obviously not a part of the customers' primary activities of using the precision tools (which are utilisation, repairing and maintaining), but are interpreted as being a potential, and attractive, market.

The cognition of these opportunities and the new value constellation associated with them, however, is also threatened by potential biases. Providing services downstream in the value chain is often far beyond the existing core competencies of the company. Also, as in the case of Fraisa (see Exhibit 10.1 and Exhibit 10.3), for example, its use of its existing reputation as a reliable manufacturer of cutting tools as a proxy for evaluating the purchasing potential of tool care is questionable. Suppliers can overcome such biases through a cognitively sophisticated and disciplined approach to decision-making. Managers are required to reassess their attitudes to satisfying customer needs related to products and services. If radical leaps are to be made, they are forced to consider markets not only in terms of the product and service offerings they sell but also what customers buy. Value is never a product or service: it is always a utility, i.e. what the product or service actually does for the customers (Drucker, 1973).

Suppliers apply an 'umbrella' strategy where seizing is concerned in order to define the boundaries of the strategic response and new value constellations. It is a strategy that allows various scenarios of value constellations and propositions to emerge. Anticipating how each scenario affects the logics of value creation (which, in turn, influences the roles of actors and their value-creating processes), suppliers mobilise other network players to participate in seizing scenarios, value propositions and value-creating processes. They thus create a learning relationship with other network players. Managers and employees, along with other business partners, become wiser in how to propose new value constellations through the formation of value networks. Suppliers learn specifically about the complex business problems encountered by their customers and gain intimate knowledge of the handling costs and various activities related to their products. Simultaneously, downstream customers become increasingly skilled in recognising the competencies of network actors that are suitable for solving their complex business challenges. The inherent learning processes help the suppliers anticipate potential value propositions for each network actor and identify which are most suitable for forming a new value constellation.

Exhibit 10.3: Scenarios at Fraisa

Fraisa envisioned potential value propositions and a new value constellation in their network using a scenario technique. Aware of the likelihood that it might collapse if only one scenario was explored, Fraisa allowed numerous scenarios to emerge. A first scenario included selling its tool care concept in cooperation with machine tool manufacturers where the service technicians of the machine tool manufacturers supported sales and ensured that service was provided. The second scenario included collaboration with providers of high-volume, low-cost, components. Such companies had already succeeded in moving from selling screws, screw accessories, dowels and plugs to integrating these components into a logistics service concept. As a provider of logistics service, Fraisa could find it beneficial to integrate tool care into its own service portfolio and to open its component portfolio to high-cost, low-volume, tools. To develop such scenarios, managers learned to anticipate or estimate the value proposition and value production logic and understand how it would influence the roles of the various actors and their value-creating processes.

The supplier in the case above is aware that one scenario might collapse and thus allowed several scenarios to emerge. Discussing various scenarios proves to be beneficial because it facilitates managerial cognition of a wide range of business opportunities. Managers are required to be flexible throughout the entire strategy process, as well as being open to discussing new aspects of the service business.

It is realised, however, that the resources and the attention spans of managers were both limited, so considering different scenarios had the potential of leading to bottlenecks and time delays in terms of implementation. Bottlenecks can be avoided if suppliers provide sufficient resources and realistic time frames. Fraisa actually considered time as not being critical for the implementation of a new value constellation and allowed schedules to be very flexible.

The suppliers in the new value constellation initiated reconfigurations in the corporate culture, human resources, organisational structures and innovation process within their respective company. They also orchestrated reconfiguration activities for other network actors. Reconfiguration is a continual process that improves subsequent operational capabilities.

Operational capabilities

Corporate values change incrementally from considering services as being add-ons to products to seeing them as a potential means of restructuring the value chain and forming new value constellations. Managers expect a more service-centred perspective of strategy to allow service competences to be translated into new value propositions via a restructuring of the processes controlling the co-creation of value within the entire value chain (Vargo and Lusch, 2004). This is conducive for establishing managerial roles that depart from, and critically reconsider, the current concepts that apply to the industry in question. Implementing new value creation processes also requires suppliers to establish clear roles for their employees in providing reliable solutions.

In the case of human resources, partner competencies are developed in order to create collaborative learning relationships with business partners and downstream customers. Suppliers deliberately recruit and develop behavioural competencies so as to learn how to provide integrated solutions quickly via a network of business partners. Learning with business partners should be rewarded: it is helpful to solve customer problems in collaboration with business partners.

Suppliers should set up specific solution teams to enhance the way in which customers and business partners perceive the solutions offered. These teams integrate products, services and partner competencies into one organisational unit, acting relatively autonomously of existing organisational functions. The size of the company means that

Table 10.2: *Summary of the dynamic capabilities associated with each approach*

		Approaches used in service business development		
Capabilities		Enhancing the relational value of existing supplier–buyer relationships	Financial value-seeking behaviour in existing and new supplier–buyer relationships	Taking a radical leap towards a new value constellation downstream in the value chain
Dynamic capabilities	Sensing	• Continuing with the propensity to sense for new opportunities timely and reactively • Making incremental improvements in the perceived customer value • Improving customer relationships when marketing opportunities arise	• Breaking with the tendency to sense for incremental improvements alone in the perceived customer value • Setting up a more counter-cyclic method of sensing • Analysing potential service needs of new customers and converting them into new financial opportunities	• Exposing sensing activities to strategic opportunities downstream in the value chain, understanding customers' consideration of total costs, new value constellations beyond the industry and existing value network boundaries • Considering the market structure that arises from innovation and learning • Substituting the current theory used for service markets • Emphasising the creation of service markets and new value propositions • Actively influencing the structure, and shaping the behaviour, of the market
	Seizing	• Balancing the costs of the services to augment the product offerings and make improvements in the quality of supplier–buyer relationship with the price premium of the product	• Defining the value associated with new services by assessing the way in which customers perceive their service needs	• Considering value propositions as utilities or in terms of how a product and/or service benefits the customer rather than separating them into product and service attributes

Reconfiguring	• Initiating reconfigurations in corporate culture, human resources and measurement systems	• Translating the customers' perception into value-based prices for each service • Verifying the financial benefits sensed; assessing whether new or existing customers are willing to demand and pay for services	• Applying 'umbrella' strategies by defining the boundaries of the strategic response and new value constellations • Allowing various scenarios of value constellations and propositions to emerge • Anticipating how each scenario will affect value creation logics and influence the roles of actors and their value-creating processes • Mobilising other network players to participate in seizing scenarios, making value propositions • Defining the role of the actors in value-creating processes • Visioning a value network that is most suitable in forming a new value constellation
		• Initiating reconfigurations in corporate culture, human resources, organisational structures and innovation processes	• Initiating reconfigurations in the corporate culture, human resources, organisational structures and innovation processes of the supplier • Orchestrating reconfiguration activities of other network actors

Table 10.3: *Summary of the operational capabilities associated with each approach*

Capabilities	Approaches for service business development		
	Enhancing the relational value of existing supplier–buyer relationships	Financial value-seeking behaviour in existing and new supplier–buyer relationships	Taking a radical leap towards a new value constellation downstream in the value chain
Operational capabilities			
Corporate culture (values and behaviour)	• Establishing a behavioural role of trusted adviser and employing a philosophy of 'whatever it takes'	• Developing corporate values away from considering services as being add-ons to products to seeing services as a potential source of revenue and profits • Establishing behavioural roles of a reliable service provider and a philosophy of 'what is paid for and valued'	• Developing corporate values away from regarding services as being add-ons to products and towards seeing them as a potential way of restructuring the value chain and forming new value constellations • Establishing managerial roles in breaking and reconsidering critically the concept currently used • Establishing employee roles in providing reliable solutions
Human resources (recruitment, development and assessment of, and compensation for, personnel)	• Recruiting; training listening and communication skills to understand the customer's expectations of the service at an early stage	• Recruiting and training in listening and communication skills to learn the nature of customer's service expectations more rapidly and to convince customers to pay for services	• Developing partnering competencies to create collaborative learning relationships with business partners and customers downstream in the value chain • Recruiting and developing behavioural competencies to learn how to provide integrated solutions rapidly through a network of business partners

	• Rewarding outstanding performance in solving customer problems and for employing the 'whatever it takes' philosophy	• Rewarding outstanding financial performance with service revenues and profits. • Rewarding the 'what is paid for and valued' philosophy	• Rewarding cooperation with business partners • Rewarding the solving of customer problems in collaboration with business partners
Organisational structures for products and services (profit/loss responsibility, organisational clarity and visibility)		• Setting up specific service teams for logistic and design services • Ascertaining profit/loss responsibilities for the service teams	• Establishing specific solution teams with integrated products, services and partner competencies • Ascertaining profit/loss responsibilities for solution teams • Strengthening inter-company collaboration with business partners
Measurement systems	• Establishing procedures for the occasional recalculation of customer profitability	• Establishing a set of financial and non-financial performance indicators for the service teams	• Establishing a set of financial and non-financial performance indicators for the solution teams
Innovation processes	• Extending the service innovation process by setting goals and assessing the financial benefits		• Opening up the innovation process to business partners • Integrating product and service innovation processes with solution innovation processes

providing solutions is cross-functional: there are various interfaces with, for example, manufacturing, sales, marketing and services, making a separate business unit unnecessary. In conformity with the second approach, suppliers who follow the third approach should also delegate profit/loss responsibilities to their solution teams (after having made the necessary changes in accounting and measurement systems) and provide them with a set of financial and non-financial performance indicators.

Finally, related to previous descriptions pertaining to visioning, mobilising and orchestrating network actors, suppliers open up the innovation process to business partners. The latter are specifically requested to participate in the development phase and to contribute in drawing up business plans, designing the system for delivery solutions and blueprinting the value activities necessary across the network as a whole. Suppliers integrate product and service innovation processes into one solution innovation process, since solutions are based on how useful the products and services are to customers and how they cope with the challenges posed by their business processes.

11 | *Service business development in small and medium OEMs*

The previous discussion of the exploitation approach is applied to small- and medium-sized OEMs (SMEMs) in this chapter. The primary goal is to provide insight into how these companies can approach service business development. As in preceding chapters, the dynamic and operational capabilities necessary for the service business development are discussed here.

11.1 The exploitation approaches used by SMEMs

Two basic approaches are possible for developing the service business of SMEMs, namely:

1. *Selling directly to a limited number of customers*: the number of customers to which an SMEM sells is rather limited; on average, three to five customers generate about 80 per cent of the revenue.
2. *Selling indirectly to a large number of customers*: an SMEM sells through distributors, who then deal with many end-users (i.e. customers). A relatively large number of customers and distributors make relatively equal contributions to the revenue.

There are, of course, companies that use a combination of these two alternatives. A company may, for example, sell one type of equipment from its product portfolio through distributors and other types directly to customers. Should this be the case, then the recommendations described in the forthcoming two sections should also be combined.

11.2 SMEMs selling directly to a limited number of customers

SMEMs that sell directly to a limited number of customers function through a matrix organisation in which employees in the manufacturing and assembly organisations report to the production function even though they are assigned to different strategic customers. The strategic customers are managed by key account teams that form the customer interface between the production and sales teams within a company: it is the key account team that maintains the existing relationship of an SMEM with a customer. Key account managers are responsible for working with customers in order to identify their needs and determine how to meet the technical requirements of the equipment. Depending on the size of the company, the account team manages either a single customer or a portfolio of two or three customers.

This organisational structure provides a distinct starting point for developing capabilities, which evolve through the following four phases (see Table 11.1 and Exhibit 11.1):

1. consolidating existing services;
2. increasing the scope of the services in the core functions;
3. increasing the scope of the key account teams;
4. orchestrating partners to broaden the solution offered to the customer.

Phase 1: consolidating existing services

Dynamic capabilities for initiating the consolidation of existing service offerings capture the sensing of services as an opportunity to augment the equipment offering. The key account team becomes aware of the fact that customers are increasingly using the service quality and reputation of SMEMs as a proxy when evaluating new equipment: they themselves then start to use service to increase the quality of their relationship with the customer. Recognising service as being an opportunity where customer relationships may be enhanced and equipment offerings differentiated is based on individual skills and attitudes associated with understanding the abstract value of services. Being aware of the fact that the opportunities provided by service allow customer relationships to be enhanced and equipment offerings differentiated, and having an understanding of the abstract value of services, do not come automatically. They emerge instead from the performance of specific tasks for evaluating the contribution of services to the quality of customer relationships. Such evaluation leads to insight into the importance of service from a customer perspective.

Phase 2: expanding the scope of services in the core functions

Expanding the scope of services in the core functions follows the first phase. Phase 2 requires dynamic capabilities for initiating and sustaining the reconfiguration of the functional responsibility for manufacturing, assembly and logistics functions. Reconfiguration of the functional responsibilities involves reappraising the job profiles of manufacturing, assembly and logistic workers.

Increasing the range of services involves assuring technical service expertise and having an appropriate customer-orientated attitude: the latter being essential in understanding individual customer needs for servicing their equipment. This attitude helps to convince customers that the service package defined suits their needs. It is interesting to note here the necessity of modifying recruiting activities: SMEMs mainly recruit production specialists ad hoc and train them on the job. On-the-job training is suitable for the installation, repair and maintenance of equipment, using formal and informal coaching programmes during which production workers are coached by experienced employees who provide services. On-the-job training is supplemented by internal seminars and classroom training on selling and delivering service.

Training production employees in service competencies initiates changes at the level of individual skills and attitudes. Employees learn to become reliable troubleshooters and performance enablers and, where the delivery of service is concerned, they react immediately to any equipment breakdowns or failures. In order to make these rapid reactions manageable, network capabilities for forecasting demands between customers and SMEMs have to be developed. These capabilities cover basic exchanges of information of scheduled service activities. Information that is exchanged via remote services enables both the company and the customer to monitor the condition of the automation equipment on a real-time basis.

Modifications in service and manufacturing priorities are guided by a reorganisation of the responsibilities held by the employees in the manufacturing, assembly and logistics departments toward the provision of service. Restructuring these responsibilities interacts with the coordination mechanisms of the interface between the key account team and production (manufacturing and assembly) and logistic functions: when the key account team customises the service elements into specific service packages, the production and logistics functions must provide service agreements and performance levels. Depending on the actual location of the customer, the logistics function provides the delivery time of the spare parts and the production function provides

Table 11.1: Capability development in SMEMs selling directly to a few strategic customers

	Phase 1: consolidating service offerings	Phase 2: expanding the scope of organisational functions	Phase 3: expanding the scope of key account teams	Phase 4: orchestrating partners to broaden the solution offered to the customer
Dynamic capabilities	• Regard services as an opportunity to enhance customer relationships • See services as an opportunity to differentiate and augment equipment offerings • Use the service provider's identity and reputation as proxy when evaluating new equipment • Pave the way to increasing the quality of customer relationships	• Reconfigure functional responsibility for manufacturing, assembly and logistics functions • Reconfigure job profiles of manufacturing, assembly and logistics workers	• Broaden the functionality of the key account team • Reconfigure the job profiles of the key account team	• Vision, mobilise and orchestrate partners to contribute to customer solutions

| Operational capabilities | • Develop individual skills and attitudes to a greater understanding of the abstract value of services
• Evaluate the contribution of services to the quality of customer relationships | • Develop values and behaviours around reliable troubleshooters and reliable performance enablers
• Expand jobs to include developing, selling and delivering services
• Extend responsibilities for manufacturing, assembly and logistics toward providing service
• Apply coordination mechanisms to the interface between key account teams and the production and logistics functions
• Improve the skill of forecasting the demands of customers and SMEMs | • Develop values and behaviours of being technical advisers to customers
• Expand jobs in the key account teams to develop learning relationships with customers
• Extend the responsibilities of the key account team to deliver specific design and construction services
• Apply coordination mechanisms to the interface between key account teams and engineering staff
• Collaborate with customers |

response and reaction times. Based on this information, key account teams establish service packages specific to the customer and then evaluate the performance from the perspective of the customer, examining factors such as uptime, mean time taken to repair and mean time between failures.

Phase 3: expanding the scope of the key account teams
The development of these cross-functional capabilities initiates the third phase: it is in Phase 3 that SMEMs reconfigure the job profiles of the members of the key account team. Each member of a key account team is compelled to adopt the values and behaviours of a technical adviser when the move is made from selling only equipment to selling customising service and equipment features to suit the individual needs of a customer. Being a technical adviser requires that customers have trust in the equipment suppliers. The modified job profiles provide the members of the key account team with an opportunity to create an in-depth understanding of the business of a particular customer; to collaborate more intensively, participate in both the formulation and implementation of solutions to the problem at hand and develop a learning relationship. The key account team should be directed towards learning about the complex business problems of the customer and gain an intimate understanding of their business needs. By complying with these sophisticated job profiles the key account team are able to offer unbiased recommendations on how the outcome desired of both the equipment and service performance can be achieved to meet the demands the customer makes on the design and operation of the equipment.

The cost of technical advice can be kept from becoming excessive if the key account team standardises elements for designing and constructing the equipment and maintenance requirements as much as possible. Collaboration between customers and technical advisers in Phase 3 concentrates on the articulated and obvious needs of the customer.

Phase 4: orchestrating partners to broaden the solution offered to the customer
The fourth phase, which addresses the broader requirements and desires of customers, entails gaining intimate knowledge of their internal operating processes, cost structures, situation and business model. Developing solutions for these broader and more detailed

needs lies beyond the scope of SMEMs. Phase 4 starts, therefore, with visioning, mobilising and orchestrating other partners to contribute to, and participate in, meeting the needs of the customer: it is a phase that has been initiated by very few SMEMs so far. Evidence of this arises mainly from examining dynamic capabilities. Dynamic capabilities for visioning, mobilising and orchestrating partners are apparent when engaging specialised engineering firms to provide a broader definition of requirements, carry out feasibility studies and customise and integrate the equipment and services into broader solutions for specific customers. Furthermore SMEMs, in collaboration with customers, mobilise vendors of logistics to manage stocks of spare parts at the customer's own site and orchestrate upstream suppliers to deliver spare parts directly to it. Suppliers and other vendors can, on the other hand, become competitors as soon as they are mobilised to participate in solving complex needs. These firms not only maintain their own equipment but also have a tendency to offer service for equipment sold by the SMEMs. Therefore orchestrating these firms to participate in resolving complex problems remains rather difficult.

Exhibit 11.1: Service business development at Hunkeler

Hunkeler, a manufacturer of high performance equipment for efficient paper and print processing, followed the sequence for developing capabilities in order to extend its service business. Initially, Hunkeler took various actions to increase the understanding of its personnel that services provide an opportunity to enhance customer relationships as well as to differentiate and augment equipment offerings. The contribution of services to the quality of customer relationships was also evaluated. The service management team, for example, discussed intensively the contribution that providing basic services for the installed base made to Hunkeler's reputation and image. The questions they discussed were:

- How should we modularise services for the installed base?
- How should we charge for the various services?
- How can we increase the predictability of service intervention and increase the capacity utilisation in the service organisation?
- How can we balance specific customer needs against standardised services?

Exhibit 11.1: *(cont.)*

The answers to these questions led to three different levels of service packages being offered, namely: basic maintenance, extended
maintenance and superior maintenance. These three service levels
were supplemented by a basic examination of the machine, educational services and troubleshooting services.

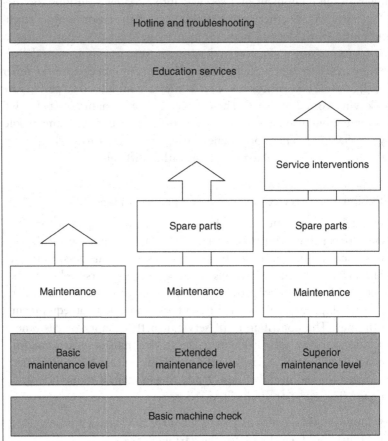

Hunkeler's service levels

In addition, Hunkeler extended the functional responsibility
for providing engineering services: it was made an integral part
of the enhanced job profiles of the key account teams. Together,

extending functional responsibility and expanding job descriptions restructured the sale phase. Instead of preparing a 'free' quotation with every technical specification, Hunkeler divided the sales phase into three sub-processes of providing a preliminary budget offer, a detailed quotation and an obligatory quotation.

- A *preliminary budget* offer describes the feasibility of the request received and provides price estimates. The customer receives a preliminary budget offer, which is free of charge, within two days.
- A *detailed quotation* states the technical recommendations and specifications. It is customised according to the requirements and applications of the customer. A detailed quotation, which is charged for, gives an indication of the cost of an obligatory quotation as well as for the machines.
- An *obligatory quotation* comprises all of the technical data and describes the technical specifications in detail. A charge is made for an obligatory quotation: should the customer purchase the machine in question, however, then it is credited against the cost of the machine.

Lately, Hunkeler has started to mobilise and orchestrate partners (such as distributors and printer manufacturers, e.g. Xerox, Sharp and Océ) to contribute to the service business.

11.3 SMEMs selling to a large number of customers via distributors

Service business development for SMEMs selling through distributors to a large number of customers proceeds in four successive stages (see Table 11.2):

1. reorganising collaboration with distributors;
2. increasing the service competence of distributors;
3. modifying potential distributors into subsidiaries;
4. increasing the scope of the tasks carried out by subsidiaries.

Phase 1: reorganising collaboration with distributors
The first phase is initiated when the SMEMs consider that their costs of delivering service are too high rather than their sensing additional

financial opportunities. For example, repair services might become increasingly unprofitable if customers are willing to pay for labour and parts only, and are unwilling to cover the travel expenses of service technicians. Travel expenses erode margins and create losses when customers are located across the globe so, in order to restrict costs, the SMEMs should mobilise their distributors to provide some of the services directly to the customers. Mobilising distributors is, therefore, one of the dynamic capabilities relevant to the first phase. Mobilising occurs when distributors sense services as being an opportunity to differentiate and augment their offerings.

After mobilising its distributors, one of the main tasks of an SMEM is to determine a potential path for transferring the responsibility for delivering service at the distributor level. This requires specific tasks to be carried out, such as the mapping of service processes and costs. These should have a solid foundation, where individual skills and attitudes are directed towards the intention of collaborating with distributors. Distributors, on the other hand, have to invest in additional resources in order to deliver the service. Such investments only succeed if SMEMs reconfigure the financial mechanisms involved, e.g. they can reward a distributor by awarding greater discounts for the spare parts used in the repair and maintenance interventions. The discounts ensure higher profit margins for the distributor which, in combination with the additional revenues gained from the repair and maintenance services, can then refinance the initial investments that were necessary to provide the service. Modified financial mechanisms lead, in general, to an extension in the contract agreements made with distributors.

Phase 2: enhancing the service competence of distributors

The second phase reveals more about the operational capabilities involved, whereas the first phase mainly exposes the dynamic capabilities relating to sensing, seizing and reconfiguring, and has only a few specific tasks relevant to operational capabilities. Dynamic capabilities embrace only reconfiguration activities, such as extending the functional responsibilities of the sales team, in order to broaden the service competence of distributors. Operational capabilities include capabilities specifically related to activities (e.g. expanding tasks that allow distributors to develop their own services, and distributors and SMEMs to develop services jointly), functional capabilities (e.g. allocating the sales team the responsibility of developing services with distributors;

giving the manufacturing and assembly functions the responsibility of assisting distributors in delivering services or knowledge-intensive services) and cross-functional capabilities (e.g. providing coordination mechanisms for the interface between the distributor and internal service support; forecasting the demands made between customers, distributors and SMEMs).

Distributors have to participate in training programmes to improve their technical expertise in order to ensure the quality of repair and maintenance services. Extensive initial training ensures that their newly-recruited service employees have both the basic technical expertise and the customer-orientated attitudes necessary for dealing with issues that arise when providing basic repair and maintenance services. Regular, ongoing training retains and increases the breadth of this expertise: providing such training requires the development of educational programmes for distributors.

Changes in responsibilities and the expansion of job profiles are based on the values and behaviours necessary for guaranteeing the service performance of distributors. Rather than regarding distributors merely as sales support they are seen as being customers with specific performance requests. The majority of SMEMs selling through distributors seem to cease the development of their service business in this phase. Only two triggers seem to motivate them in continuing: the first is dissatisfaction with efforts made by their distributors in developing the service business and the second is sensing new business opportunities moving downstream in the value chain.

Phases 3 and 4: modifying potential distributors into subsidiaries and enhancing job profiles in subsidiaries

These two triggers initiate Phase 3 and 4 and thereby change the relationship with the customer: the relationships SMEMs have with distributors and customers are replaced by direct relationships between sales subsidiaries and customers. Once SMEMs succeed with this replacement, their service capability development resembles the approach whereby they sell directly to a limited number of customers, in a similar phase of expanding jobs in the organisational functions. In contrast to those selling directly to a limited number of customers, SMEMs selling through distributors to a large number of customers might sell to many customers via their newly-established sales subsidiaries and not to just a few customers. Hence, these SMEMs do not have key

Table 11.2: *Capability development in SMEMs selling via distributors to a large number of customers*

	Phase 1: reorganising collaboration with distributors	Phase 2: enhancing the service competence of distributors	Phase 3: modifying potential distributors into subsidiaries	Phase 4: enhancing job profiles in the sales function of subsidiaries
Dynamic capabilities	• Use consolidation as a way of reducing costs • See services as an opportunity for differentiating and augmenting distributor offerings • Find paths for enhancing service competencies of distributors • Introduce mechanisms and competencies for developing distributors	• Widen functional sales responsibility to increase the service competence of distributors • Reconfigure service processes between distributors and subsidiaries	• Sense opportunities to move farther down the value chain • Identify potential ways of convincing distributors to become a subsidiary • Identify potential ways of overcoming internal resistance • Reconfigure the sales network	• Establish service at the subsidiary level
Operational capabilities	• Approach distributors with the intent of entering into collaboration • Introduce suitable behaviour for developing a learning relationship with distributors	• Develop the values and behaviour that enhance the service performance of distributors • Increase the scope of job profiles to develop the service provided by distributors	• Use entrepreneurial behaviour to invest in modifications in the sales network • Recruit service and sales staff from the distributors	• Develop values and behaviour toward being reliable trouble-shooters, performance enablers and technical advisers • Educate how to develop, sell and deliver services

- Extend contractual arrangements with distributors
- Map service processes and costs

- Increase the scope of job profiles to allow distributors and SMEMs to develop services jointly
- Extend responsibilities for sales towards service development with distributors
- Extend responsibilities for manufacturing and assembly functions to assist distributors in delivering service and knowledge-intensive services
- Coordinate mechanisms for developing the interface between distributors and internal service support
- Improve the skill of forecasting the demands of the customer, distributor and SMEM

- Transfer service knowledge to the new subsidiary
- Transfer service responsibilities to the subsidiary
- Extend the breadth of services
- Standardise the service elements
- Increase the scope of job profiles of the service staff in the new subsidiaries

- Improve forecasting the service demand between customers and the subsidiaries of SMEMs
- Develop standardising procedures in order to standardise service elements at the subsidiary level

account teams: they have, instead, sales teams in the subsidiaries that deal with a relatively large number of customers. Any service activities are therefore directed resolutely toward standardisation of the service offering and service delivery process rather than customising services to meet the needs of individual customers. SMEMs that had reached this phase offer standard repair and maintenance services with predefined service performance levels. Customers requesting specific solution are often referred to specialised providers of service.

12 | *Summary*

This chapter summarises the contents of this book and presents some ideas and suggestions for future research.

12.1 Highlights

How manufacturers of capital goods can succeed in service business development is the general question that is addressed. The various chapters concentrate on answering the following specific questions:

- What are the dynamic capabilities necessary for service business development?
- Which patterns can be identified when service strategies are changed?
- What are appropriate alignments of service strategies with organisational variables for operational capabilities?
- What are the potential network approaches for manufacturing companies planning on extending their service business?
- How should organisational variables (operational capabilities) be adapted for international markets?
- How can suppliers develop their service business?
- How can small- and medium-sized OEMs in particular develop their service business?

The relationship between dynamic capabilities and the way in which manufacturing companies develop their service business are identified in Chapter 3. Service business can be developed through using either an exploitation or exploration approach:

- *Exploitation of service opportunities*: the business logic here becomes incrementally more service-orientated through the extension of the service offering in the field of the customer's primary activities. Companies can 'exploit' the service business opportunities by following three phases: (1) integrating basic services into the price of the product, (2) separating the product from the service, thereby increasing service profits and revenues, and (3) utilising the expansion in service in the customer's primary activity chain.

- *Exploration of service opportunities*: the notion 'exploration' suggests that companies take a radical leap to a new strategic state which focuses on services addressing the customers' adjacent activity chain. Companies can 'explore' new service opportunities by following three phases: (1) integrating basic services into the price of the product, (2) creating a new value constellation, and (3) utilising the expansion in service in the customer's primary and adjacent activity chains.

Chapter 4 includes a case study that describes how Bosch Packaging employed the exploitation approach. Chapter 5 offers a case study of Hilti using the exploration approach, which deepens understanding as to how dynamic capabilities around sensing service opportunities and threats, seizing the sensed opportunities and reconfiguring the operational capabilities contributed to taking the leap in moving from products to solutions. The dynamic capabilities described enabled Hilti to challenge the assumptions that had previously been made about its existing competition and deviate from the dominant industrial recipe. Hilti's dynamic capabilities reshaped existing markets by changing the nature of the competition. It looked beyond the boundaries of competition defined by convention in order to discover uncontested market space and seek radically superior value, which has rendered competition irrelevant.

The exploitation approach is described in Chapter 6, which also discusses various service strategies supporting the development of service business. The chapter explains, specifically, four patterns of changes that can be made in the service strategy employed. These are:

- from a customer service strategy to an after-sales service strategy;
- from an after-sales service strategy to a customer support service strategy;
- from a customer support service strategy to a development partner;
- from a customer support service strategy to an outsourcing partner.

These four changes in the service strategy used lay the foundation for becoming a solution provider. Understanding how companies can survive using each service strategy and as being a solution provider is discussed in Chapter 7, which describes the operational capabilities that are necessary and provides guidelines for how the characteristics of operational capabilities can be aligned to the actual service strategies. The modifications of the operational capabilities discussed include key aspects such as:

- corporate culture;
- human resource management;
- organisational structures;
- service development processes;
- IT support for the service business.

Considering these key aspects, Chapter 7 describes the operational capabilities required for an after-sales service strategy, a customer support service strategy, a development partner, an outsourcing partner as well as a solution provider.

Chapter 8 describes four network approaches that may be employed in service business development, namely:

- vertical after-sales service network;
- horizontal outsourcing service network;
- vertical life-cycle service network;
- horizontal solution network.

Modifying operational capabilities is not restricted to the homeland of the company in question: it should be considered for international markets, too. Chapter 9 therefore discusses global approaches to the development of service business and includes elements such as domestic and foreign factors in the global organisational structure, organisational distinctiveness, proximity to customers, organisational functions supporting the service business and behavioural orientation (ethnocentric, polycentric and geocentric).

Four global approaches for service business development are then introduced:

- integrated and ethnocentric approach;
- integrated and polycentric approach;
- separated and polycentric approach;
- separated and geocentric approach.

The first two of these approaches specifically fit the after-sales service strategy, whereas the third is associated with the customer-support service strategy. The fourth approach is suitable for the development and outsourcing partner strategy as well as for solution providers.

The Chinese market is becoming increasingly important: Chapter 9 also suggests how companies can modify their human resource management and logistic processes to suit the very specific conditions that pertain to China.

While these recommendations apply mainly to companies positioned as OEMs, Chapter 10 deals with suppliers moving towards services and explains three different approaches:

- enhancing relational value to the existing supplier–buyer relationship;
- adopting financial value-seeking behaviour in existing and new supplier–buyer relationships;
- taking a radical leap towards a new value constellation downstream in the value chain.

Finally, Chapter 11 discusses how the recommendations described in Chapters 6 to 9 can be used by small- and medium-sized OEMs. There are two approaches for service business development that may be utilised, depending on whether such OEMs sell directly to a few customers, or indirectly to many. In the first approach, small- and medium-sized OEMs selling directly to a few customers can follow these four phases to develop their service business:

- Phase 1: consolidating service offerings.
- Phase 2: enhancing job profiles in organisational functions.
- Phase 3: enhancing job profiles in the key account teams.
- Phase 4: orchestrating partners to broaden customer solutions.

In the second approach, small- and medium-sized OEMs selling indirectly to many customers can follow these four phases:

- Phase 1: rearranging collaboration with distributors.
- Phase 2: enhancing the service competence of distributors.
- Phase 3: modifying potential distributors into subsidiaries.
- Phase 4: enhancing job profiles in the sales function of subsidiaries.

Altogether, the contents of each chapter offer comprehensive guidelines for managers and researchers seeking recommendations of how to develop a service business.

12.2 Recommendations for further research

It should be stated that this book has at least two limitations. Firstly, the manufacturing companies studied are mostly situated in Western European countries, so they have high labour costs and extensive technical experience. Secondly, the companies offer mostly capital goods, which require their customers to make large investments, and are positioned in a business-to-business context.

These shortcomings should form the starting point for future research. Newly-industrialised countries, such as Brazil, China, India, Mexico and Russia (Reynoso, 2010) are recommended for conducting research in. Although such countries are experiencing strong growth in their manufacturing industries, the idiosyncrasies surrounding labour costs, cultural characteristics and manufacturing capabilities would certainly provide fertile ground for developing theories rather than testing existing theories on services in manufacturing companies. Qualitative research methods based on narrative, longitudinal and case study approaches would therefore be most suitable. Once a more elaborate theory has been built for manufacturing companies in newly-industrialised countries moving towards services, researchers should then formulate and test their hypotheses empirically. Furthermore, research should also investigate how companies positioned in both business-to-business and business-to-consumer (e.g. electricity or energy providers) can extend their service business.

In line with recent calls for more interdisciplinary perspectives on research of services (Maglio and Spohrer, 2008), our major concern for future research is that previous contributions often neglect more general management theories, which include resource-based views, capability-driven competitive advantages, strategy processes, making organisational changes and altering company boundaries. The shift in the total offering from pure products to combinations of products and services, for example, should be considered from the perspective of the boundary of the firm (Santos and Eisenhardt, 2005). More detailed insights in operational and dynamic capabilities necessary for moving from products to services could contribute to understanding capability-driven competitive advantages (Barney, 1991; Teece, 2007), whereas traditional literature on strategy processes and organisational change might offer insights into successive hurdles and barriers for extending the service business (Brax, 2005; Kowalkowksi et al., 2011). Future research can use such management theories to extend and diversify their contributions to reach beyond the service and marketing research community.

Bibliography

Allmendinger, G. and Lombreglia, R. (2005). 'Four strategies for the age of smart services', *Harvard Business Review* 83 (10): 131–45.

Antioco, M., Moenaert, R. K., Lindgreen, A. and Wetzels, M. (2008). 'Organizational antecedents to and consequences of service business orientations in manufacturing companies', *Journal of the Academy of Marketing Science* 36 (3): 337–58.

Ashforth, B. and Lee, R. T. (1990). 'Defensive behaviour in organizations: a preliminary model', *Human Relations* 43: 621–48.

Auguste, B., Harmon, E. and Pandit, V. (2006). 'The right service strategies for product companies', *McKinsey Quarterly* 1: 40–52.

Baines, T. S., Lightfoot, H. W., Benedettini, O. and Kay, J. M. (2009). 'The servitization of manufacturing: a review of literature and reflection on future challenges', *Journal of Manufacturing Technology Management* 20 (5): 547–67.

Barney, J. (1991). 'Firm resources and sustained competitive advantage', *Journal of Management,* 17 (1): 99–120.

Bartlett, C. A. and Wozny, M. (1999). 'GE's two-decade transformation: Jack Welch's leadership', *Harvard Business School Cases*: Reference no: 9-399-150.

Baveja, S. S., Gilbert, J. and Ledingham, D. (2004). 'From products to services: why it's not so simple', *Harvard Management Update* 9 (4): 3–5.

Belz, C., Schuh, G., Groos, A. and Reinecke, S. (1997). *Industrie als Dienstleister*. St. Gallen: Thexis.

Bitner, M. J., Ostrom, A. and Morgan, F. (2008). 'Service blueprinting: a practical technique for service innovation', *California Management Review* 50 (3): 66–94.

Bitzer, A. and Abele, E. (2004). 'Universitäre und gewerbliche Ausbildung im chinesischen Werkzeugmaschinenbau – Zusammenfassung der Ergebnisse einer Studie des PTW der TU Darmstadt', *ZWF – Zeitschrift für wirtschaftlichen Fabrikbetrieb* 11: 609–13.

Bowen, D. E., Siehl, C. and Schneider, B. (1989). 'A framework for analyzing customer service orientations in manufacturing', *Academy of Management Review* 14 (1): 75–95.

Bowen, J. (1990). 'Development of a taxonomy of services to gain strategic marketing insights', *Journal of the Academy of Marketing Science* 18 (1): 43–9.

Brax, S. (2005). 'A manufacturer becoming service provider – challenges and a paradox', *Managing Service Quality* 15 (2): 142–55.

Brown, S. W., Gustafsson, A. and Witell, L. (2009). 'Beyond products', *Wall Street Journal*, June 22.

Burckhardt Compression (2009). *Annual Report 2008*.

Cepeda, G. and Vera, D. (2007). 'Dynamic capabilities and operational capabilities: a knowledge management perspective', *Journal of Business Research* 60 (5): 426–37.

Chandler, A. D. (1990). *Scale and Scope: The Dynamics of Industrial Capitalism*. Cambridge, MA: Belknap Press of Harvard University Press.

Chase, R. B. (1981). 'The customer contact approach to services: theoretical bases and practical extensions', *Operations Research* 29 (4): 698–706.

Cohen, M., Agrawal, N. and Agrawal, V. (2006). 'Winning in the aftermarket', *Harvard Business Review* 84 (5): 129–38.

Cooper, R. and Edgett, S. J. (1999). *Product Development for the Service Sector: Lessons from Market Leaders*. Cambridge, MA: Perseus Books.

Cornet, E., Katz, R., Molloy, R., Schädler, J., Sharma, D. and Tipping, A. (2000). *Customer Solutions: From Pilots to Profits*. New York: Booz Allen & Hamilton.

Davies, A. (2004). 'Moving base into high-value integrated solutions: a value stream approach', *Industrial and Corporate Change* 13 (5): 727–56.

Davies, A. and Brady, T. (2000). 'Organisational capabilities and learning in complex product systems: towards repeatable solutions', *Research Policy* 29 (7–8): 931–53.

Davies, A., Brady, T. and Hobday, M. (2007). 'Organizing for solutions: systems seller vs. systems integrator', *Industrial Marketing Management* 36 (2): 183–93.

Day, G. S. (2006). 'Aligning the organization with the market', *Sloan Management Review* 48 (1): 41–9.

De Brentani, U. (2001). 'Innovative versus incremental new business services: different keys for achieving success', *Journal of Product Innovation Management* 18 (3): 169–87.

Dickies, H. F. (1951). 'ABC inventory analysis shoots for dollars, not pennies', *Factory Management and Maintenance* 109: 92–4.

Dörner, N., Gassmann, O. and Gebauer, H. (2011). 'Service innovation: why is it so difficult to accomplish?', *Journal of Business Strategy* 32 (3): 37–46.

Drucker, P. F. (1973). *Management: Tasks, Responsibilities, Practices*. New York: Harper & Row.

Easingwood, C. J. (1986). 'New product development for service companies', *Journal of Product Innovation Management* 3 (4): 264–75.

Edvardsson, B. and Olsson, J. (1996). 'Key concepts in new service development', *The Service Industries Journal* 16 (2): 140–64.

Eisenhardt, K. M. and Martin, J. A. (2000). 'Dynamic capabilities: what are they?', *Strategic Management Journal* 21 (10–11): 1105–21.

Fischer, T., Gebauer, H., Ren, G., Gregory M. and Fleisch, E. (2010). 'Exploitation and exploration in service business development? Insights from a dynamic capability perspective', *Journal of Service Management* 21 (5): 591–624.

Fleisch, E. and Mattern, F. (eds.) (2005). *Das Internet der Dinge: Ubiquitous Com-puting und RFID in der Praxis*. Berlin: Springer.

Fouraker, L. E. and Stopford, J. M. (1968). 'Organization structure and multinational strategy', *Administrative Science Quarterly* 13 (1): 47–64.

Galbraith, J. R. (2002). 'Organizing to deliver solutions', *Organizational Dynamics* 31 (2): 194–207.

(2005). *Designing the Customer-centric Organization: A Guide to Strategy, Structure and Process*. San Francisco: Jossey-Bass.

Gavetti, G., Levinthal, D. A. and Rivkin, J. W. (2005). 'Strategy making in novel and complex worlds: the power of analogy', *Strategic Management Journal* 26 (8): 691–712.

Gebauer, H. (2008). 'Identifying service strategies in product manufacturing companies by exploring environment–strategy configurations', *Industrial Marketing Management* 37 (3): 278–91.

Gebauer, H. and Fleisch, E. (2007). 'An investigation of the relationship between behavioral processes, motivation, investments in the service business and service revenue', *Industrial Marketing Management* 36 (3): 337–48.

Gebauer, H., Fleisch, E. and Friedli, T. (2005). 'Overcoming the service paradox in manufacturing companies', *European Management Journal* 23 (1): 14–26.

Gebauer, H., Pütz, F., Fischer, T. and Fleisch, E. (2009). 'Service orientation of organizational structures', *Journal of Relationship Marketing* 8 (2): 103–26.

Gebauer, H., Edvardsson, B., Gustafsson, A. and Witell, L. (2010). 'Match or mismatch: strategy structure configurations in the service business of manufacturing companies', *Journal of Service Research* 13 (2): 198–215.

Gershenfeld, N., Krikorian, R. and Cohen, D. (2004). 'The internet of things', *Scientific American*, 291 (4): 76–81.

Gerstner, L. V. (2002). *Who Says Elephants Can't Dance?* New York: Harper Business.

Gibson, J. L., Ivanecevich, J. M., Donnelly, J. H. and Konopaske, R. (2006). *Organizations – Behavior, Structure and Processes.* 12th edn. New York: McGraw-Hill Irwin.

Glueck, J. J., Koudal, P. and Vaessen, W. (2007). 'The service revolution – manufacturing's missing crown jewel', *Deloitte Review*: 22–33.

Grönroos, C. (1990). *Service Management and Marketing: Managing the Moments of Truth in Service Competition.* Lexington: Lexington Books.

(1999). 'Internationalization strategies for services', *Journal of Services Marketing* 13 (4–5): 290–7.

Grönroos, C. and Helle, P. (2010). 'Adopting a service logic in manufacturing. Conceptual foundation and metrics for mutual value creation', *Journal of Service Management* 21 (5): 564–90.

Gummesson, E. (1994). 'Service management: an evaluation and the future', *International Journal of Service Industry Management* 5 (1): 77–96.

Hänggi, R. (2004). 'Service Innovation in der Industrie – SIG Pack Services', presented at *Business for Innovation: Innovating for Business – VIII. Technologiemanagement Tagung ITEM-HSG St. Gallen*, 3 March.

Harreld, B., O'Reilly, C. and Tushman, M. (2007). 'Dynamic capabilities at IBM: driving strategy into action', *California Management Review* 49 (4): 21–43.

Heskett, J. L., Sasser, W. E. and Schlesinger, L. A. (1997). *The Service Profit Chain: How Leading Companies Link Profit and Growth to Loyalty, Satisfaction, and Value.* New York: Free Press.

Hill, C., Hitt, M. A. and Hoskisson, R. E. (1992). 'Cooperative versus competitive structures in related and unrelated diversified firms', *Organization Science* 3 (4): 501–21.

Hilti (2004). *Benchmarking Project: Profitable Customer Relationships through Integrated Service Management.* St. Gallen: TECTEM.

Hobday, M., Davies, A. and Prencipe, A. (2005). 'Systems integration: a core capability of the modern corporation', *Industrial and Corporate Change* 14 (6): 1109–43.

Holmström, J., Hoover, W. E. Jr., Eloranta, E. and Vasara, A. (1999). 'Using value reengineering to implement breakthrough solutions for customers', *International Journal of Logistics Management* 10 (2): 1–12.

Holmström, J., Brax, S. and Ala-Risku, T. (2010). 'Comparing provider-customer constellations of visibility-based service', *Journal of Service Management* 21 (5): 675–92.

Homburg, C., Günther, C. and Fassnacht, M. (2000a). 'Wenn Industrieunternehmen zu Dienstleistern werden – Lernen von den Besten', Working Paper of the University Mannheim.

Homburg, C., Workman, J. P. and Jensen, O. (2000b). 'Fundamental changes in marketing organization: the movement toward a customer-focused organizational structure', *Journal of the Academy of Marketing Science* 28 (4): 459–78.

Homburg, C., Fassnacht M. and Günther C. (2003). 'The role of soft factors in implementing a service-oriented strategy in industrial marketing companies', *Journal of Business-to-Business Marketing* 10 (2): 723–51.

Hong, P., Noh, J. and Hwang, W. (2006). 'Global supply chain strategy: a Chinese market perspective', *Journal of Enterprise Information Management* 19 (3): 320–33.

Hünerberg, R. and Hüttmann, A. (2003). 'Performance as a basis for price-setting in the capital goods industry: concepts and empirical evidence', *European Management Journal* 21 (6): 717–30.

Hypko, P., Tilebein, M. and Gleich, R. (2010). 'Clarifying the concept of performance-based contracting in manufacturing industries: a research synthesis', *Journal of Service Management* 21 (5): 625–55.

IBM (2001). *Annual Report*.

(2004 to 2010). *IBM Annual Reports 2004 to 2010*.

Jacob, F. and Ulaga, W. (2008). 'The transition from product to service in business markets: an agenda for academic inquiry', *Industrial Marketing Management* 37 (3): 247–53.

Jaworski, B., Kohli, A. and Sahay, A. (2000). 'Market-driven versus driving markets', *Journal of the Academy of Marketing Science* 28 (1): 45–54.

Jiang, B. (2002). 'How international firms are coping with supply chain issues in China', *Supply Chain Management: An International Journal* 7 (4): 184–8.

Johnson, M. and Mena, C. (2008). 'Supply chain management for servitised products: a multi-industry case study', *International Journal of Production Economics* 114 (1): 27–39.

Johnstone, S., Dainty, A. and Wilkinson, A. (2008). 'In search of "product-service": evidence from aerospace, construction, and engineering', *Service Industries Journal* 26 (6): 1–14.

Kahneman, D., Slovic, P. and Tversky, A. (1982). *Judgement under Uncertainty: Heuristics and Biases*. Cambridge University Press.

Kellogg, D. L. and Nie, W. (1995). 'A framework for strategic service management', *Journal of Operations Management* 13 (4): 323–37.

Kindström, D., Kowalkowski, C. and Sandberg, E. (2009). 'A dynamic capabilities approach to service infusion in manufacturing', in Stauss, B., Brown, S. W., Edvardsson, B. and Johnston, R. (eds.) *QUIS 11 – Moving Forward With Service Quality*. Wolfsburg: Ingolstadt School of Management, pp. 331–40.

Kinkel, S., Jung Erceg, P. and Lay, G. (eds.) (2003). *Controlling produktbegleitender Dienstleistungen. Methoden und Praxisbeispiele zur Kosten- und Erlössteuerung*. Heidelberg: Physica-Verlag.

Kotler, P. (1994). *Marketing Management: Analysis, Planning, Implementation and Control*. 8th edn. Englewood Cliffs: Prentice Hall.

Kotler, P. and Keller, K. L. (2005). *Marketing Management*. 12th edn. Upper Saddle River: Prentice Hall.

Kowalkowski, C., Kindström, D. and Gebauer, H. (2010). 'ICT as a catalyst for service business orientation', *Proceedings of the 17th Annual CBIM Academic Workshop*, San Juan, Puerto Rico.

Kowalkowski, C., Kindström, D., Brashear Alejandro, T., Brege, S. and Biggemann, S. (2011). 'Service infusion as agile incrementalism in action', *Journal of Business Research*, forthcoming.

Lay, G., Schroeter, M. and Biege, S. (2009). 'Service-based business concepts: a typology for business-to-business markets', *European Management Journal* 27 (6): 442–55.

Maglio, P. P. and Spohrer, J. (2008). 'Fundamentals of service science', *Journal of the Academy of Marketing Science* 36 (1): 18–20.

Magna (2004 to 2010). *Annual Reports 2004 to 2010*.

Malleret, V. (2006). 'Value creation through service offers', *European Management Journal* 24 (1): 106–16.

March, J. G. (1991). 'Exploration and exploitation in organizational learning', *Organization Science* 2 (1): 71–87.

Martin, C. R., Jr. and Horne, D. A. (1992). 'Restructuring towards a service orientation: the strategic challenges', *International Journal of Service Industry Management* 3 (1): 25–38.

Mathieu, V. (2001a). 'Service strategies within the manufacturing sector: benefits, costs and partnership', *International Journal of Service Industry Management* 12 (5): 451–75.

(2001b). 'Product services: from a service supporting the product to a service supporting the client', *Journal of Business and Industrial Marketing* 16 (1): 39–58.

Matthyssens, P. and Vandenbempt, K. (1998). 'Creating competition advantage in industrial services', *Journal of Business and Industrial Marketing* 13 (4/5): 339–55.

(2008). 'Moving from basic offerings to value-added solutions: strategies, barriers and alignment', *Industrial Marketing Management* 37 (3): 316–28.

(2010). 'Service addition as business market strategy: identification of transition trajectories', *Journal of Service Management* 21 (5): 693–714.

Meiren, T. (2006). *Service Engineering im Trend*. Stuttgart: Fraunhofer IRB Verlag.

Mercer (2003). *Service im Maschinenbau – Ungenutzte Chancen im Servicegeschäft*. Mercer Management Consulting.

Michel, S., Brown, S. W. and Gallan, A. S. (2008). 'Service-logic innovations: how to innovate customers, not products', *California Management Review* 50 (3): 49–65.

Mintzberg, H. and Waters, J. (1985). 'Of strategies, deliberate and emergent', *Strategic Management Journal* 6 (3): 257–72.

Mintzberg, H. and Westley, F. (1992). 'Cycles of organizational change', *Strategic Management Journal* 13 (S2): 39–59.

Möller, K. (2006). 'Role of competences in creating customer value: a value-creation logic approach', *Industrial Marketing Management* 35 (8): 913–24.

Möller, K., Rajala, A. and Svahn, S. (2005). 'Strategic business nets – their type and management', *Journal of Business Research* 58 (9): 1274–84.

Neely, A. (2008). 'Exploring the financial consequences of the servitization of manufacturing', *Operations Management Research* 1 (2): 103–18.

Neu, W. A. and Brown, S. W. (2005). 'Forming successful business-to-business services in goods-dominant firms', *Journal of Service Research* 8 (1): 3–17.

  (2008). 'Manufacturers forming successful complex business services: designing an organization to fit the market', *International Journal of Service Industry Management* 19 (2): 232–51.

Noch, R. (1995). *Dienstleistungen im Investitionsgüter-Marketing – Strategien und Umsetzung*. Munich: FGM.

Normann, R. (2001). *Reframing Business: When the Map Changes the Landscape*. Chichester: Wiley.

Oliva, R. and Kallenberg, R. (2003). 'Managing the transition from products to services', *International Journal of Service Industry Management* 14 (2): 160–72.

O'Reilly, C. A. and Tushman, M. L. (2007). 'Ambidexterity as a dynamic capability: resolving the innovator's dilemma', Research Paper No. 1963, *Research Paper Series*, Stanford Graduate School of Business.

Pawar, K.S., Beltagui, A. and Riedel, J. C. (2009). 'The PSO triangle: designing product, service and organisation to create value', *International Journal of Operations & Production Management* 29 (5): 468–93.

Penttinen, E. and Palmer, J. (2007). 'Improving firm positioning through enhanced offerings and buyer–seller relationships', *Industrial Marketing Management* 36 (5): 552–64.

Perlmutter, H. V. (1969). 'The tortuous evolution of the multinational enterprise', *Columbia Journal of World Business* 4 (1): 9–18.

Porter, M. E. (1985). *Competitive Advantage*. New York: The Free Press.

Potts, G. W. (1988). 'Exploiting your product's life cycle', *Harvard Business Review* 66 (5): 32–5.

Powell, T. C. (1992). 'Organizational alignment as competitive advantage', *Strategic Management Journal* 13 (2): 119–34.

Raddats, C. and Easingwood, C. (2010). 'Services growth options for B2B product-centric businesses', *Industrial Marketing Management* 39 (8): 1334–45.

Ramírez, R. (1999). 'Value co-production: intellectual origins and implications for practice and research', *Strategic Management Journal* 20 (1): 49–65.

Reinartz, W. and Ulaga, W. (2008). 'How to sell services more profitably', *Harvard Business Review* 86 (5): 90–6.

Ren, G. and Gregory, M. (2007). 'Servitization in manufacturing companies – a conceptualization, critical review and research agenda', *Proceedings of the 16th Annual Frontiers in Service Conference*, San Francisco, CA, 4–7 October.

Reynoso, J. (2010). 'Identifying service orientation roles in manufacturing', *Proceedings of AMA SERVSIG International Conference*, Porto, Portugal, p. 130.

Roland Berger (2010). *Industrieservice in Deutschland – Status Quo und zukünftige Entwicklung*. Munich: Roland Berger Strategy Consultants.

Saaksvuori, A. and Immonen, A. (2008). *Product Lifecycle Management*. Berlin: Springer.

Sandberg, R., and Werr, A. (2003). 'The three challenges of corporate consulting', *MIT Sloan Management Review* 44 (3): 59–66.

Santos, F. M. and Eisenhardt, K. M. (2005). 'Oganizational boundaries and theories of organization', *Organization Science* 16 (5): 491–508.

Sawhney, M. (2006). 'Going beyond the product, defining, designing and delivering customer solutions', in Lusch, R. and Vargo, S. (eds.) *The Service-Dominant Logic of Marketing: Dialog, Debate and Directions*, New York: M. E. Sharp, pp. 365–80.

Sawhney, M., Balasubramanian, S. and Krishan, V. (2004). 'Creating growth with services', *Sloan Management Review* 45 (2): 34–43.

Schmenner, R. W. (1986). 'How can service businesses survive and prosper?', *Sloan Management Review* 27 (3): 21–32.

  (2009). 'Manufacturing, service, and their integration: some history and theory', *International Journal of Operations & Production Management* 29 (5): 431–43.

Schuh, G., Friedli, T. and Gebauer, H. (2004). *Fit for Service – Industrie als Dienstleister*. Munich: Hanser.

Senge, P. (1990). *The Fifth Discipline: The Art and Practice of the Learning Organization*. New York: Doubleday Currency.

Shah, D., Rust, R. T., Parasuraman, A., Staelin, R. and Day, G. S. (2006). 'The path to customer centricity', *Journal of Service Research* 9 (2): 113–24.

Sheth, J. N. and Sharma, A. (2008). 'The impact of the product to service shift in industrial markets and the evolution of the sales organization', *Industrial Marketing Management* 37 (3): 260–9.

Siemens (2006). *Annual Report*.

Simon, H. (1992). 'Service policies of German manufacturers – critical factors in international competition', *European Management Journal* 10 (4): 404–11.

(1993). *Industrielle Dienstleistungen*. Stuttgart: Schäffer-Poeschel.

SKF (2004 to 2010). *Annual Report 2004 to 2010*.

Slater, S. F. and Narver, J. C. (1995). 'Market orientation and the learning organization', *Journal of Marketing* 59 (3): 63–74.

(2000). 'Intelligence generation and superior customer value', *Journal of the Academy of Marketing Science* 28 (1): 120–7.

Storbacka, K. (2011). 'A solution business model: capabilities and management practices for integrated solutions', *Industrial Marketing Management* 40 (5): 699–711.

Storbacka, K., Ryals, L., Davies, I. A. and Nenonen, S. (2009). 'The changing role of sales: viewing sales as a strategic, cross-functional process', *European Journal of Marketing* 43 (7/8): 890–906.

Teece, D. J. (2007). 'Explicating dynamic capabilities: the nature and microfoundations of (sustainable) enterprise performance', *Strategic Management Journal* 28 (13): 1319–50.

Thomas, A. and Schenk, E. (2001). *Beruflich in China. Trainingsprogramm für Manager, Fach- und Führungskräfte*. 2nd edn. Göttingen: Vandenhoeck & Ruprecht.

Tukker, A. (2004). 'Eight types of product service system; eight ways to sustainability? Experiences from SUSPRONET', *Business Strategy and the Environment* 13 (4): 246–60.

Tuli, K. R., Kohli, A. K. and Bharadwaj, S. G. (2007). 'Rethinking customer solutions: from product bundles to relational processes', *Journal of Marketing* 71 (3): 1–17.

Ulaga, W. and Eggert, A. (2006). 'Value-based differentiation in business relationships: gaining and sustaining key supplier status', *Journal of Marketing* 70 (1): 119–36.

Ulaga, W. and Reinartz, W. (2011). 'Hybrid offerings: how manufacturing firms combine goods and services successfully', *Journal of Marketing* 75 (6): 5–23.

Vandenbosch, M. and Dawar, N. (2002). 'Beyond better products: capturing value in customer interactions', *MIT Sloan Management Review* 43 (4): 35–42.

Vandermerwe, S. and Chadwick, M. (1989). 'The internationalization of service', *The Services Industries Journal* 9 (1): 79–93.

Vandermerwe, S. and Rada, J. (1988). 'Servitization of business: adding value by adding services', *European Management Journal* 6 (4): 314–24.

Vargo, S. L. and Lusch, R. F. (2004). 'Evolving to a new dominant logic for marketing', *Journal of Marketing* 68 (1): 1–17.

VDMA (2004). *Serviceleistungen im Maschinen-und Anlagenbau – Statisches Jahrbuch*. Frankfurt am Main: VDMA-Verlag.

   (2008). *Dienstleistungsmanagement in der Investitionsgüterindustrie: Services erfolgreich entwickeln, steuern und vertreiben*. Frankfurt am Main: VDMA-Verlag.

Wärtsilä (2010). *Annual Report*.

Wernerfelt, B. (1984). 'A resource-based view of the firm', *Strategic Management Journal* 5 (2): 171–80.

Windahl, C. and Lakemond, E. (2010). 'Integrated solutions from a service-centered perspective: applicability and limitations in the capital goods industry', *Industrial Marketing Management* 39 (8): 1278–90.

Windahl, C., Andersson, P., Berggren, C. and Nehler, C. (2004). 'Manufacturing firms and integrated solutions: characteristics and implications', *European Journal of Innovation Management* 7 (3): 218–28.

Wise, R. and Baumgartner, P. (1999). 'Go downstream: the new imperative in manufacturing', *Harvard Business Review* 77 (5): 133–41.

Wouters, J. P. (2004). 'Customer service strategy options: a multiple case study in a B2B setting', *Industrial Marketing Management* 33 (7): 583–92.

Index

ABB, 6, 143, 188
after-sales service provider, 28, 131,
    136, 137, 146
Alfa Laval, 213

behavioural orientation, 83, 220
Bilfinger Berger, 211
Bosch Packaging, 106, 139,
    193, 212
Bucher Foodtech, 148
Bühler Die Casting, 178
Burckhardt Compression, 27
business consulting, 28
business network, 199, 264
    horizontal, 200, 207, 215
    vertical, 199, 204, 213
Bystronic Glass, 170

capacity utilisation, 134
Carl Zeiss IMT, 165
China, 234
cognitive phenomena
    disbelief in the economic potential,
        48
    overemphasis on obvious and
        tangible characteristics, 48
    risk aversion, 49
Comau Group, 25
corporate culture, 81, 264
corporate values, 146, 153, 167, 182,
    261
cost centre, 220, 224
customer activity chain
    adjacent, supplementary customer
        activities, 54, 116, 123
    primary customer activities, 54, 123
customer needs, 86
    complexity, 46
customer proximity, 149, 158, 174,
    186, 218

centralised service units, 218
    decentralised service units, 218
customer service, 3, 73
customer service provider, 131, 136
customer support service provider, 28,
    132, 137, 153
customs regulations, 243

Deutz, 149
development partner, 28, 132, 138,
    167
distributors, 11, 37, 205
    distributor collaboration, 275
    service competence, 276
dominant design, 92
downstream analysis, 50
downstream in the value chain, 2, 16
Dürr, 26
dynamic capabilities, 23, 91, 98, 214,
    253, 258, 271, 279

economies of scale, 66, 211
economies of skill, 66
employee roles, 146, 153,
    167, 182
Endress+Hauser, 159
Ericsson Operating Systems, 7, 137,
    173, 195, 197
Escatec, 257
ethnocentric, 83, 220
exploitation, 87, 89, 91, 106, 122, 267
exploration, 88, 89, 98, 113

first-level support, 217, 226
Fraisa, 251, 260

General Electric, 7, 10, 24, 28, 29, 143
geocentric, 83, 220, 230
GF AgieCharmilles, 156, 204, 245
global service approach, 217

Heidelberg, 30, 161
horizontal outsourcing service
   network, 201, 207
horizontal solution network,
   201, 215
human resource management, 81, 82,
   233, 234, 264
Hunkeler, 273

IBM, 16, 18, 23, 27
information and communication
   technologies (ICT), 86
installed base, 2, 47, 211
integrated and ethnocentric approach,
   220
integrated and polycentric approach,
   223
integration of product and service
   organisation, 84, 101
inter-firm collaboration, 149, 158,
   173, 185
intermediary services, 76
internal resistance, 97
investment cycle, 14
IT-support, 69, 81, 151, 164,
   179, 188

key account team, 268, 272

learning relationship, 170
life-cycle cost analysis, 50
losing face, 237

Magna, 34, 176
market entry
   direct, 33, 86, 218
   indirect, 33, 86, 218
Mettler-Toledo, 154, 194
Mikron, 136, 151

operational capabilities, 68, 81, 141,
   152, 168, 180, 190, 192, 206,
   210, 214, 216, 253, 254, 256,
   261, 271, 279
operational services, 28, 76
orchestration, 206, 214, 216, 266, 273
organisational capabilities, 43
organisational distinctiveness, 84, 148,
   172, 185
organisational structures, 81, 264

original equipment manufacturer
   (OEM), 12, 33, 34
   small- and medium-sized OEM, 37,
   205, 267
outsourcing, 5
outsourcing partner, 28, 132,
   139, 182
outsourcing specialist, 207

performance enablers, 83, 269
performance-based business logic,
   15, 144
   pay-per-performance, 200
personal relations, 239
personnel compensation, assessment
   and rewards, 147, 155, 172, 185,
   237
personnel recruitment and training,
   147, 153, 171, 184, 234, 236
planned strategy, 95, 105
polycentric, 83, 220, 223, 227
post-customs clearance, 244, 246
price premium, 249, 254
pricing, 135, 255
product life cycle, 48
product manufacturer, 5, 6
product services, 73
product-related services, 3
product-service systems, 2, 33
profit-and-loss responsibility, 83, 227

reconfiguration, 27, 29, 57, 97, 104,
   120, 209, 214, 254, 262
reliable troubleshooters, 83
risk, 5, 75, 93, 100, 135
Rolls-Royce, 7, 143

second-level support, 217, 229
seizing, 27, 53, 97, 103, 117, 209, 253,
   256, 262
sensing, 27, 46, 97, 103, 116, 206,
   209, 216, 253, 255, 259, 262
separated and geocentric approach,
   229
separated and polycentric approach,
   227
separation of product and service
   organisation, 84, 93
service as a product, 73
service culture, 111

service development process, 81, 150,
    159, 175, 186
service export, 33, 86
service factory, 121
service hub, 229
service innovation process, 264
service jungle, 21
service offerings, 2, 217
    advanced services, 3, 44
    comprehensive services, 72
    distribution control, 72
    embedded services, 72
    integrated solutions, 72
    product-related services, 55
service opportunity matrix, 53, 123
service paradox, 21, 22, 62
service pricing, 69, 100
service profitability, 12, 13, 46, 61, 134
service provider, 5, 7
service revenue, 9, 10, 11, 47, 134, 233
service strategies, 80, 123, 129
    after-sales service, 76
    after-sales service provider, 125
    customer service provider, 125
    customer support service providers,
        125
    development partner, 126
    maintenace offerings, 56
    operational offerings, 56
    outsourcing partner, 127
    performance offerings, 57
    rental offerings, 57
    service engagement, 56
    service extension, 56
    service partner, 76
    service penetration, 56
    service transformation, 56
    solution partner, 76
    supplementary service provider, 127
    value partner, 76
service strategy changes, 131, 133
servitisation, 2
servitisation failures, 21

Siemens, 30
SKF, 35
solution provider, 143, 192
solution selling process, 196
spare parts business, 233, 239
spare parts logistics, 245
    bonded and non-bonded warehouse,
        243, 246
    direct export, 241
    local warehouses, 241
stage-gate model, 69
strategic capabilities, 23
Sulzer Innotec, 174
supplier–buyer relationship, 31, 207,
    248
suppliers, 22, 34, 248
system integrators, 199
system sellers, 199
systems integration, 2, 28, 76

temporary borrowing, 244, 246
third-level support, 217
ThyssenKrupp, 25
transition line, 58
troubleshooters, 269
Trumpf, 137, 158
trusted advisers, 83, 167

umbrella strategy, 99, 259, 262

value constellation, 90, 100, 105, 118,
    249, 250, 251, 252, 258
value creation, 16
value proposition, 124, 205
vertical after-sales service network,
    201, 204
vertical life-cycle solution network,
    201, 213
Voith, 182, 209

Wärtsilä, 32

Xerox, 30

Printed in the United States
By Bookmasters